THE AMAZING SPIDER-MAN
NEW AVENGERS

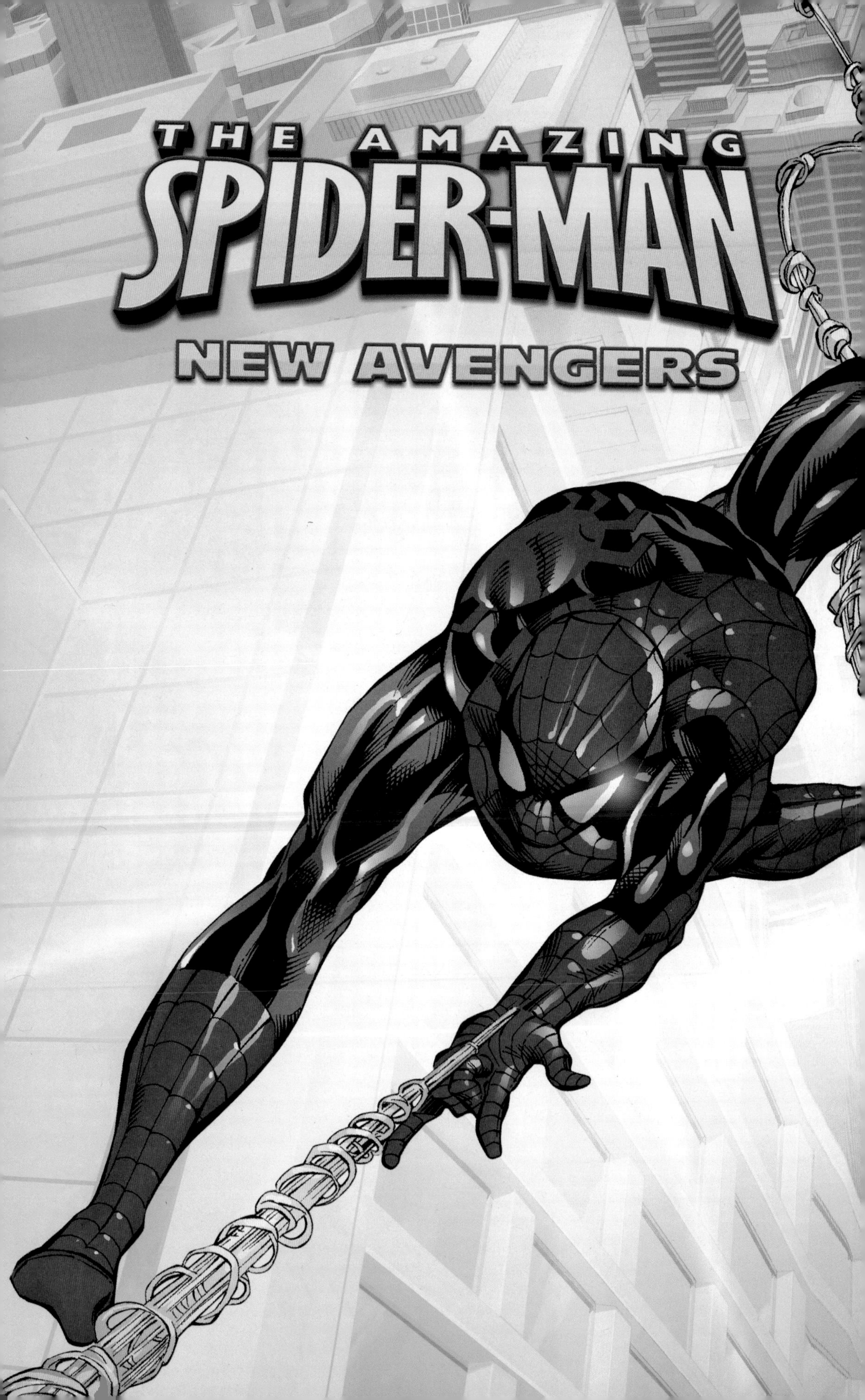
THE AMAZING
SPIDER-MAN
NEW AVENGERS

writer
J. MICHAEL STRACZYNSKI

penciler
MIKE DEODATO JR.

inker
JOE PIMENTEL

finishes
(Issue #521, pgs. 5-9 & 14 and
Issue #522 pgs. 11-18)
TOM PALMER

colorist
MATT MILLA

letterer
**VIRTUAL CALLIGRAPHY'S
CORY PETIT**

cover art
**MIKE DEODATO JR.,
KAARE ANDREWS,
TERRY DODSON
& TONY HARRIS**

associate editor
WARREN SIMONS

editor
AXEL ALONSO

collection editor
JENNIFER GRÜNWALD

senior editor, special projects
JEFF YOUNGQUIST

director of sales
DAVID GABRIEL

production
JERRY KALINOWSKI

book designer
MEGHAN KERNS

creative director
TOM MARVELLI

editor in chief
JOE QUESADA

publisher
DAN BUCKLEY

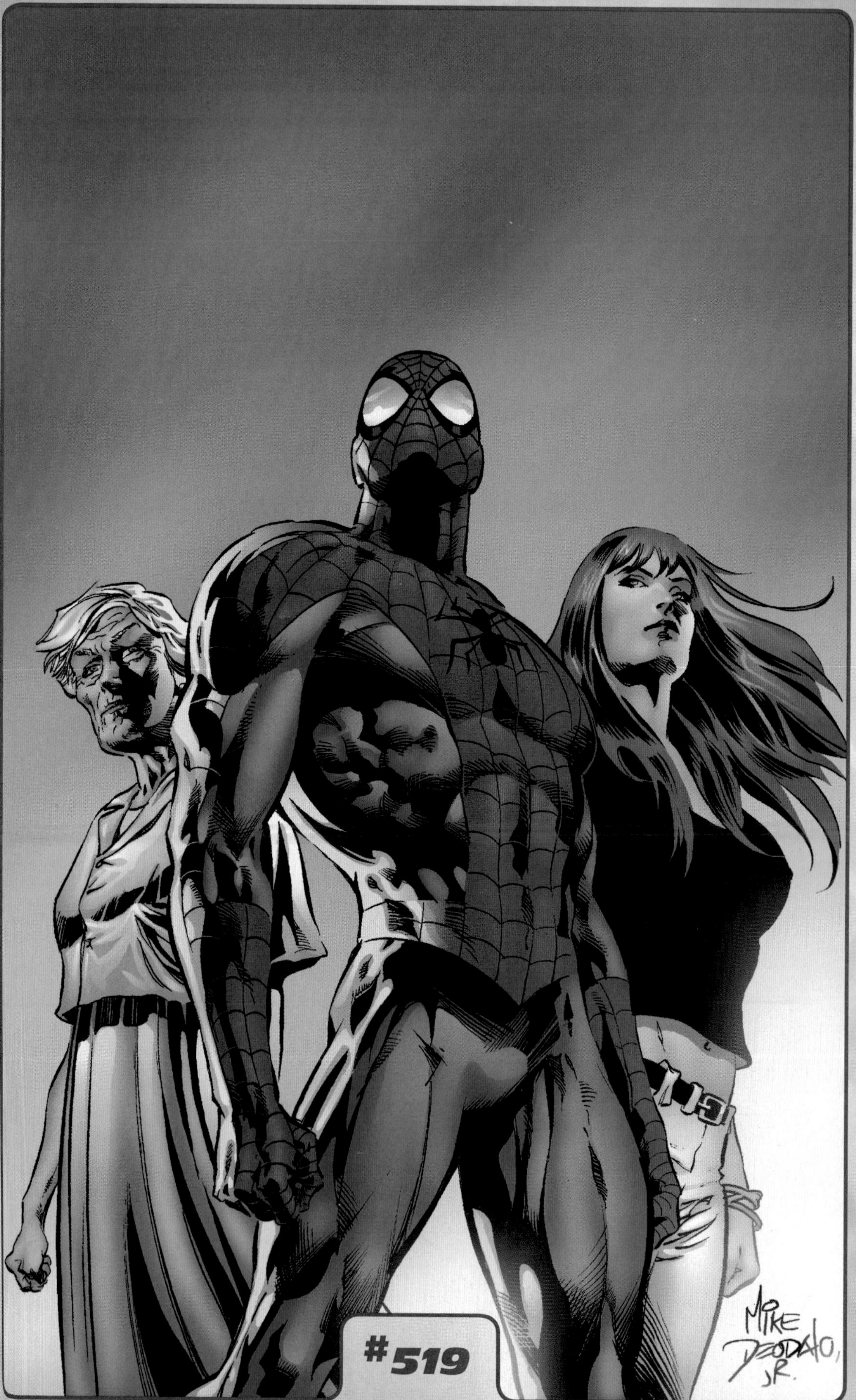
#519
MIKE DEODATO, JR.

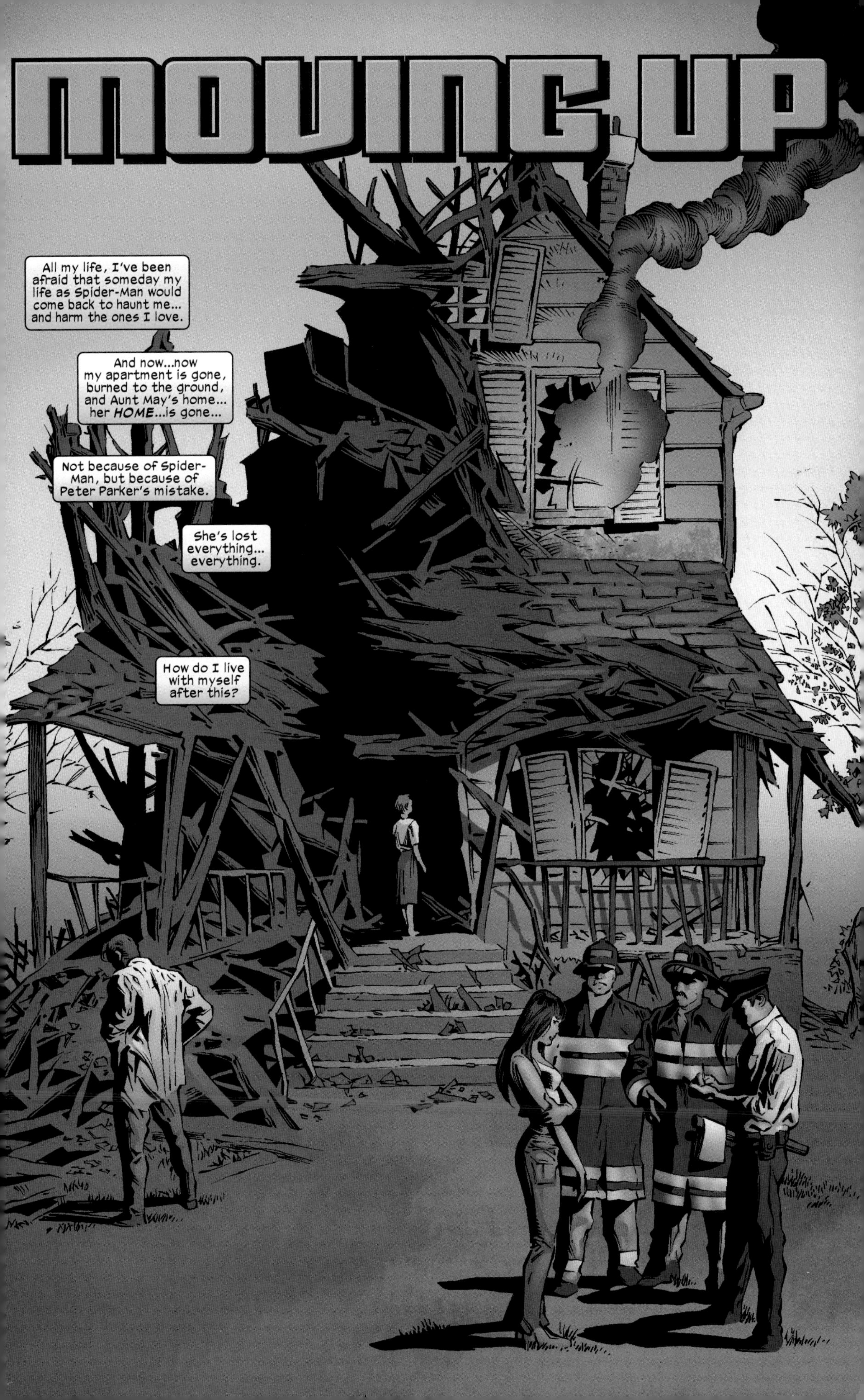
MOVING UP
All my life, I've been afraid that someday my life as Spider-Man would come back to haunt me... and harm the ones I love.
And now...now my apartment is gone, burned to the ground, and Aunt May's home... her HOME...is gone...
Not because of Spider-Man, but because of Peter Parker's mistake.
She's lost everything... everything.
How do I live with myself after this?

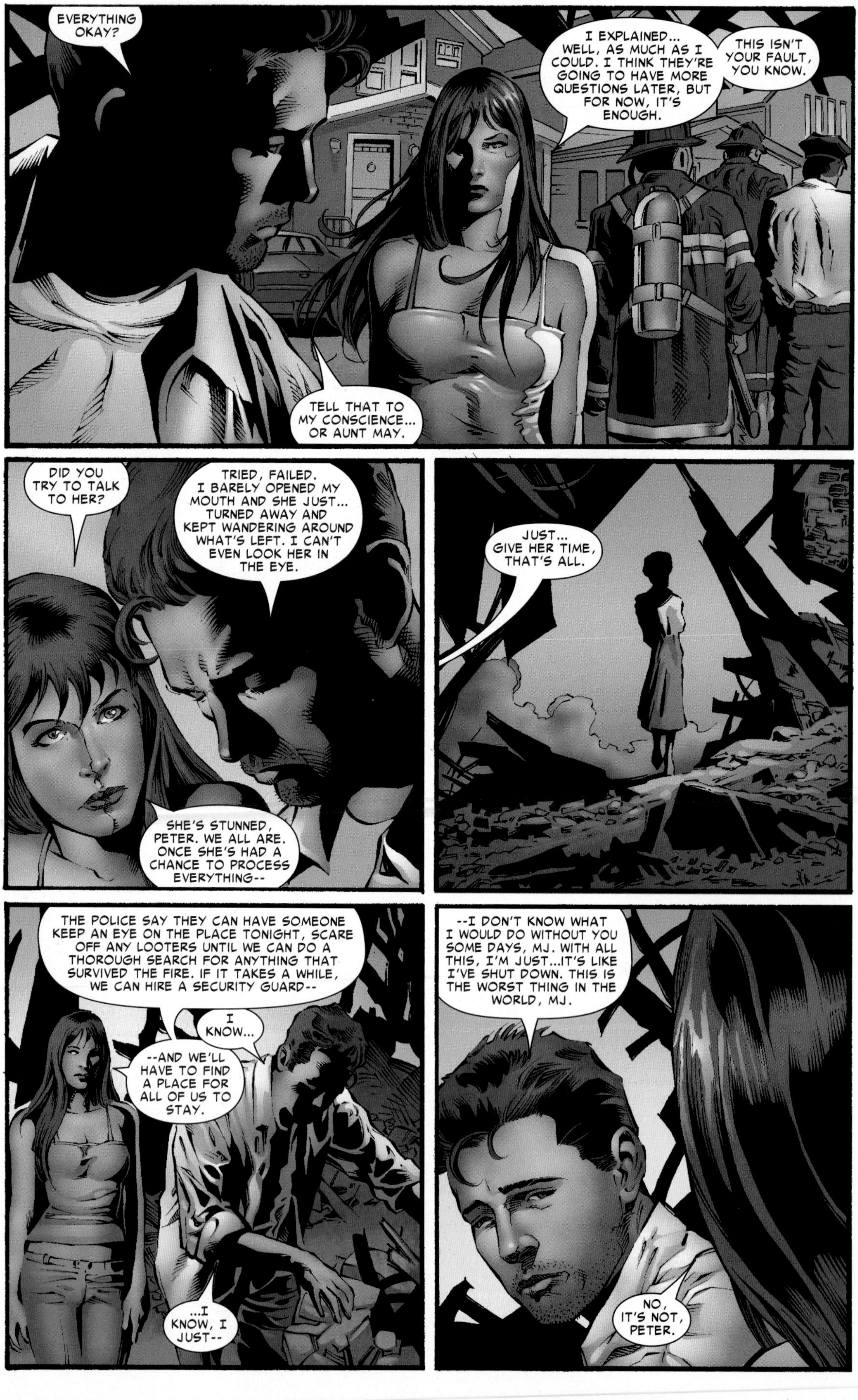
EVERYTHING OKAY?
I EXPLAINED... WELL, AS MUCH AS I COULD. I THINK THEY'RE GOING TO HAVE MORE QUESTIONS LATER, BUT FOR NOW, IT'S ENOUGH.
THIS ISN'T YOUR FAULT, YOU KNOW.
TELL THAT TO MY CONSCIENCE... OR AUNT MAY.
DID YOU TRY TO TALK TO HER?
TRIED, FAILED. I BARELY OPENED MY MOUTH AND SHE JUST... TURNED AWAY AND KEPT WANDERING AROUND WHAT'S LEFT. I CAN'T EVEN LOOK HER IN THE EYE.
SHE'S STUNNED, PETER. WE ALL ARE. ONCE SHE'S HAD A CHANCE TO PROCESS EVERYTHING--
JUST... GIVE HER TIME, THAT'S ALL.
THE POLICE SAY THEY CAN HAVE SOMEONE KEEP AN EYE ON THE PLACE TONIGHT, SCARE OFF ANY LOOTERS UNTIL WE CAN DO A THOROUGH SEARCH FOR ANYTHING THAT SURVIVED THE FIRE. IF IT TAKES A WHILE, WE CAN HIRE A SECURITY GUARD--
I KNOW...
--AND WE'LL HAVE TO FIND A PLACE FOR ALL OF US TO STAY.
...I KNOW, I JUST--
--I DON'T KNOW WHAT I WOULD DO WITHOUT YOU SOME DAYS, MJ. WITH ALL THIS, I'M JUST...IT'S LIKE I'VE SHUT DOWN. THIS IS THE WORST THING IN THE WORLD, MJ.
NO, IT'S NOT, PETER.

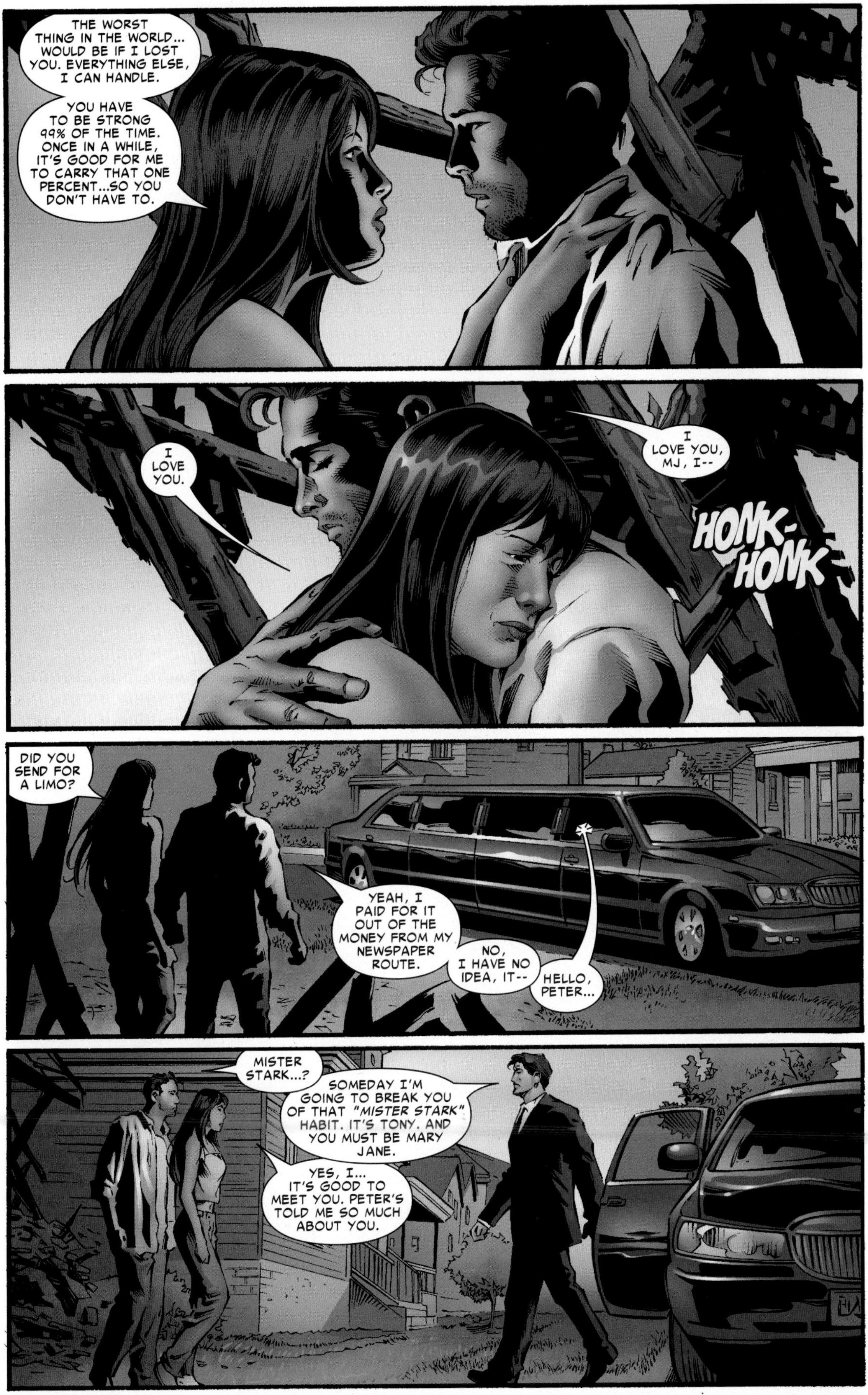
THE WORST THING IN THE WORLD... WOULD BE IF I LOST YOU. EVERYTHING ELSE, I CAN HANDLE.
YOU HAVE TO BE STRONG 99% OF THE TIME. ONCE IN A WHILE, IT'S GOOD FOR ME TO CARRY THAT ONE PERCENT...SO YOU DON'T HAVE TO.
I LOVE YOU.
I LOVE YOU, MJ, I--
HONK-HONK
DID YOU SEND FOR A LIMO?
YEAH, I PAID FOR IT OUT OF THE MONEY FROM MY NEWSPAPER ROUTE.
NO, I HAVE NO IDEA, IT--
HELLO, PETER...
MISTER STARK...?
SOMEDAY I'M GOING TO BREAK YOU OF THAT "MISTER STARK" HABIT. IT'S TONY. AND YOU MUST BE MARY JANE.
YES, I... IT'S GOOD TO MEET YOU. PETER'S TOLD ME SO MUCH ABOUT YOU.

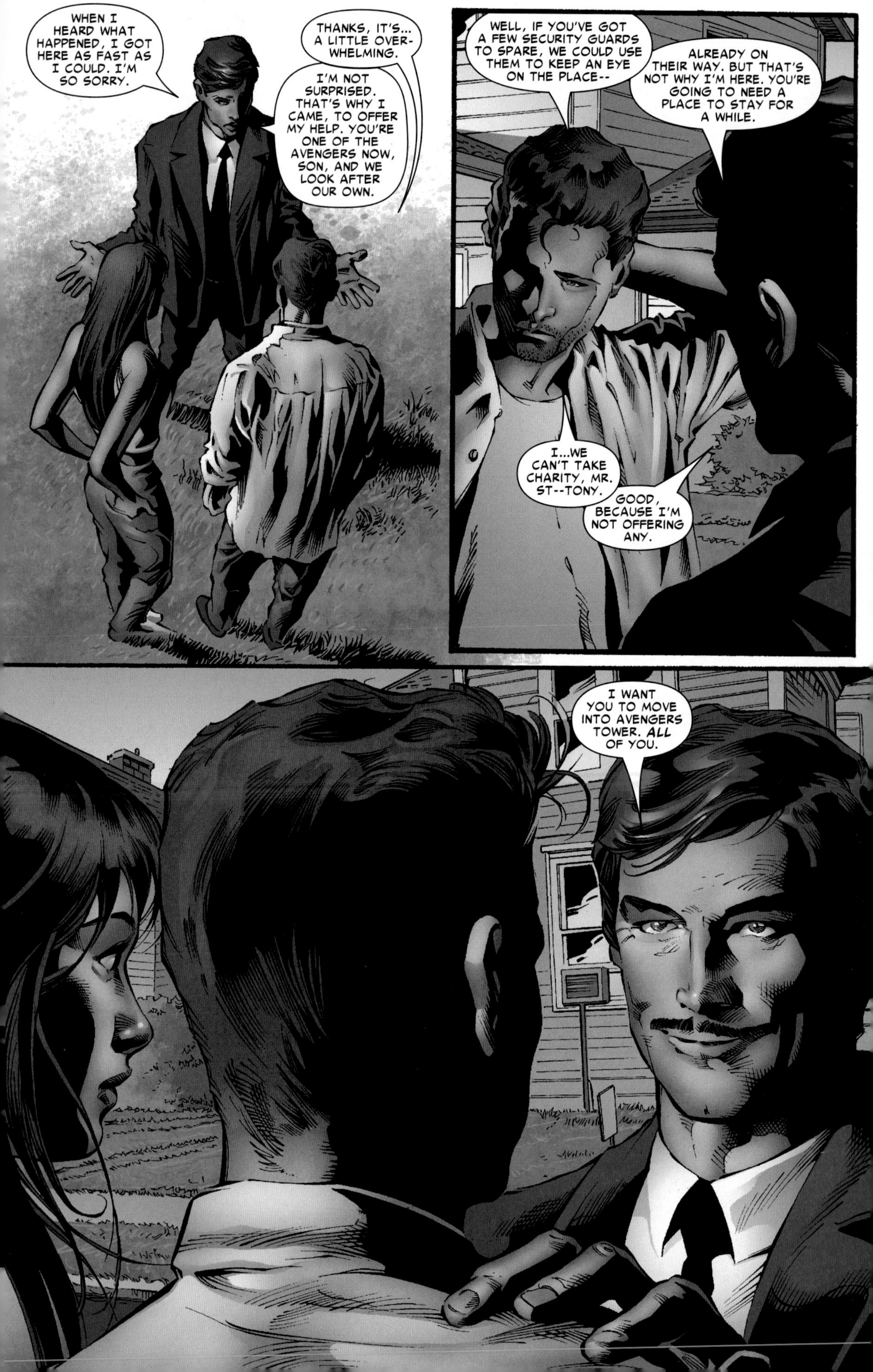
WHEN I HEARD WHAT HAPPENED, I GOT HERE AS FAST AS I COULD. I'M SO SORRY.
THANKS, IT'S... A LITTLE OVER-WHELMING.
I'M NOT SURPRISED. THAT'S WHY I CAME, TO OFFER MY HELP. YOU'RE ONE OF THE AVENGERS NOW, SON, AND WE LOOK AFTER OUR OWN.
WELL, IF YOU'VE GOT A FEW SECURITY GUARDS TO SPARE, WE COULD USE THEM TO KEEP AN EYE ON THE PLACE--
ALREADY ON THEIR WAY. BUT THAT'S NOT WHY I'M HERE. YOU'RE GOING TO NEED A PLACE TO STAY FOR A WHILE.
I...WE CAN'T TAKE CHARITY, MR. ST--TONY.
GOOD, BECAUSE I'M NOT OFFERING ANY.
I WANT YOU TO MOVE INTO AVENGERS TOWER. *ALL* OF YOU.

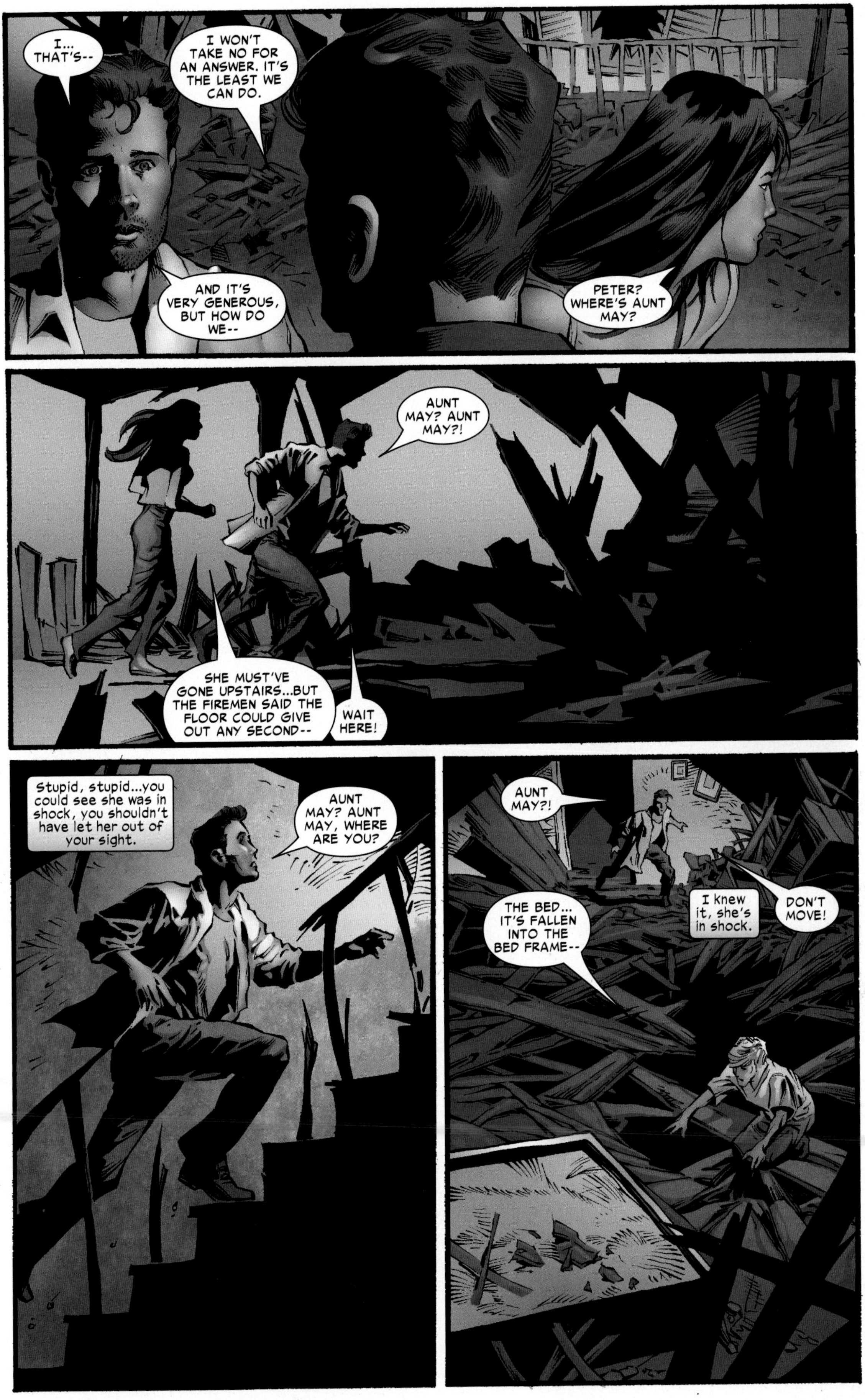
I... THAT'S--
I WON'T TAKE NO FOR AN ANSWER. IT'S THE LEAST WE CAN DO.
AND IT'S VERY GENEROUS, BUT HOW DO WE--
PETER? WHERE'S AUNT MAY?
AUNT MAY? AUNT MAY?!
SHE MUST'VE GONE UPSTAIRS...BUT THE FIREMEN SAID THE FLOOR COULD GIVE OUT ANY SECOND--
WAIT HERE!
Stupid, stupid...you could see she was in shock, you shouldn't have let her out of your sight.
AUNT MAY? AUNT MAY, WHERE ARE YOU?
AUNT MAY?!
THE BED... IT'S FALLEN INTO THE BED FRAME--
I knew it, she's in shock.
DON'T MOVE!

OKAY, NOW JUST STAY THERE, AND I'LL--

YOU HAVE TO HELP ME WITH THE BED.

THERE'S NOTHING TO CLEAN UP, AUNT MAY, NO POINT TO MAKING THE BED, IT'S GONE, IT'S--

PETER--

--I'M NOT SENILE, I'M NOT IN SHOCK, AND I KNOW WHAT I'M DOING. NOW PLEASE LIFT THE BED.

YES, MA'AM.

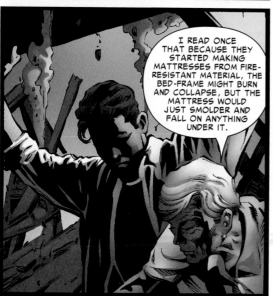

I READ ONCE THAT BECAUSE THEY STARTED MAKING MATTRESSES FROM FIRE-RESISTANT MATERIAL, THE BED-FRAME MIGHT BURN AND COLLAPSE, BUT THE MATTRESS WOULD JUST SMOLDER AND FALL ON ANYTHING UNDER IT.

AND THAT'S WHEN I DECIDED TO KEEP IT HERE... JUST IN CASE.

DECIDED TO KEEP WHAT HERE, AUNT MAY? I--

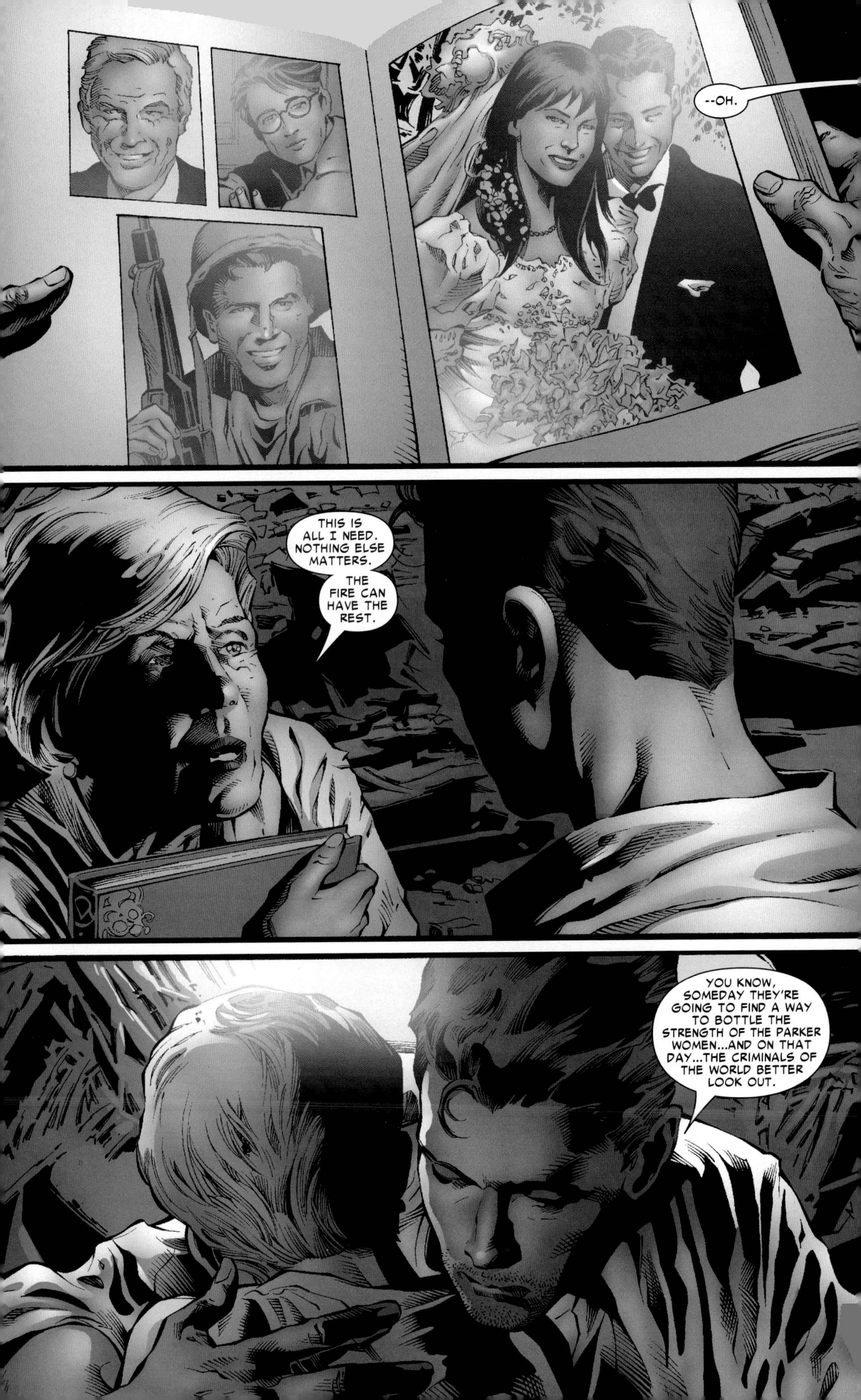
--OH.
THIS IS ALL I NEED. NOTHING ELSE MATTERS.
THE FIRE CAN HAVE THE REST.
YOU KNOW, SOMEDAY THEY'RE GOING TO FIND A WAY TO BOTTLE THE STRENGTH OF THE PARKER WOMEN...AND ON THAT DAY...THE CRIMINALS OF THE WORLD BETTER LOOK OUT.

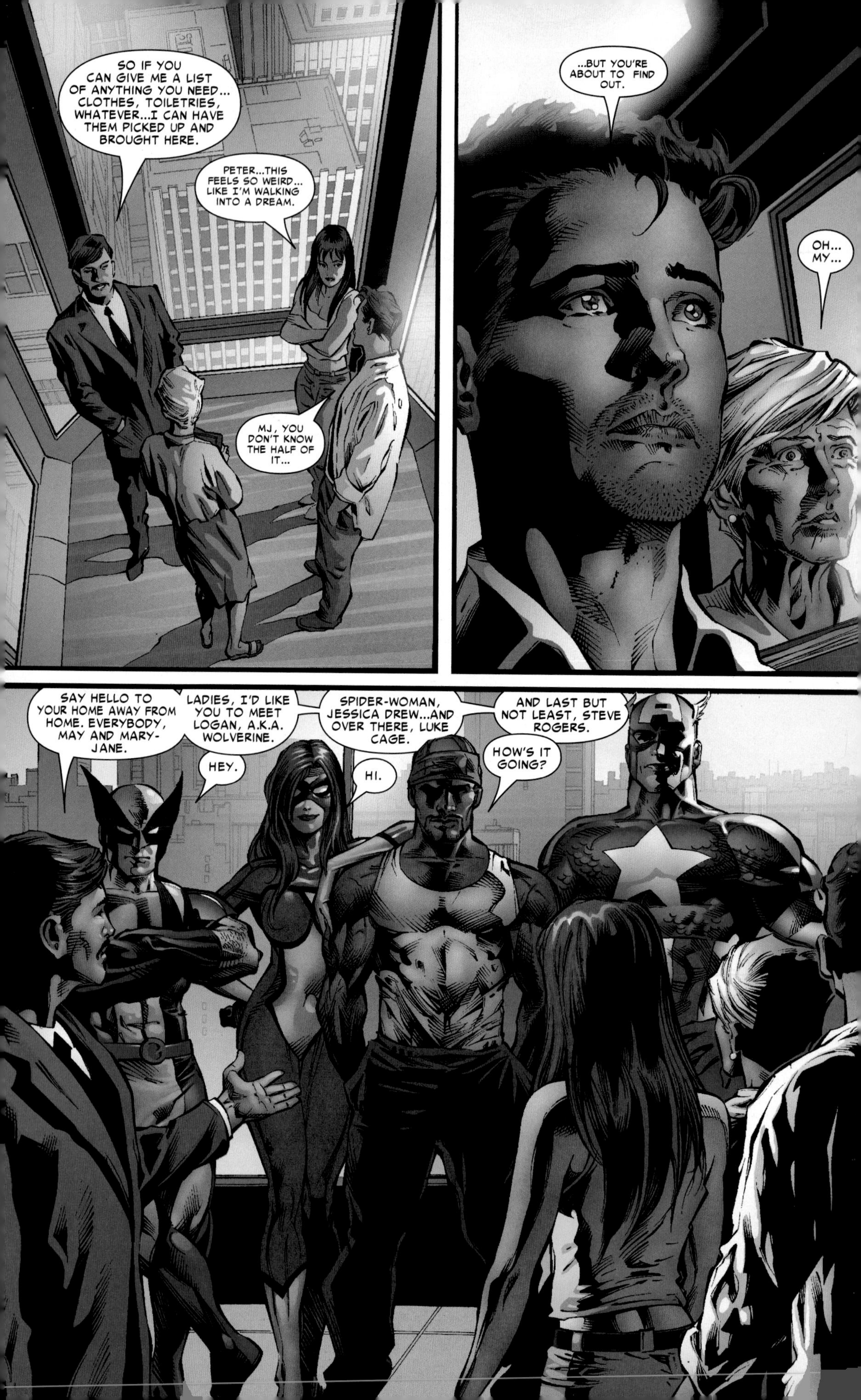
SO IF YOU CAN GIVE ME A LIST OF ANYTHING YOU NEED... CLOTHES, TOILETRIES, WHATEVER...I CAN HAVE THEM PICKED UP AND BROUGHT HERE.
PETER...THIS FEELS SO WEIRD... LIKE I'M WALKING INTO A DREAM.
MJ, YOU DON'T KNOW THE HALF OF IT...
...BUT YOU'RE ABOUT TO FIND OUT.
OH... MY...
SAY HELLO TO YOUR HOME AWAY FROM HOME. EVERYBODY, MAY AND MARY-JANE.
LADIES, I'D LIKE YOU TO MEET LOGAN, A.K.A. WOLVERINE.
HEY.
SPIDER-WOMAN, JESSICA DREW...AND OVER THERE, LUKE CAGE.
HI.
AND LAST BUT NOT LEAST, STEVE ROGERS.
HOW'S IT GOING?

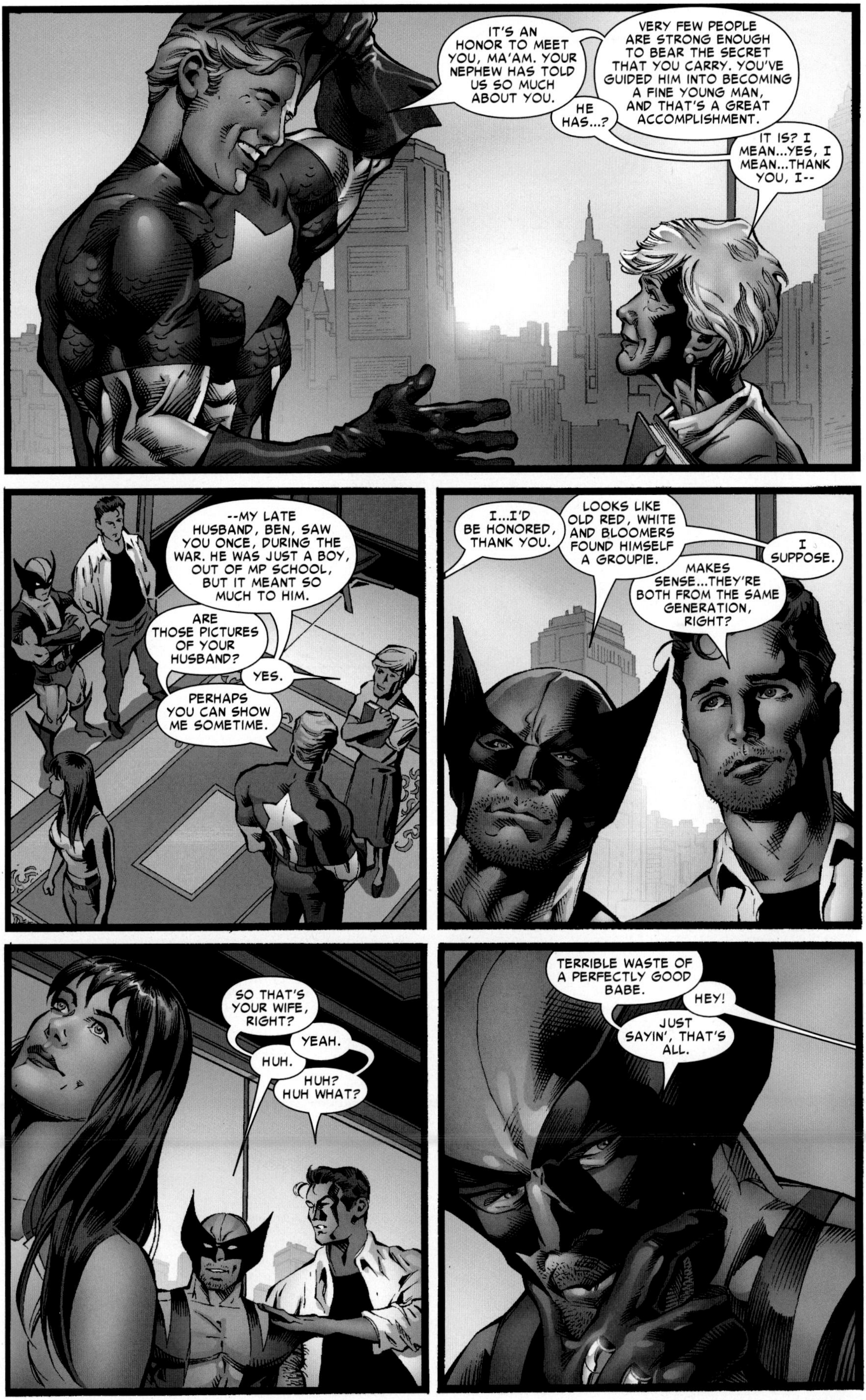
IT'S AN HONOR TO MEET YOU, MA'AM. YOUR NEPHEW HAS TOLD US SO MUCH ABOUT YOU.
HE HAS...?
VERY FEW PEOPLE ARE STRONG ENOUGH TO BEAR THE SECRET THAT YOU CARRY. YOU'VE GUIDED HIM INTO BECOMING A FINE YOUNG MAN, AND THAT'S A GREAT ACCOMPLISHMENT.
IT IS? I MEAN...YES, I MEAN...THANK YOU, I--
--MY LATE HUSBAND, BEN, SAW YOU ONCE, DURING THE WAR. HE WAS JUST A BOY, OUT OF MP SCHOOL, BUT IT MEANT SO MUCH TO HIM.
ARE THOSE PICTURES OF YOUR HUSBAND?
YES.
PERHAPS YOU CAN SHOW ME SOMETIME.
I...I'D BE HONORED, THANK YOU.
LOOKS LIKE OLD RED, WHITE AND BLOOMERS FOUND HIMSELF A GROUPIE.
I SUPPOSE.
MAKES SENSE...THEY'RE BOTH FROM THE SAME GENERATION, RIGHT?
SO THAT'S YOUR WIFE, RIGHT?
YEAH.
HUH.
HUH? HUH WHAT?
TERRIBLE WASTE OF A PERFECTLY GOOD BABE.
HEY!
JUST SAYIN', THAT'S ALL.

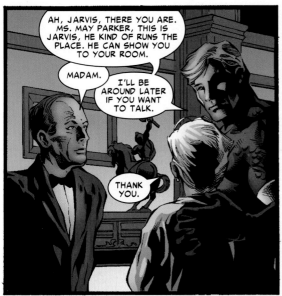

AH, JARVIS, THERE YOU ARE. MS. MAY PARKER, THIS IS JARVIS, HE KIND OF RUNS THE PLACE. HE CAN SHOW YOU TO YOUR ROOM.

MADAM.

I'LL BE AROUND LATER IF YOU WANT TO TALK.

THANK YOU.

IF YOU'LL COME THIS WAY. YOUR ROOM IS JUST DOWN THE HALL AND TO THE RIGHT.

THANK YOU... I'M AFRAID I'M SHAKING LIKE A LEAF. THESE PEOPLE, THEY--

WELL, THEY'RE JUST SO--

YES, AMAZING, AREN'T THEY?

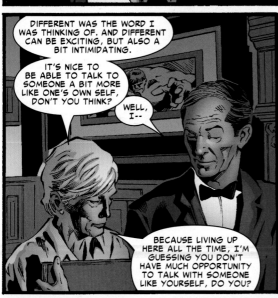

DIFFERENT WAS THE WORD I WAS THINKING OF. AND DIFFERENT CAN BE EXCITING, BUT ALSO A BIT INTIMIDATING.

IT'S NICE TO BE ABLE TO TALK TO SOMEONE A BIT MORE LIKE ONE'S OWN SELF, DON'T YOU THINK?

WELL, I--

BECAUSE LIVING UP HERE ALL THE TIME, I'M GUESSING YOU DON'T HAVE MUCH OPPORTUNITY TO TALK WITH SOMEONE LIKE YOURSELF, DO YOU?

TO TELL YOU THE TRUTH, MADAM, NO, I DON'T. AND IT'S QUITE REFRESHING, I MUST SAY, MS. PARKER.

PLEASE... CALL ME MAY.

OF COURSE.

"THIS IS OUR ROOM?"

YEAH... APPARENTLY TONY RAN OUT OF THE REALLY *NICE* ROOMS, SO WE'LL HAVE TO MAKE DO WITH THIS OLD THING.

WOW. IT'S JUST...

WOW. IT'S GORGEOUS.

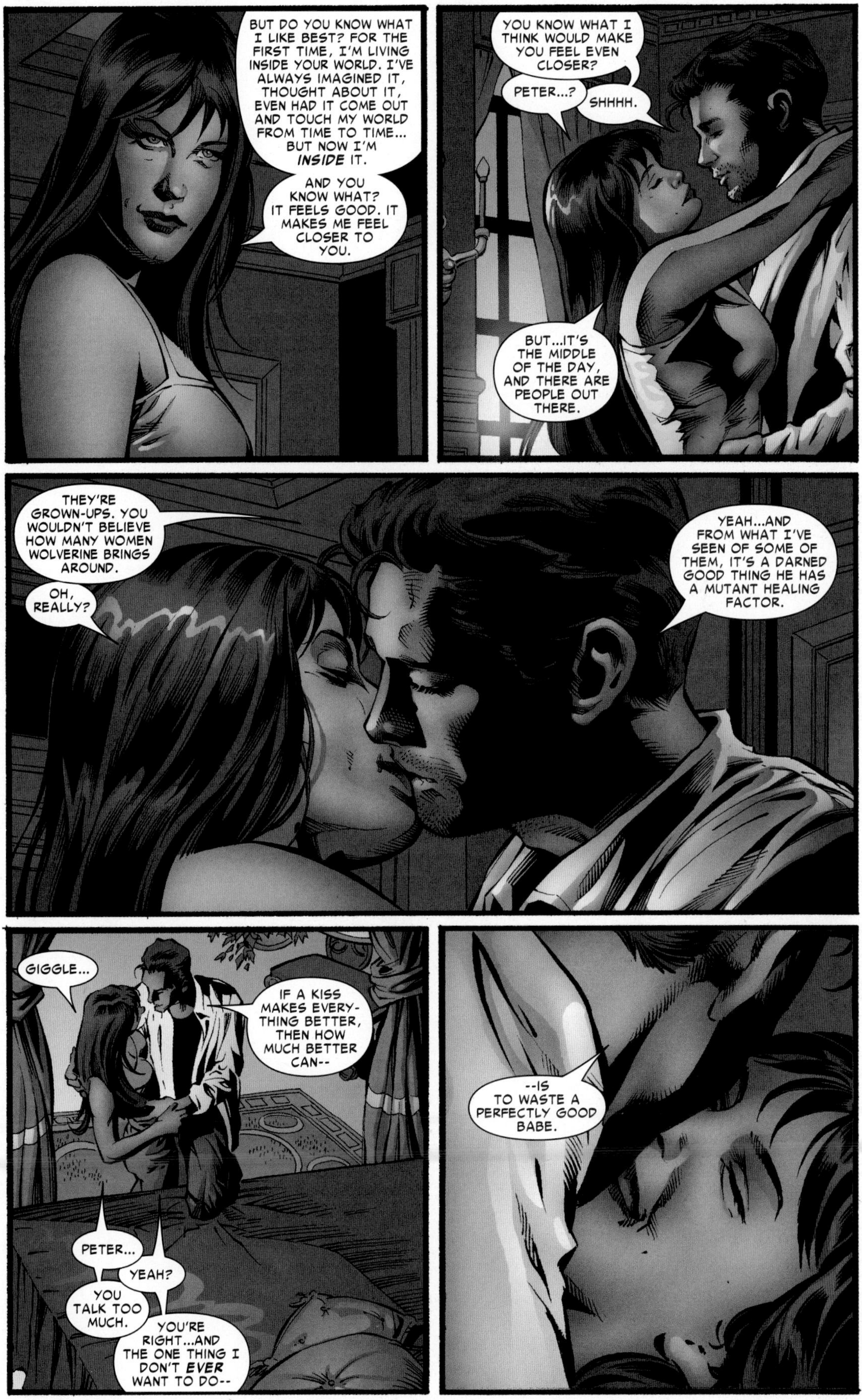

BUT DO YOU KNOW WHAT I LIKE BEST? FOR THE FIRST TIME, I'M LIVING INSIDE YOUR WORLD. I'VE ALWAYS IMAGINED IT, THOUGHT ABOUT IT, EVEN HAD IT COME OUT AND TOUCH MY WORLD FROM TIME TO TIME... BUT NOW I'M *INSIDE* IT.
AND YOU KNOW WHAT? IT FEELS GOOD. IT MAKES ME FEEL CLOSER TO YOU.
YOU KNOW WHAT I THINK WOULD MAKE YOU FEEL EVEN CLOSER?
PETER...?
SHHHH.
BUT...IT'S THE MIDDLE OF THE DAY, AND THERE ARE PEOPLE OUT THERE.
THEY'RE GROWN-UPS. YOU WOULDN'T BELIEVE HOW MANY WOMEN WOLVERINE BRINGS AROUND.
OH, REALLY?
YEAH...AND FROM WHAT I'VE SEEN OF SOME OF THEM, IT'S A DARNED GOOD THING HE HAS A MUTANT HEALING FACTOR.
GIGGLE...
IF A KISS MAKES EVERY-THING BETTER, THEN HOW MUCH BETTER CAN--
PETER...
YEAH?
YOU TALK TOO MUCH.
YOU'RE RIGHT...AND THE ONE THING I DON'T *EVER* WANT TO DO--
--IS TO WASTE A PERFECTLY GOOD BABE.

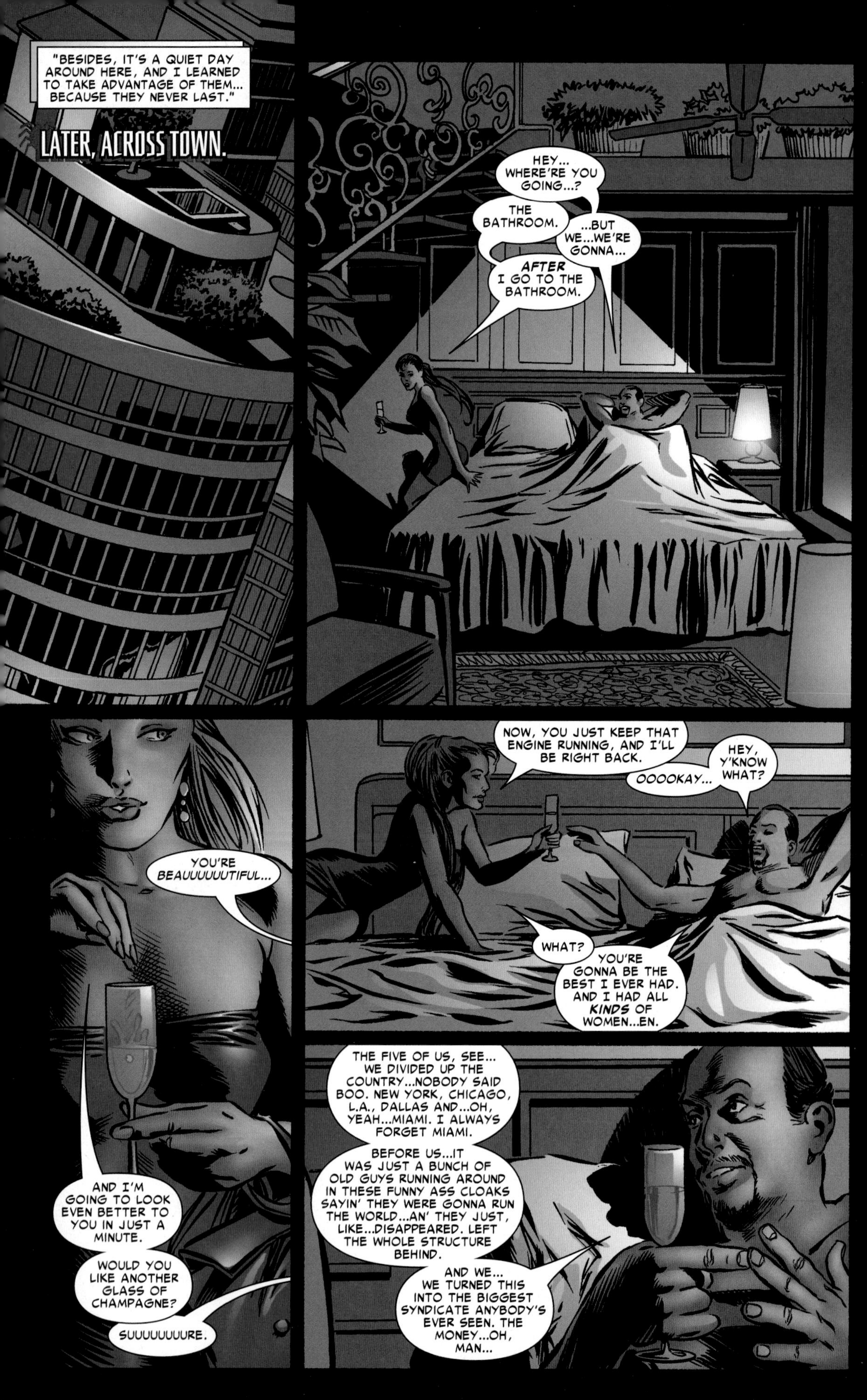
"BESIDES, IT'S A QUIET DAY AROUND HERE, AND I LEARNED TO TAKE ADVANTAGE OF THEM... BECAUSE THEY NEVER LAST."
LATER, ACROSS TOWN.
HEY... WHERE'RE YOU GOING...?
THE BATHROOM.
...BUT WE...WE'RE GONNA...
AFTER I GO TO THE BATHROOM.
YOU'RE BEAUUUUUUTIFUL...
AND I'M GOING TO LOOK EVEN BETTER TO YOU IN JUST A MINUTE.
WOULD YOU LIKE ANOTHER GLASS OF CHAMPAGNE?
SUUUUUUUURE.
NOW, YOU JUST KEEP THAT ENGINE RUNNING, AND I'LL BE RIGHT BACK.
OOOOKAY...
HEY, Y'KNOW WHAT?
WHAT?
YOU'RE GONNA BE THE BEST I EVER HAD. AND I HAD ALL KINDS OF WOMEN...EN.
THE FIVE OF US, SEE... WE DIVIDED UP THE COUNTRY...NOBODY SAID BOO. NEW YORK, CHICAGO, L.A., DALLAS AND...OH, YEAH...MIAMI. I ALWAYS FORGET MIAMI.
BEFORE US...IT WAS JUST A BUNCH OF OLD GUYS RUNNING AROUND IN THESE FUNNY ASS CLOAKS SAYIN' THEY WERE GONNA RUN THE WORLD...AN' THEY JUST, LIKE...DISAPPEARED. LEFT THE WHOLE STRUCTURE BEHIND.
AND WE... WE TURNED THIS INTO THE BIGGEST SYNDICATE ANYBODY'S EVER SEEN. THE MONEY...OH, MAN...

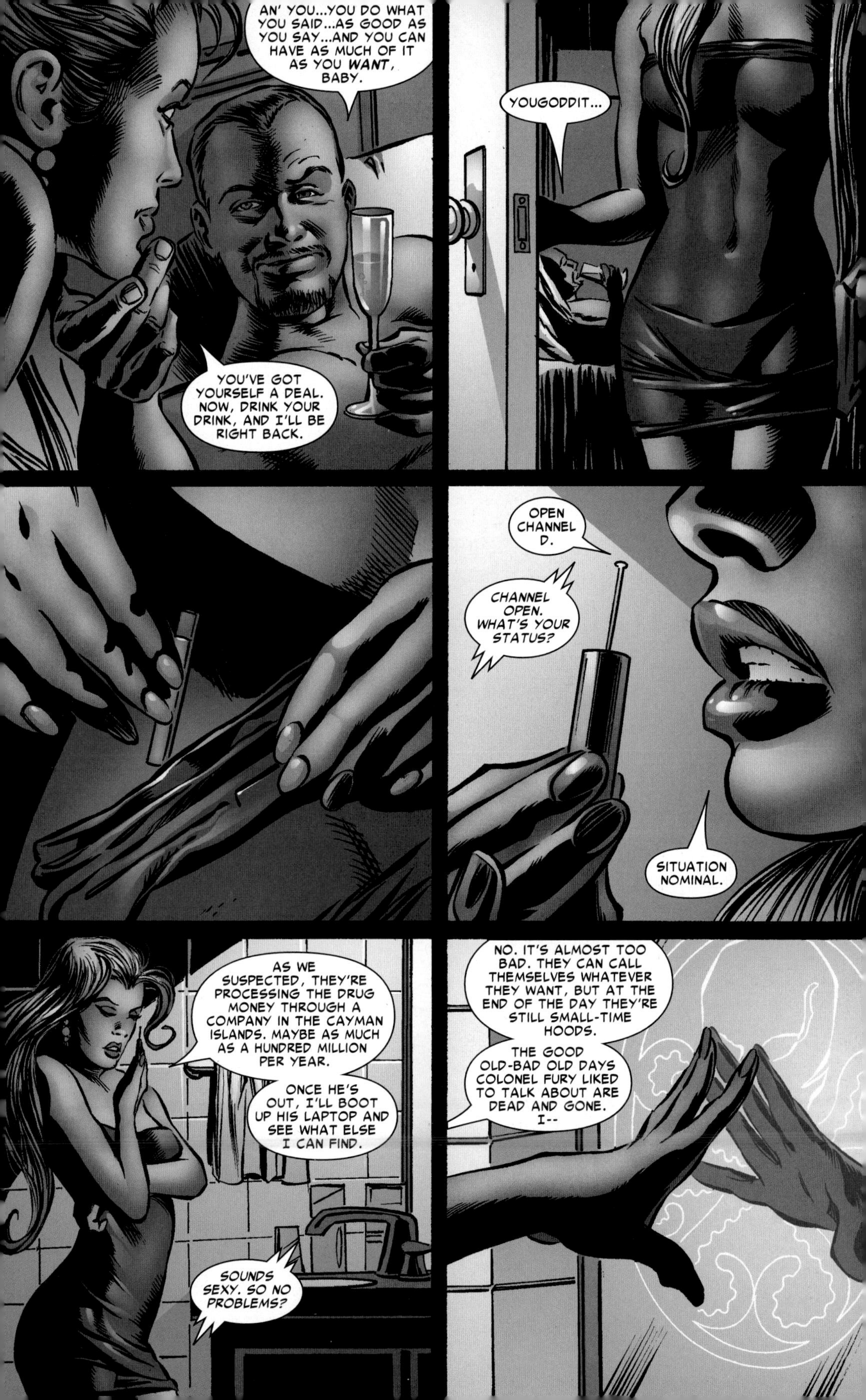

AN' YOU...YOU DO WHAT YOU SAID...AS GOOD AS YOU SAY...AND YOU CAN HAVE AS MUCH OF IT AS YOU *WANT*, BABY.
YOU'VE GOT YOURSELF A DEAL. NOW, DRINK YOUR DRINK, AND I'LL BE RIGHT BACK.
YOUGODDIT...
OPEN CHANNEL D.
CHANNEL OPEN. WHAT'S YOUR STATUS?
SITUATION NOMINAL.
AS WE SUSPECTED, THEY'RE PROCESSING THE DRUG MONEY THROUGH A COMPANY IN THE CAYMAN ISLANDS. MAYBE AS MUCH AS A HUNDRED MILLION PER YEAR.
ONCE HE'S OUT, I'LL BOOT UP HIS LAPTOP AND SEE WHAT ELSE I CAN FIND.
SOUNDS SEXY. SO NO PROBLEMS?
NO. IT'S ALMOST TOO BAD. THEY CAN CALL THEMSELVES WHATEVER THEY WANT, BUT AT THE END OF THE DAY THEY'RE STILL SMALL-TIME HOODS.
THE GOOD OLD-BAD OLD DAYS COLONEL FURY LIKED TO TALK ABOUT ARE DEAD AND GONE. I--

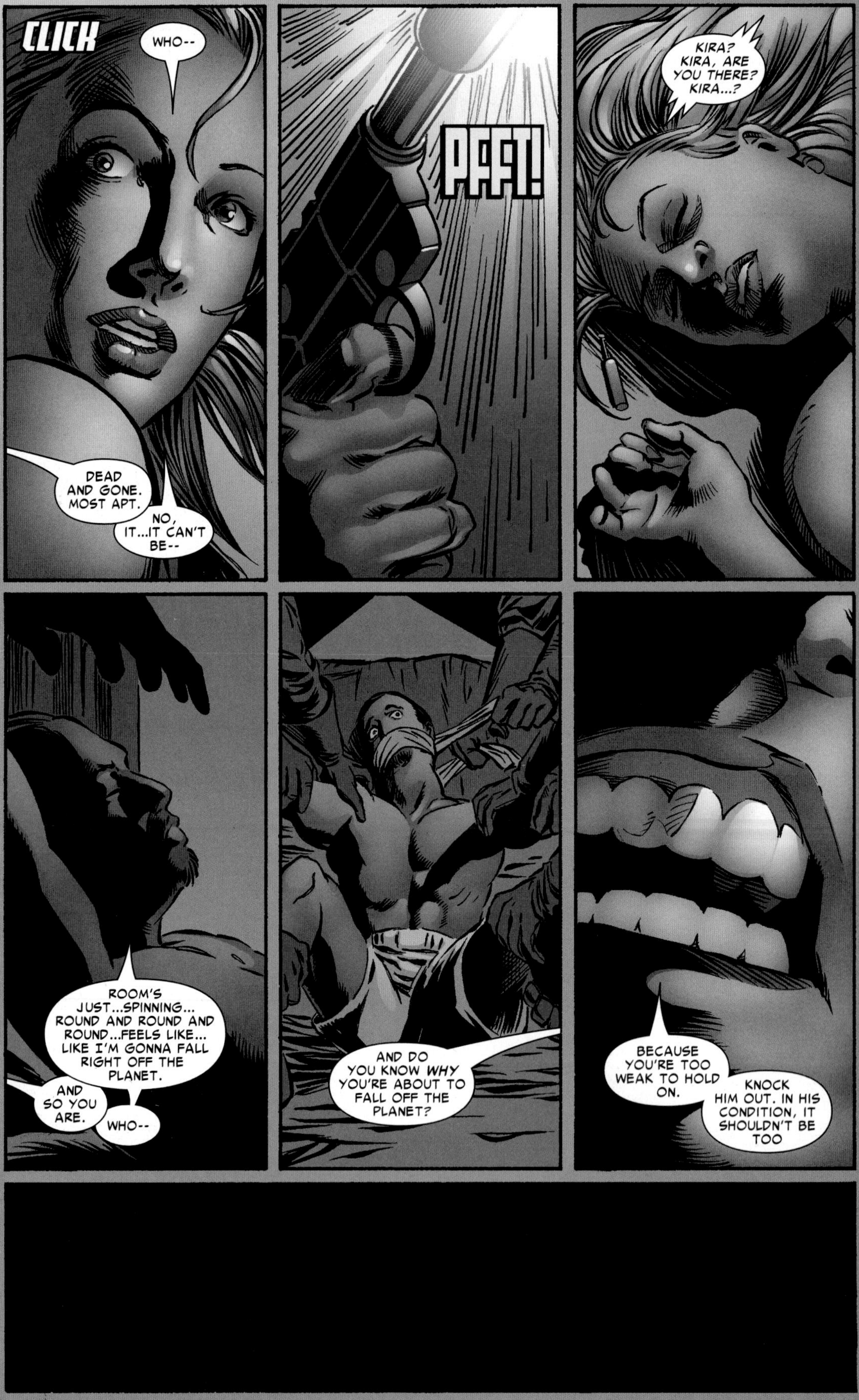
CLICK
WHO--
DEAD AND GONE. MOST APT.
NO, IT...IT CAN'T BE--
PFFT!
KIRA? KIRA, ARE YOU THERE? KIRA...?
ROOM'S JUST...SPINNING... ROUND AND ROUND AND ROUND...FEELS LIKE... LIKE I'M GONNA FALL RIGHT OFF THE PLANET.
AND SO YOU ARE.
WHO--
AND DO YOU KNOW WHY YOU'RE ABOUT TO FALL OFF THE PLANET?
BECAUSE YOU'RE TOO WEAK TO HOLD ON.
KNOCK HIM OUT. IN HIS CONDITION, IT SHOULDN'T BE TOO

...MMM MMMMMMF FFFFF...

MMM MMMMPP PHHH!

AH, I SEE THE LAST OF YOU IS AWAKE AT LAST.

NOW WE CAN BEGIN.

BY NOW, I'M SURE THAT EVEN THE SLOWEST OF YOU HAS COME TO REALIZE THAT YOU WILL NEVER LEAVE THIS ROOM ALIVE. THE QUESTION YOU CAN'T UNRAVEL IS--

--WHO IS DOING THIS TO YOU?

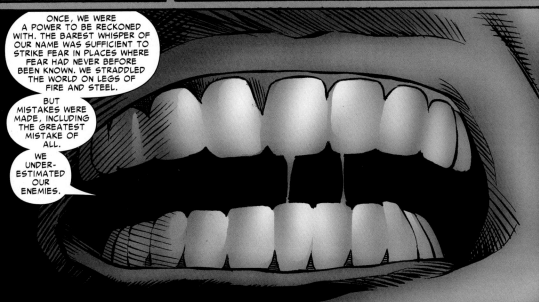

ONCE, WE WERE A POWER TO BE RECKONED WITH. THE BAREST WHISPER OF OUR NAME WAS SUFFICIENT TO STRIKE FEAR IN PLACES WHERE FEAR HAD NEVER BEFORE BEEN KNOWN. WE STRADDLED THE WORLD ON LEGS OF FIRE AND STEEL.

BUT MISTAKES WERE MADE, INCLUDING THE GREATEST MISTAKE OF ALL.

WE UNDER-ESTIMATED OUR ENEMIES.

WE WERE DEFEATED, REPEATEDLY, AND WITH DEFEAT COMES A LOSS OF RESPECT, A TERMINUS OF FEAR.

IN FIGHTING BACK, WE EXHAUSTED OUR RESOURCES, BECAUSE WE HAD NOT COMPENSATED FOR THE STRENGTH OF OUR OPPOSITION. IN THE END, WE HAD ONLY TWO CHOICES.

TERMINATION...OR TRANSFORMATION.

THUS...WE DISAPPEARED--

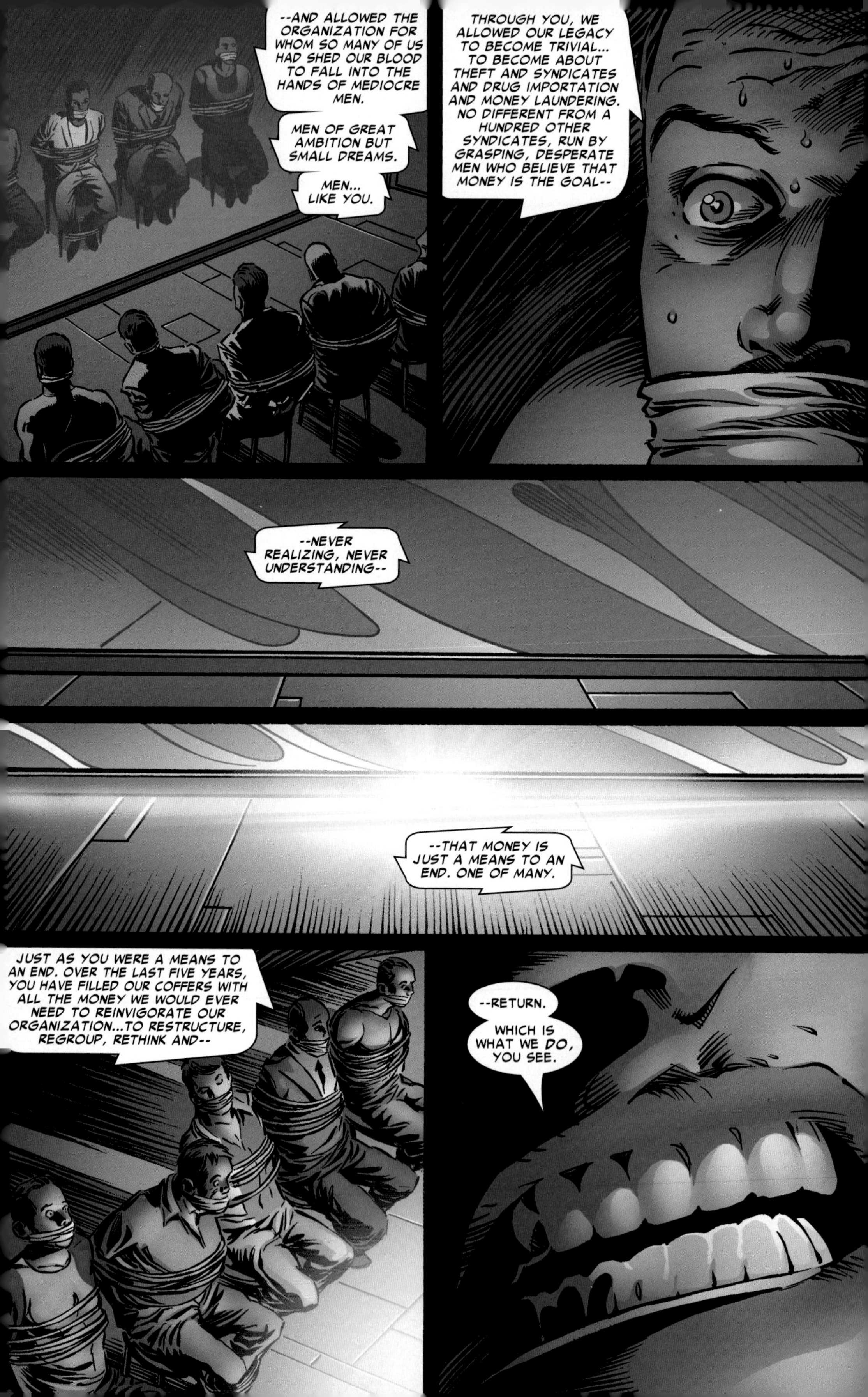
--AND ALLOWED THE ORGANIZATION FOR WHOM SO MANY OF US HAD SHED OUR BLOOD TO FALL INTO THE HANDS OF MEDIOCRE MEN.
MEN OF GREAT AMBITION BUT SMALL DREAMS.
MEN... LIKE YOU.
THROUGH YOU, WE ALLOWED OUR LEGACY TO BECOME TRIVIAL... TO BECOME ABOUT THEFT AND SYNDICATES AND DRUG IMPORTATION AND MONEY LAUNDERING. NO DIFFERENT FROM A HUNDRED OTHER SYNDICATES, RUN BY GRASPING, DESPERATE MEN WHO BELIEVE THAT MONEY IS THE GOAL--
--NEVER REALIZING, NEVER UNDERSTANDING--
--THAT MONEY IS JUST A MEANS TO AN END. ONE OF MANY.
JUST AS YOU WERE A MEANS TO AN END. OVER THE LAST FIVE YEARS, YOU HAVE FILLED OUR COFFERS WITH ALL THE MONEY WE WOULD EVER NEED TO REINVIGORATE OUR ORGANIZATION...TO RESTRUCTURE, REGROUP, RETHINK AND--
--RETURN.
WHICH IS WHAT WE DO, YOU SEE.

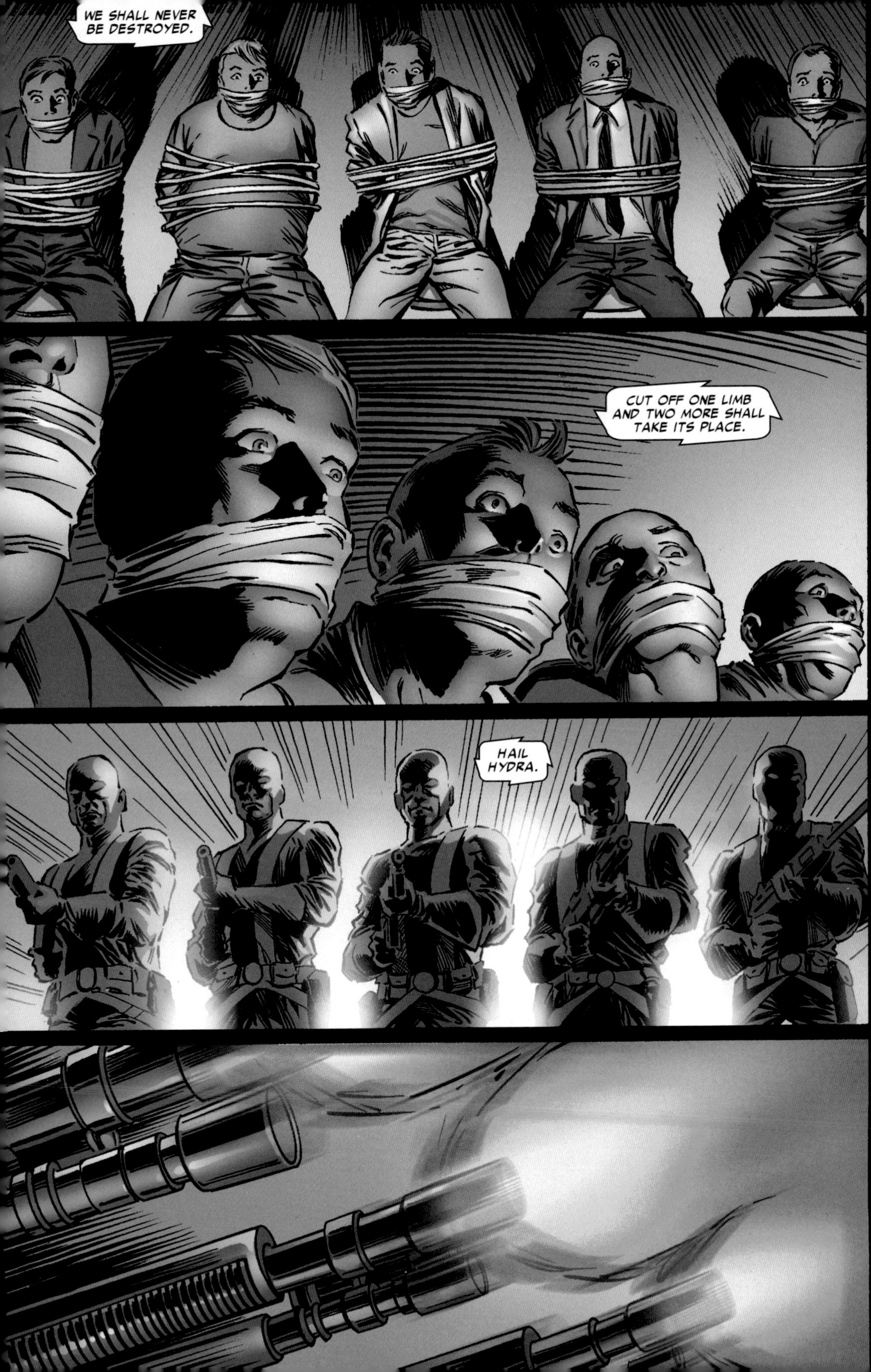
WE SHALL NEVER BE DESTROYED.
CUT OFF ONE LIMB AND TWO MORE SHALL TAKE ITS PLACE.
HAIL HYDRA.

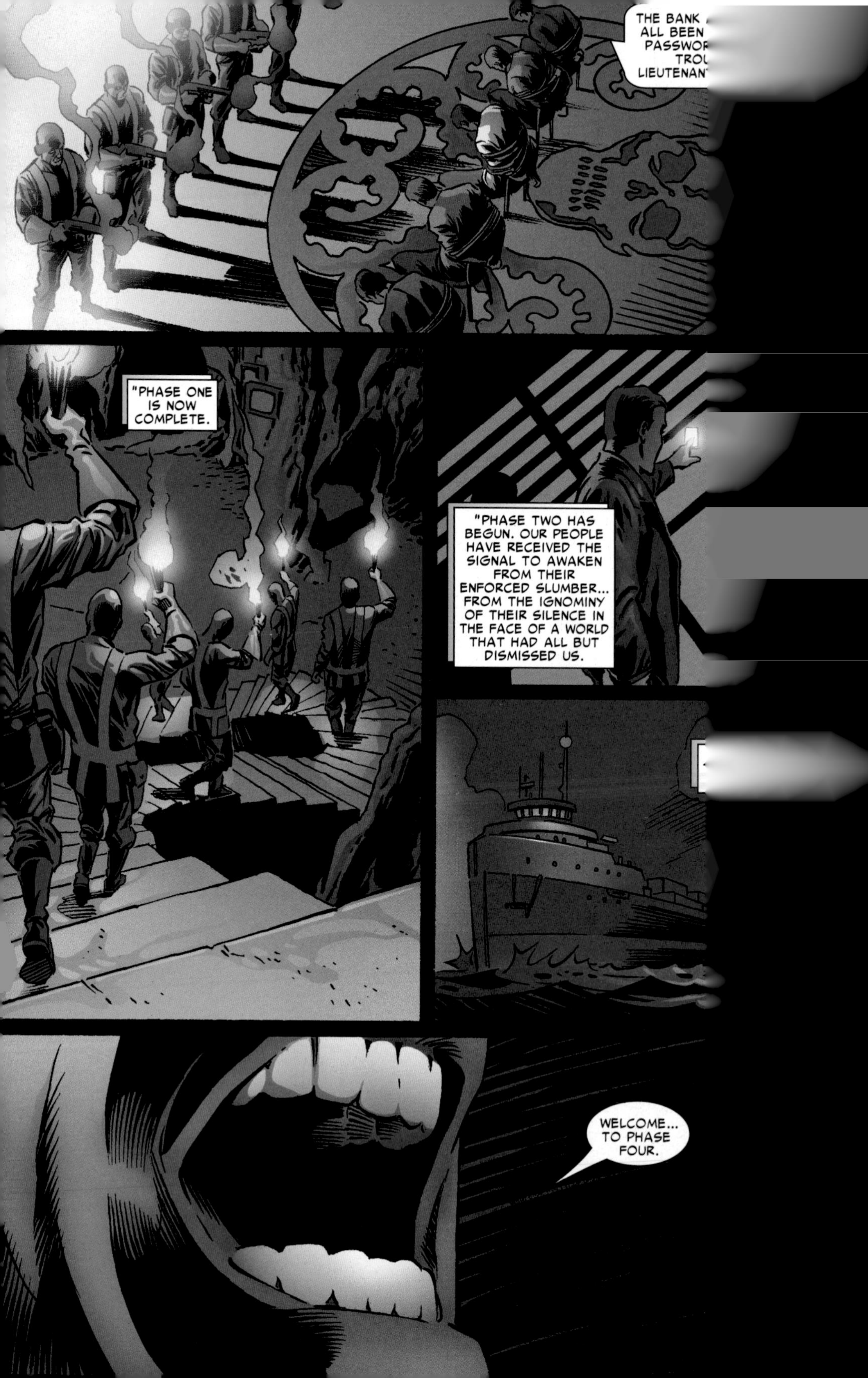
THE BANK
ALL BEEN
PASSWOR
TROU
LIEUTENANT
"PHASE ONE IS NOW COMPLETE.
"PHASE TWO HAS BEGUN. OUR PEOPLE HAVE RECEIVED THE SIGNAL TO AWAKEN FROM THEIR ENFORCED SLUMBER... FROM THE IGNOMINY OF THEIR SILENCE IN THE FACE OF A WORLD THAT HAD ALL BUT DISMISSED US.
WELCOME... TO PHASE FOUR.

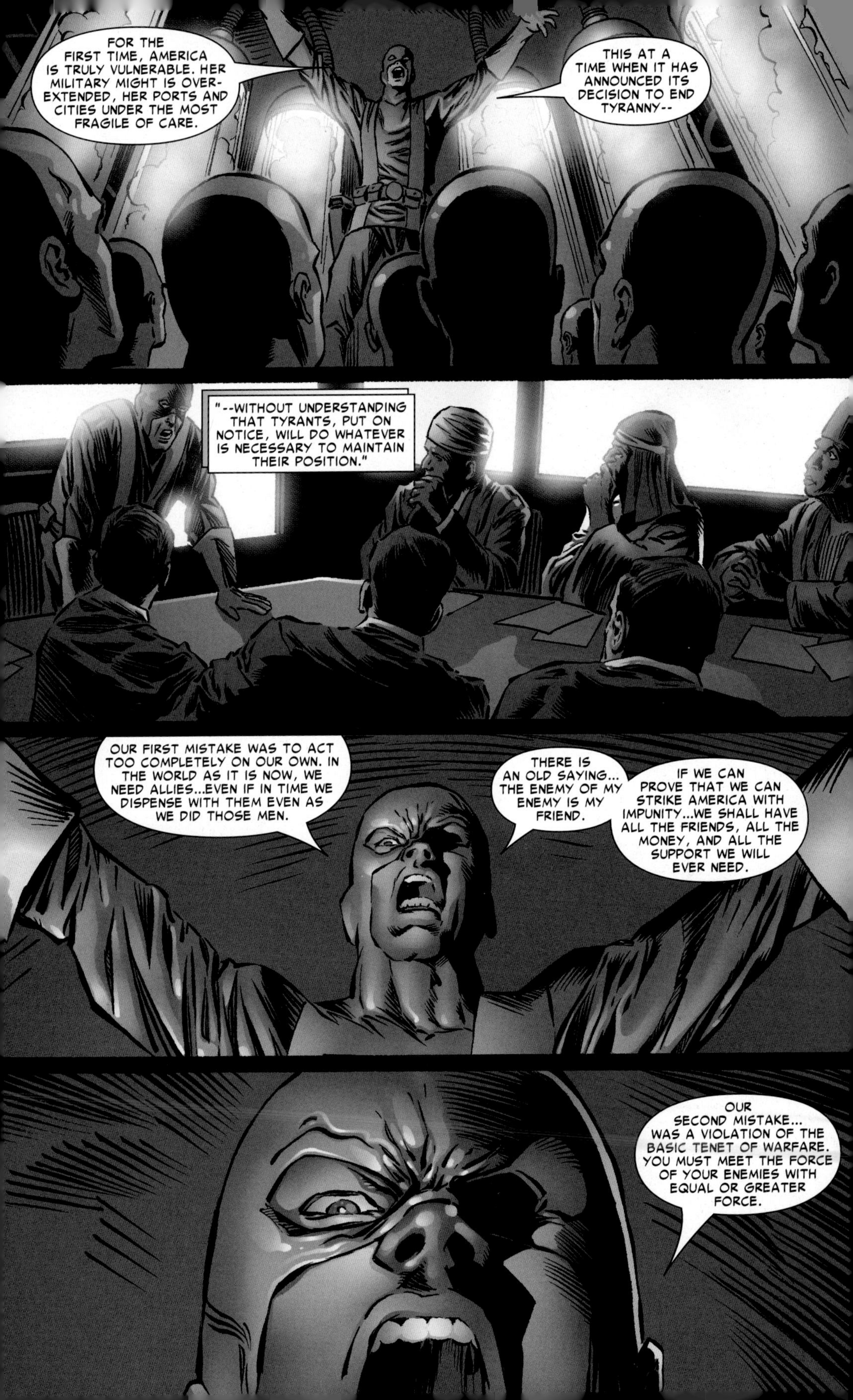

FOR THE FIRST TIME, AMERICA IS TRULY VULNERABLE. HER MILITARY MIGHT IS OVER-EXTENDED, HER PORTS AND CITIES UNDER THE MOST FRAGILE OF CARE.
THIS AT A TIME WHEN IT HAS ANNOUNCED ITS DECISION TO END TYRANNY--
"--WITHOUT UNDERSTANDING THAT TYRANTS, PUT ON NOTICE, WILL DO WHATEVER IS NECESSARY TO MAINTAIN THEIR POSITION."
OUR FIRST MISTAKE WAS TO ACT TOO COMPLETELY ON OUR OWN. IN THE WORLD AS IT IS NOW, WE NEED ALLIES...EVEN IF IN TIME WE DISPENSE WITH THEM EVEN AS WE DID THOSE MEN.
THERE IS AN OLD SAYING... THE ENEMY OF MY ENEMY IS MY FRIEND.
IF WE CAN PROVE THAT WE CAN STRIKE AMERICA WITH IMPUNITY...WE SHALL HAVE ALL THE FRIENDS, ALL THE MONEY, AND ALL THE SUPPORT WE WILL EVER NEED.
OUR SECOND MISTAKE... WAS A VIOLATION OF THE BASIC TENET OF WARFARE. YOU MUST MEET THE FORCE OF YOUR ENEMIES WITH EQUAL OR GREATER FORCE.

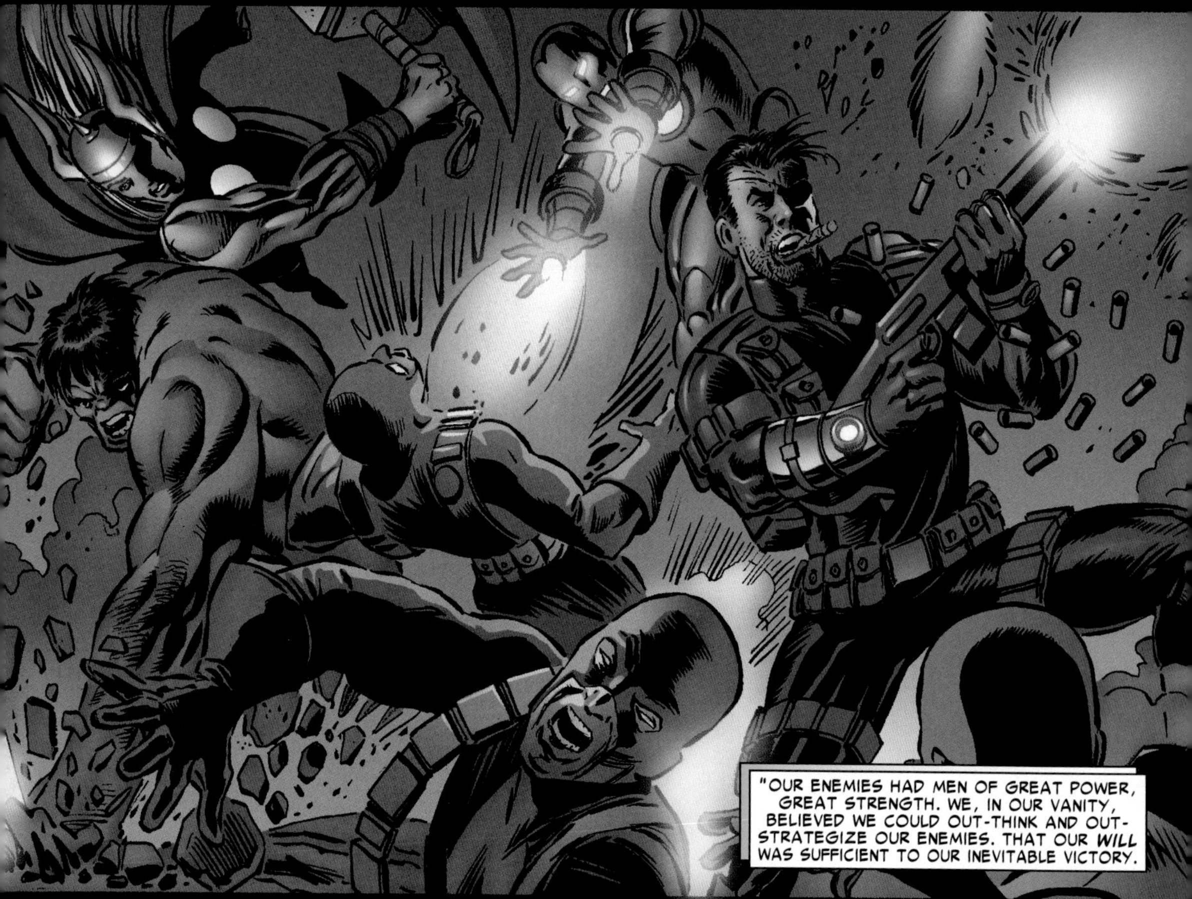
"OUR ENEMIES HAD MEN OF GREAT POWER, GREAT STRENGTH. WE, IN OUR VANITY, BELIEVED WE COULD OUT-THINK AND OUT-STRATEGIZE OUR ENEMIES. THAT OUR *WILL* WAS SUFFICIENT TO OUR INEVITABLE VICTORY.

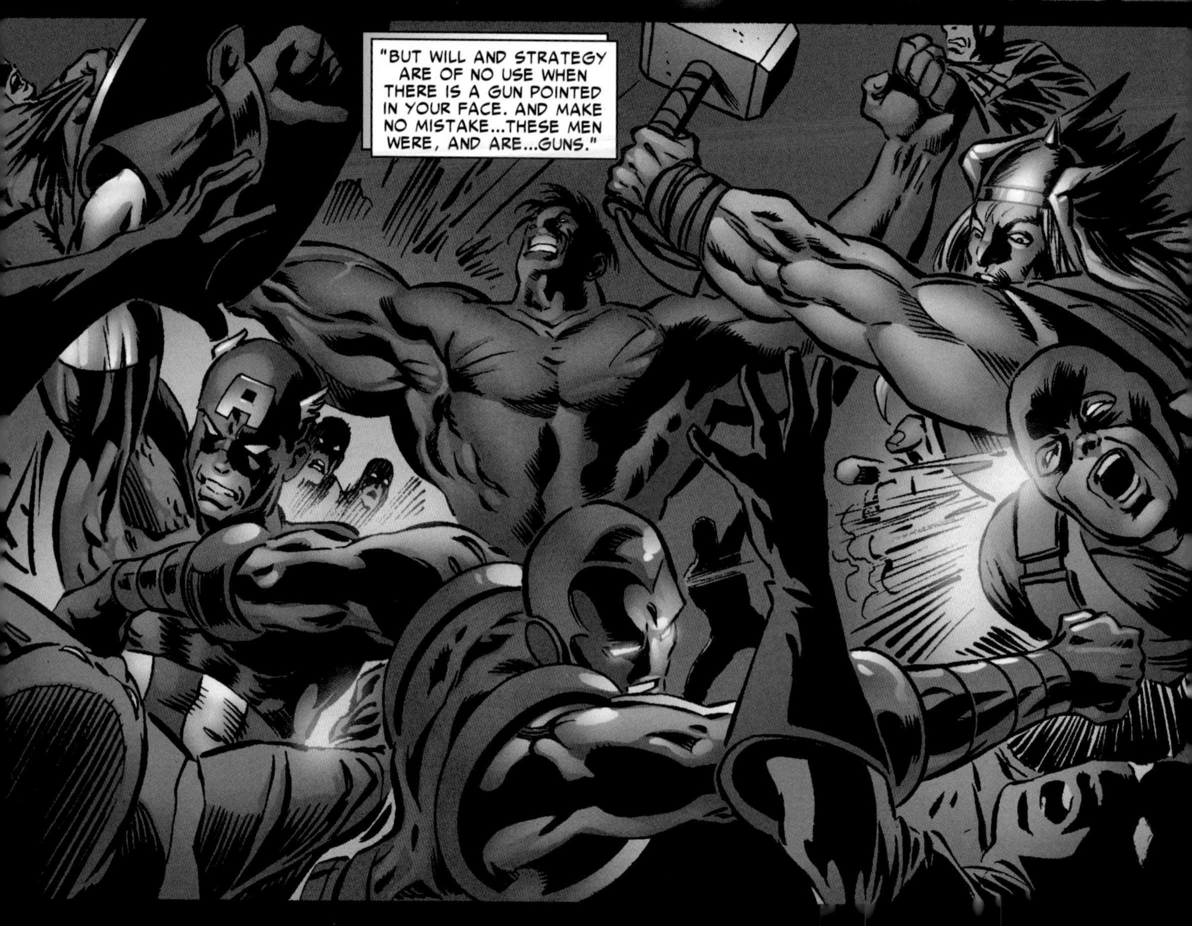
"BUT WILL AND STRATEGY ARE OF NO USE WHEN THERE IS A GUN POINTED IN YOUR FACE. AND MAKE NO MISTAKE...THESE MEN WERE, AND ARE...GUNS."

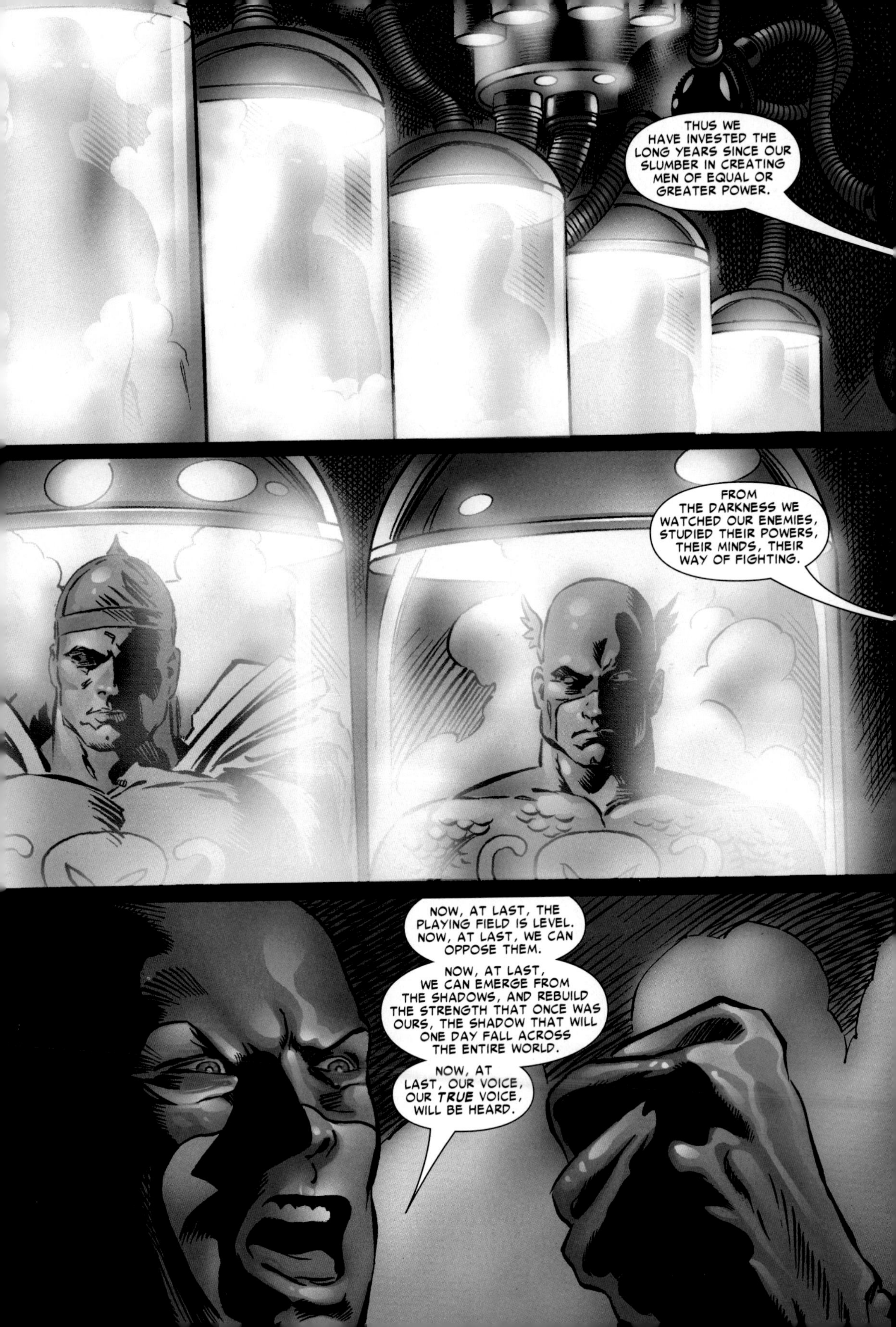
THUS WE HAVE INVESTED THE LONG YEARS SINCE OUR SLUMBER IN CREATING MEN OF EQUAL OR GREATER POWER.
FROM THE DARKNESS WE WATCHED OUR ENEMIES, STUDIED THEIR POWERS, THEIR MINDS, THEIR WAY OF FIGHTING.
NOW, AT LAST, THE PLAYING FIELD IS LEVEL. NOW, AT LAST, WE CAN OPPOSE THEM.
NOW, AT LAST, WE CAN EMERGE FROM THE SHADOWS, AND REBUILD THE STRENGTH THAT ONCE WAS OURS, THE SHADOW THAT WILL ONE DAY FALL ACROSS THE ENTIRE WORLD.
NOW, AT LAST, OUR VOICE, OUR *TRUE* VOICE, WILL BE HEARD.

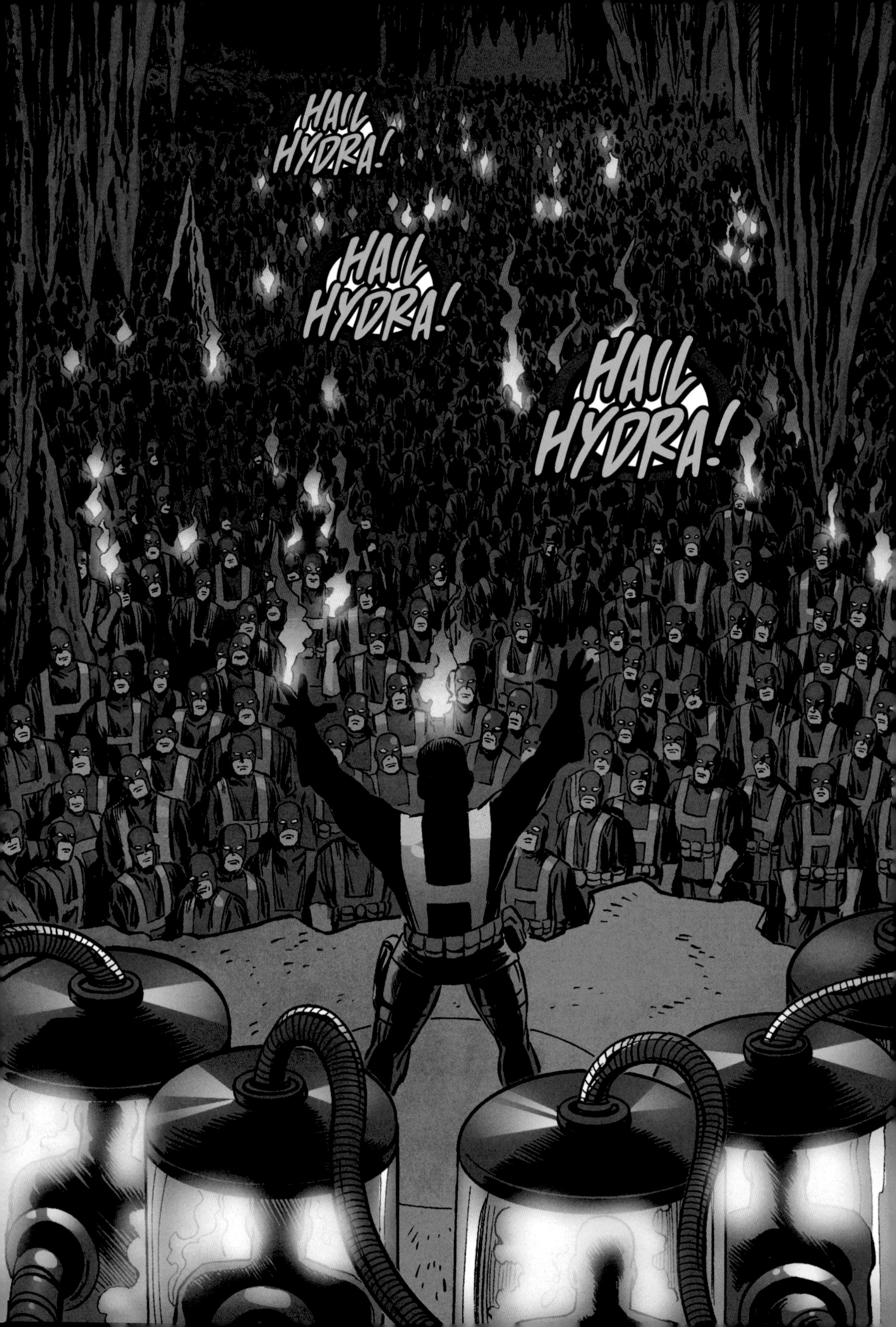
HAIL HYDRA!
HAIL HYDRA!
HAIL HYDRA!

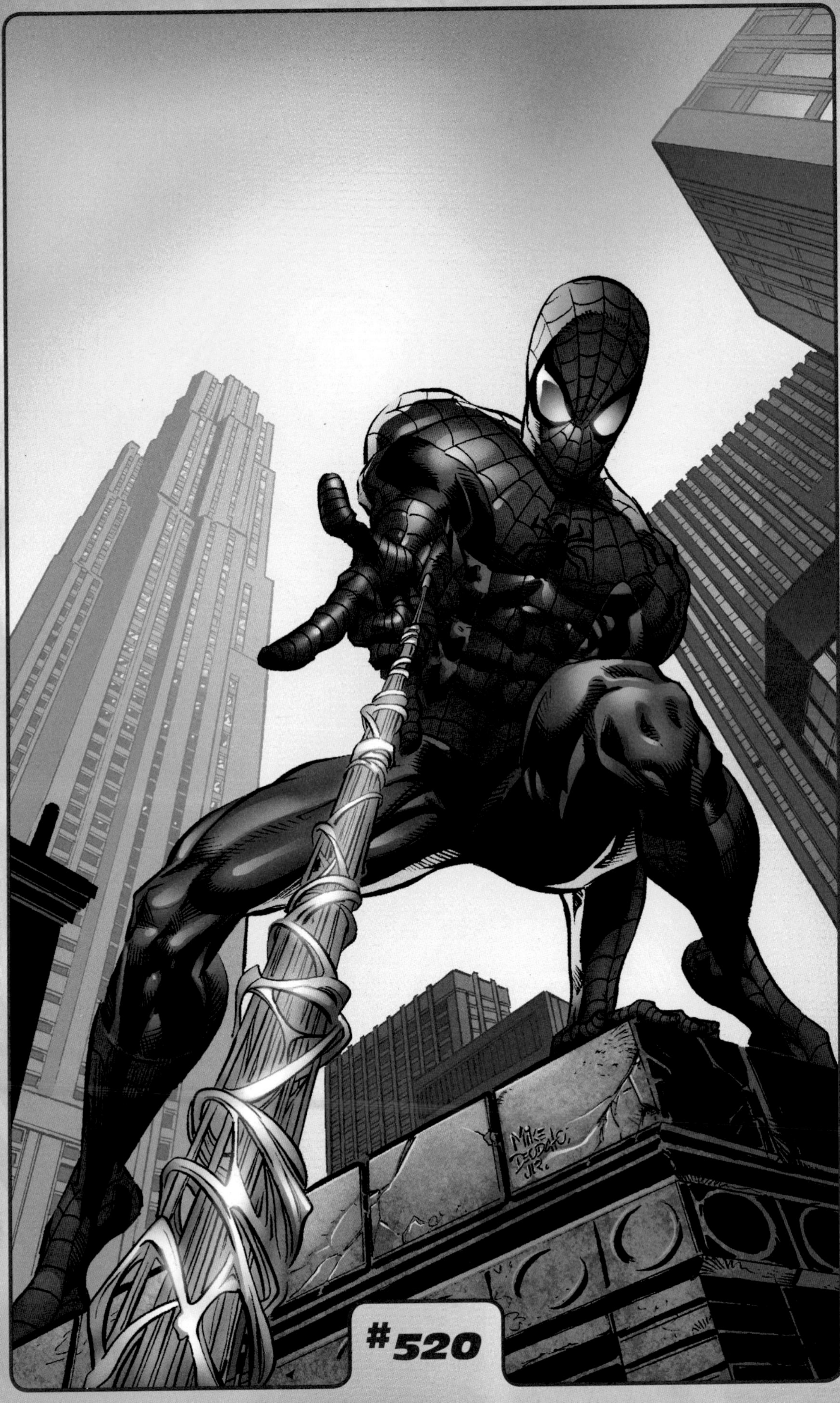
MIKE DEODATO JR.
#520

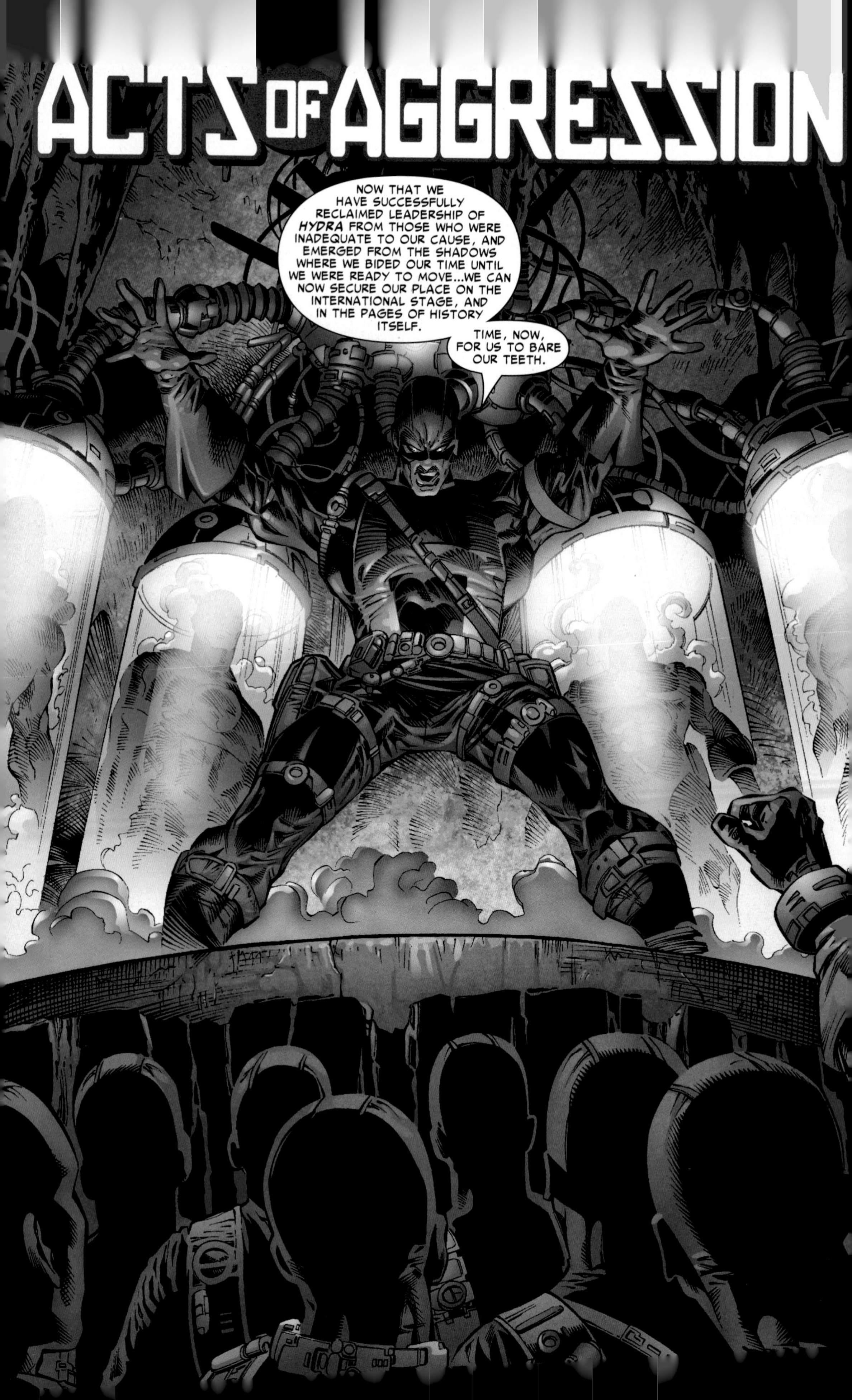
ACTS OF AGGRESSION
NOW THAT WE HAVE SUCCESSFULLY RECLAIMED LEADERSHIP OF HYDRA FROM THOSE WHO WERE INADEQUATE TO OUR CAUSE, AND EMERGED FROM THE SHADOWS WHERE WE BIDED OUR TIME UNTIL WE WERE READY TO MOVE...WE CAN NOW SECURE OUR PLACE ON THE INTERNATIONAL STAGE, AND IN THE PAGES OF HISTORY ITSELF.
TIME, NOW, FOR US TO BARE OUR TEETH.

AND THIS TIME, WE HAVE THE TACTICAL POWER TO SUPPORT OUR STRATEGIC AIMS.

UNLOCK TUBES ONE THROUGH FOUR.

FOUR TARGETS...AND FOUR FISTS TO STRIKE ON OUR BEHALF.

EACH THE RESULT OF MILLIONS OF DOLLARS IN WEAPONS DEVELOPMENT, AND YEARS OF RESEARCH INTO OUR ENEMIES.

FORCE AGAINST FORCE. IT IS THE OLDEST PRINCIPLE OF MARTIAL ARTS, AND THE CENTRAL RULE OF PHYSICS.

FOR EVERY ACTION, THERE IS AN EQUAL AND OPPOSITE REACTION.

MEET OUR FORCE. OUR REACTION. OUR... WARRIORS. HAIL HYDRA!

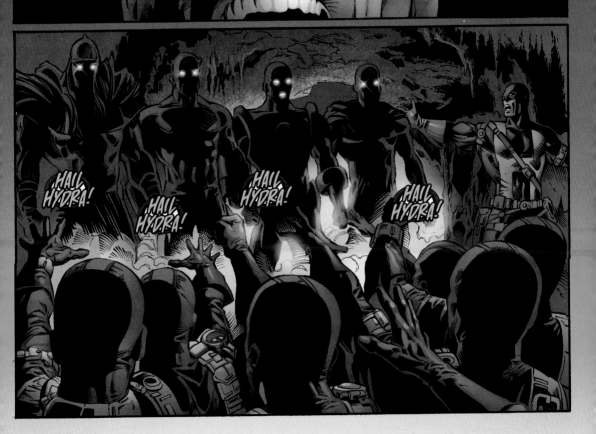

HAIL HYDRA!

HAIL HYDRA!

HAIL HYDRA!

HAIL HYDRA!

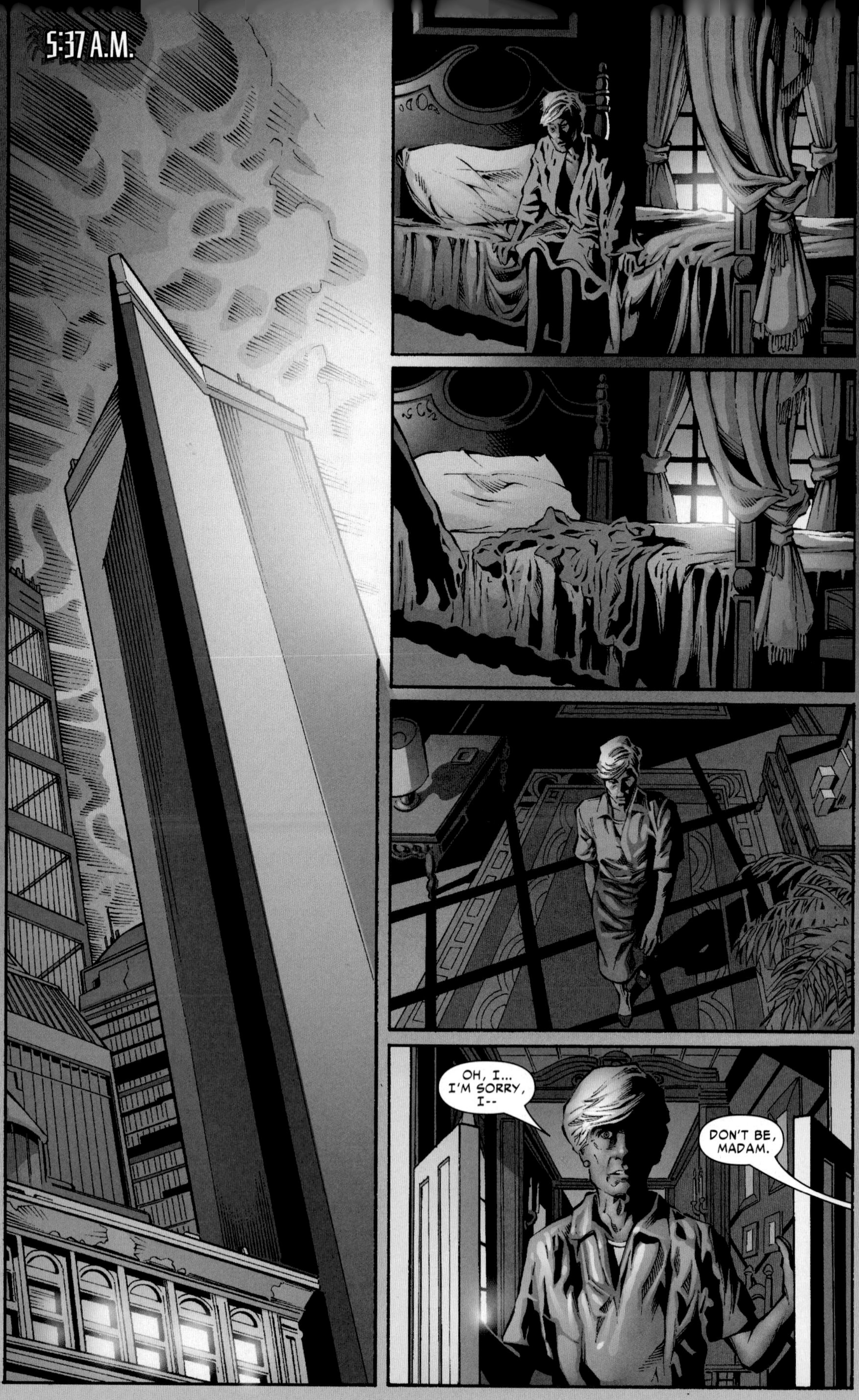
5:37 A.M.
OH, I... I'M SORRY, I--
DON'T BE, MADAM.

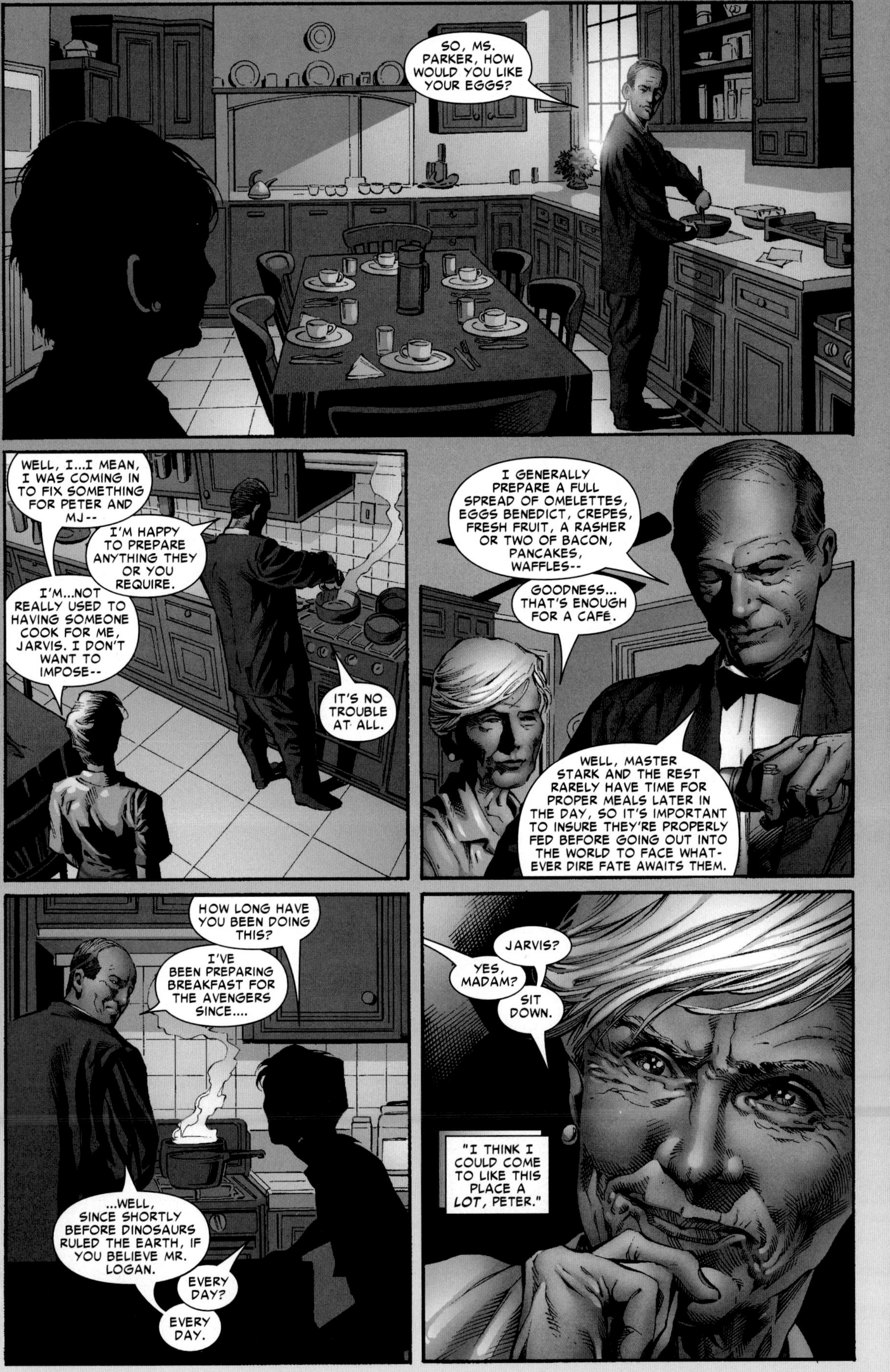
SO, MS. PARKER, HOW WOULD YOU LIKE YOUR EGGS?
WELL, I...I MEAN, I WAS COMING IN TO FIX SOMETHING FOR PETER AND MJ--
I'M HAPPY TO PREPARE ANYTHING THEY OR YOU REQUIRE.
I'M...NOT REALLY USED TO HAVING SOMEONE COOK FOR ME, JARVIS. I DON'T WANT TO IMPOSE--
IT'S NO TROUBLE AT ALL.
I GENERALLY PREPARE A FULL SPREAD OF OMELETTES, EGGS BENEDICT, CREPES, FRESH FRUIT, A RASHER OR TWO OF BACON, PANCAKES, WAFFLES--
GOODNESS... THAT'S ENOUGH FOR A CAFÉ.
WELL, MASTER STARK AND THE REST RARELY HAVE TIME FOR PROPER MEALS LATER IN THE DAY, SO IT'S IMPORTANT TO INSURE THEY'RE PROPERLY FED BEFORE GOING OUT INTO THE WORLD TO FACE WHAT-EVER DIRE FATE AWAITS THEM.
HOW LONG HAVE YOU BEEN DOING THIS?
I'VE BEEN PREPARING BREAKFAST FOR THE AVENGERS SINCE....
...WELL, SINCE SHORTLY BEFORE DINOSAURS RULED THE EARTH, IF YOU BELIEVE MR. LOGAN.
EVERY DAY?
EVERY DAY.
JARVIS?
YES, MADAM?
SIT DOWN.
"I THINK I COULD COME TO LIKE THIS PLACE A LOT, PETER."

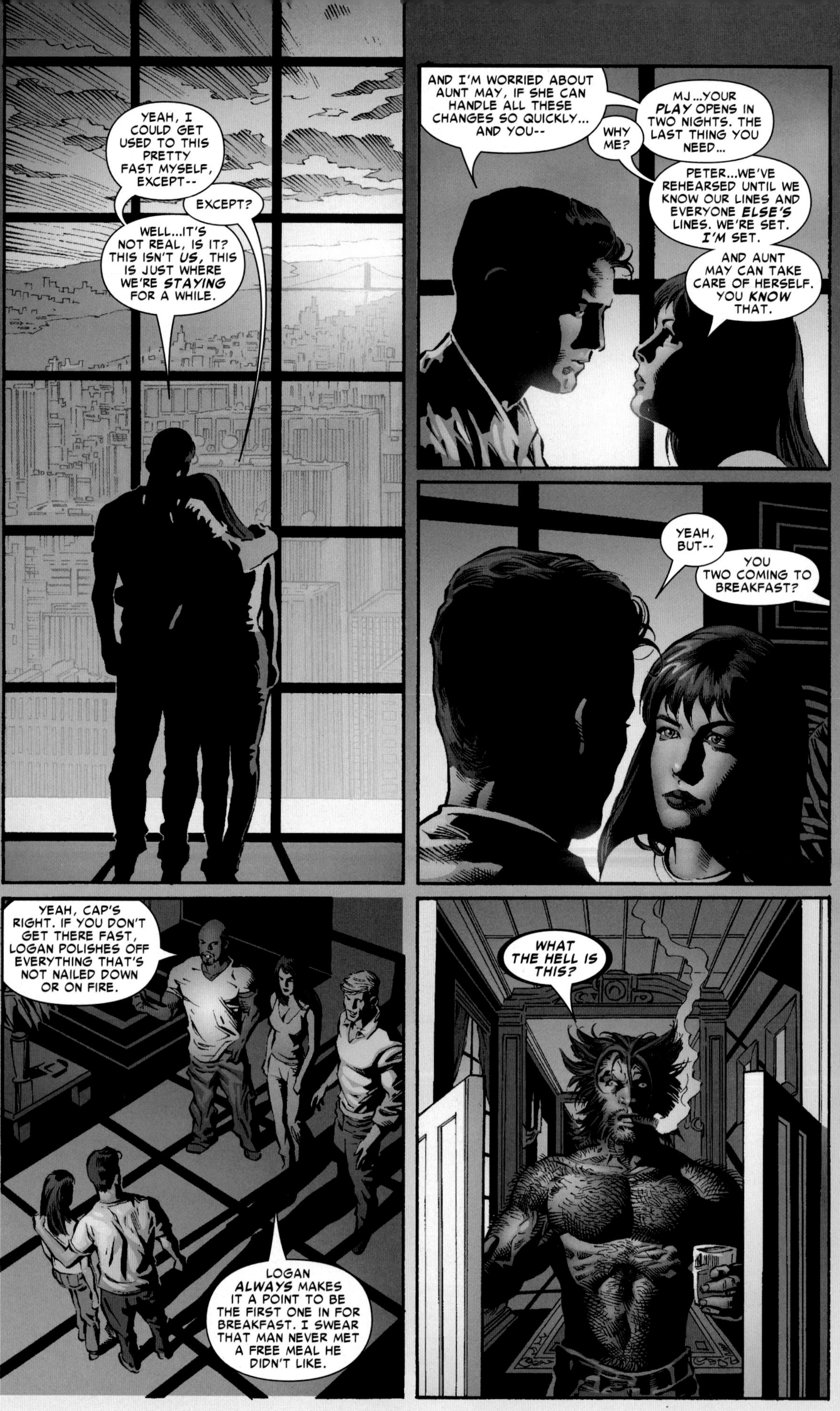
YEAH, I COULD GET USED TO THIS PRETTY FAST MYSELF, EXCEPT--
EXCEPT?
WELL...IT'S NOT REAL, IS IT? THIS ISN'T US, THIS IS JUST WHERE WE'RE STAYING FOR A WHILE.
AND I'M WORRIED ABOUT AUNT MAY, IF SHE CAN HANDLE ALL THESE CHANGES SO QUICKLY... AND YOU--
MJ...YOUR PLAY OPENS IN TWO NIGHTS. THE LAST THING YOU NEED...
WHY ME?
PETER...WE'VE REHEARSED UNTIL WE KNOW OUR LINES AND EVERYONE ELSE'S LINES. WE'RE SET. I'M SET.
AND AUNT MAY CAN TAKE CARE OF HERSELF. YOU KNOW THAT.
YEAH, BUT--
YOU TWO COMING TO BREAKFAST?
YEAH, CAP'S RIGHT. IF YOU DON'T GET THERE FAST, LOGAN POLISHES OFF EVERYTHING THAT'S NOT NAILED DOWN OR ON FIRE.
LOGAN ALWAYS MAKES IT A POINT TO BE THE FIRST ONE IN FOR BREAKFAST. I SWEAR THAT MAN NEVER MET A FREE MEAL HE DIDN'T LIKE.
WHAT THE HELL IS THIS?

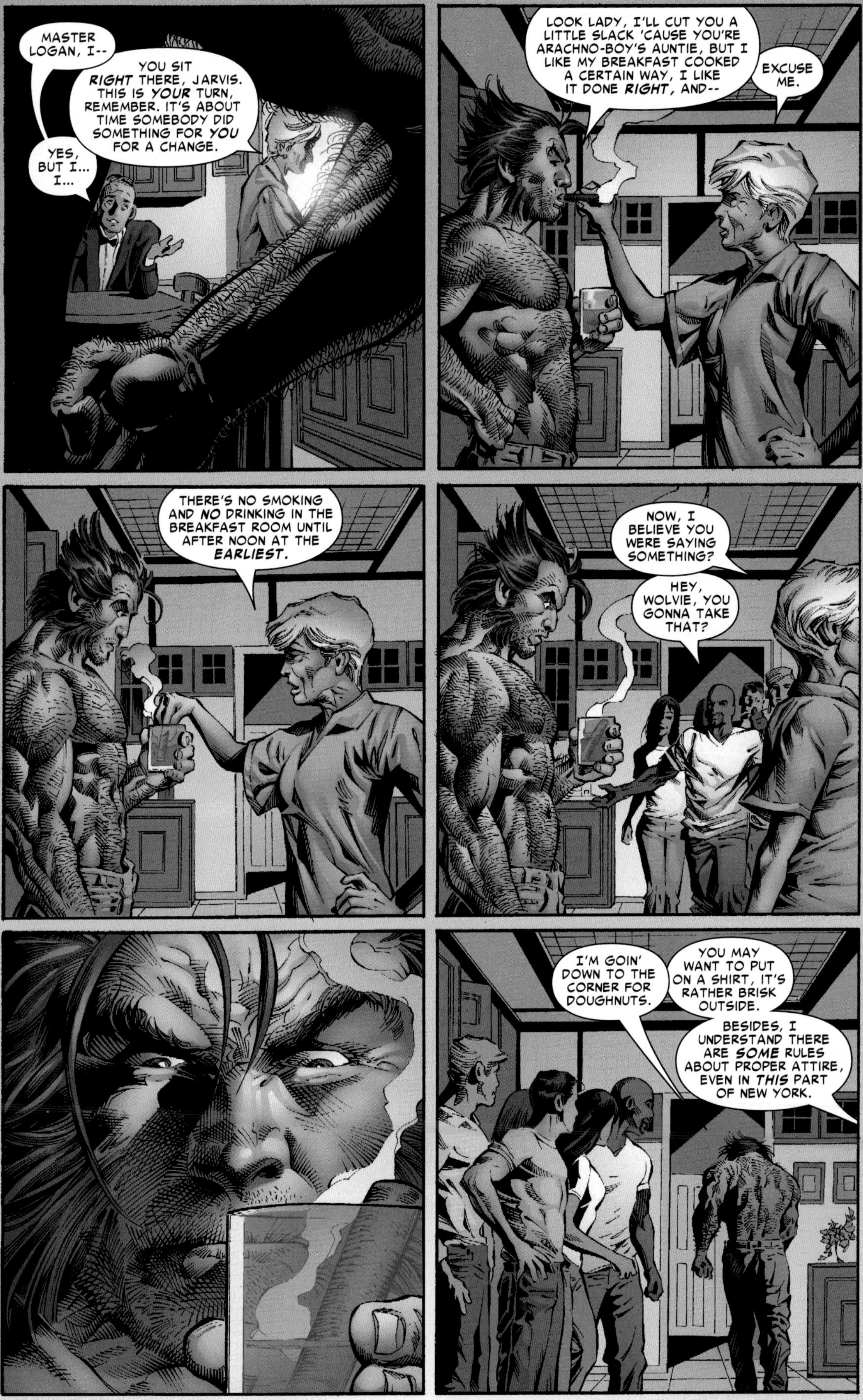
MASTER LOGAN, I--
YOU SIT RIGHT THERE, JARVIS. THIS IS YOUR TURN, REMEMBER. IT'S ABOUT TIME SOMEBODY DID SOMETHING FOR YOU FOR A CHANGE.
YES, BUT I... I...
LOOK LADY, I'LL CUT YOU A LITTLE SLACK 'CAUSE YOU'RE ARACHNO-BOY'S AUNTIE, BUT I LIKE MY BREAKFAST COOKED A CERTAIN WAY, I LIKE IT DONE RIGHT, AND--
EXCUSE ME.
THERE'S NO SMOKING AND NO DRINKING IN THE BREAKFAST ROOM UNTIL AFTER NOON AT THE EARLIEST.
NOW, I BELIEVE YOU WERE SAYING SOMETHING?
HEY, WOLVIE, YOU GONNA TAKE THAT?
I'M GOIN' DOWN TO THE CORNER FOR DOUGHNUTS.
YOU MAY WANT TO PUT ON A SHIRT, IT'S RATHER BRISK OUTSIDE.
BESIDES, I UNDERSTAND THERE ARE SOME RULES ABOUT PROPER ATTIRE, EVEN IN THIS PART OF NEW YORK.

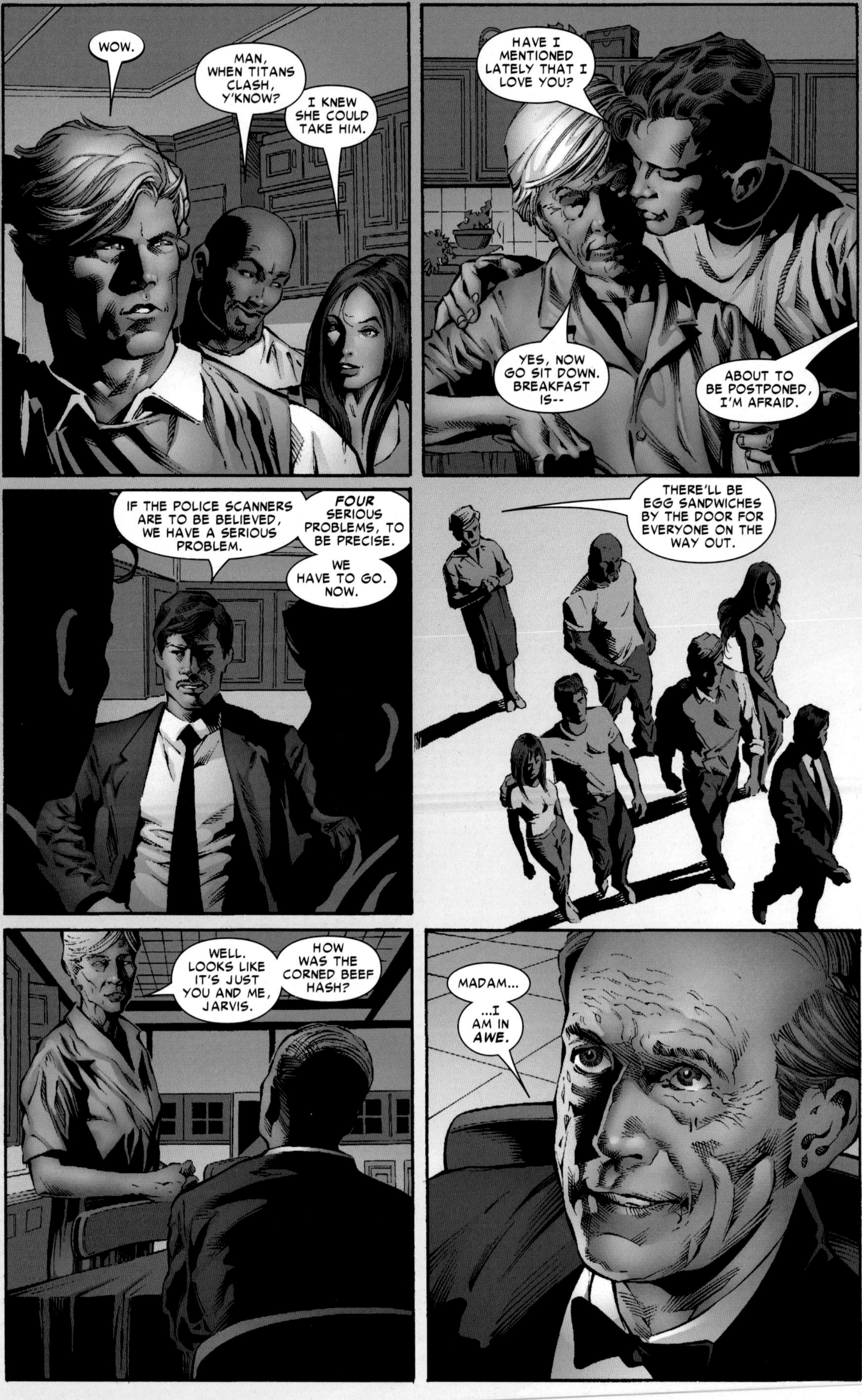
WOW.
MAN, WHEN TITANS CLASH, Y'KNOW?
I KNEW SHE COULD TAKE HIM.
HAVE I MENTIONED LATELY THAT I LOVE YOU?
YES, NOW GO SIT DOWN. BREAKFAST IS--
ABOUT TO BE POSTPONED, I'M AFRAID.
IF THE POLICE SCANNERS ARE TO BE BELIEVED, WE HAVE A SERIOUS PROBLEM.
FOUR SERIOUS PROBLEMS, TO BE PRECISE.
WE HAVE TO GO. NOW.
THERE'LL BE EGG SANDWICHES BY THE DOOR FOR EVERYONE ON THE WAY OUT.
WELL. LOOKS LIKE IT'S JUST YOU AND ME, JARVIS.
HOW WAS THE CORNED BEEF HASH?
MADAM...
...I AM IN *AWE*.

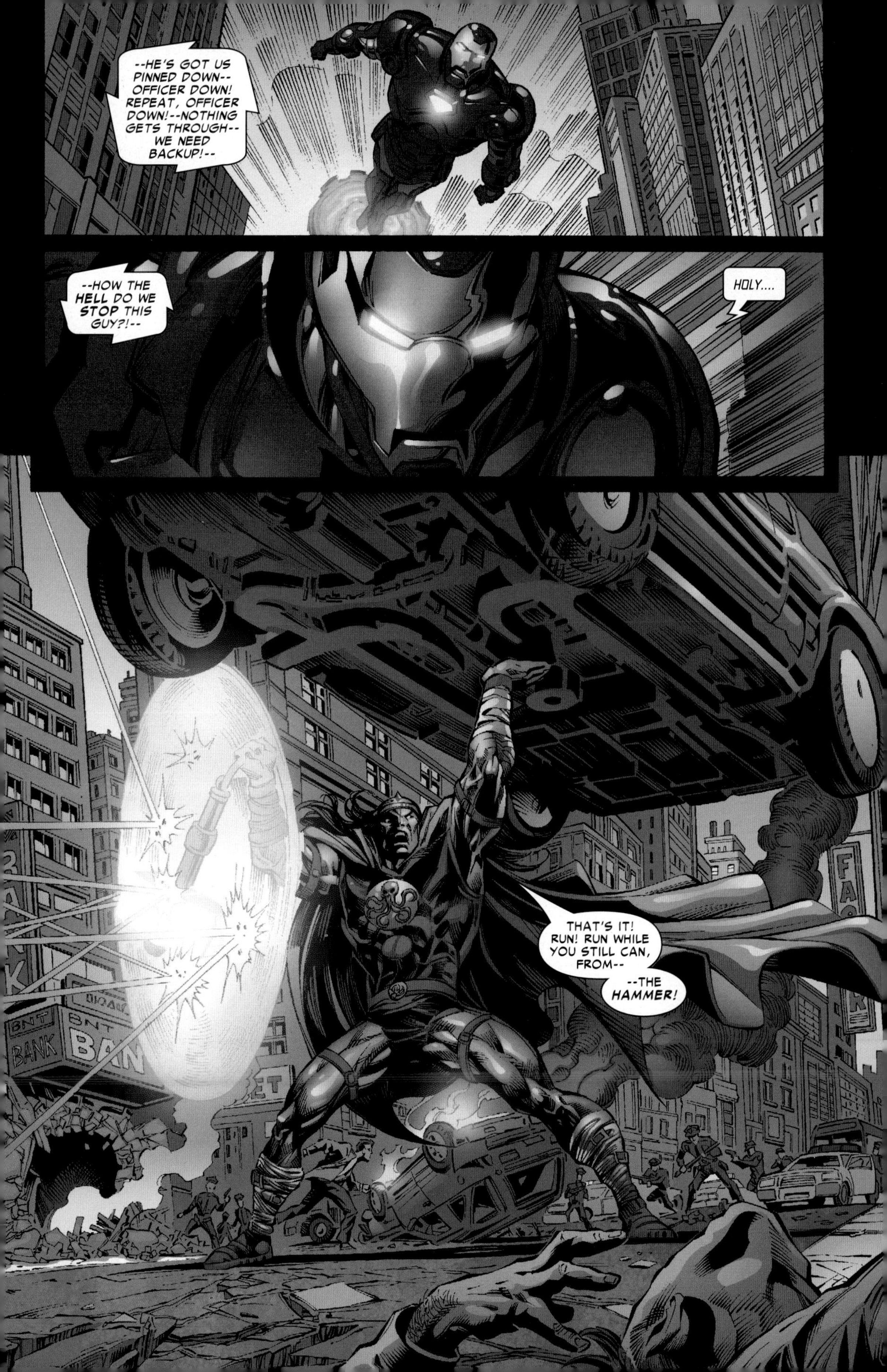
--HE'S GOT US PINNED DOWN-- OFFICER DOWN! REPEAT, OFFICER DOWN!--NOTHING GETS THROUGH-- WE NEED BACKUP!--
--HOW THE HELL DO WE STOP THIS GUY?!--
HOLY....
THAT'S IT! RUN! RUN WHILE YOU STILL CAN, FROM--
--THE HAMMER!
BNT BANK

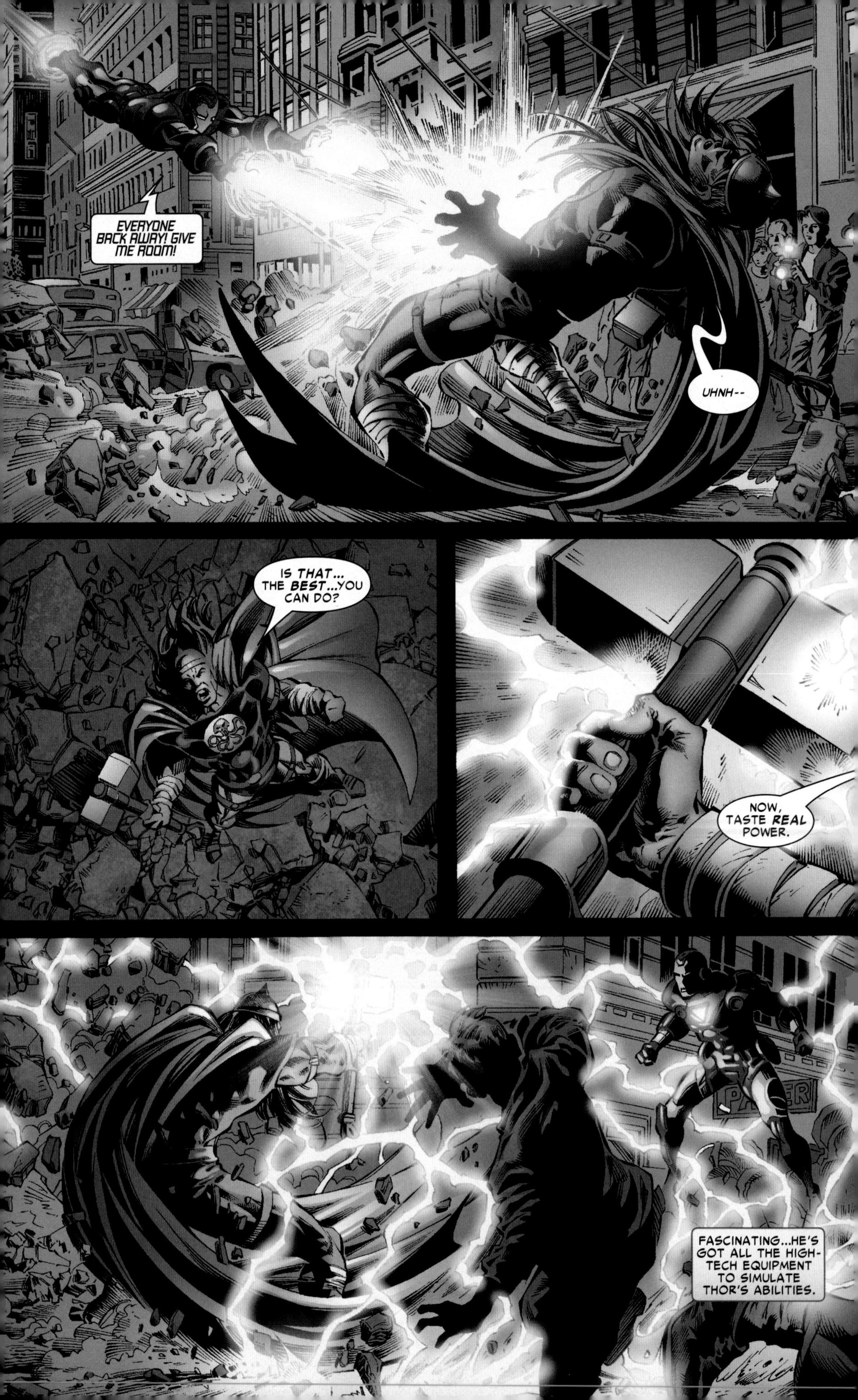
EVERYONE BACK AWAY! GIVE ME ROOM!
UHNH--
IS THAT... THE BEST...YOU CAN DO?
NOW, TASTE REAL POWER.
PAPER
FASCINATING...HE'S GOT ALL THE HIGH-TECH EQUIPMENT TO SIMULATE THOR'S ABILITIES.

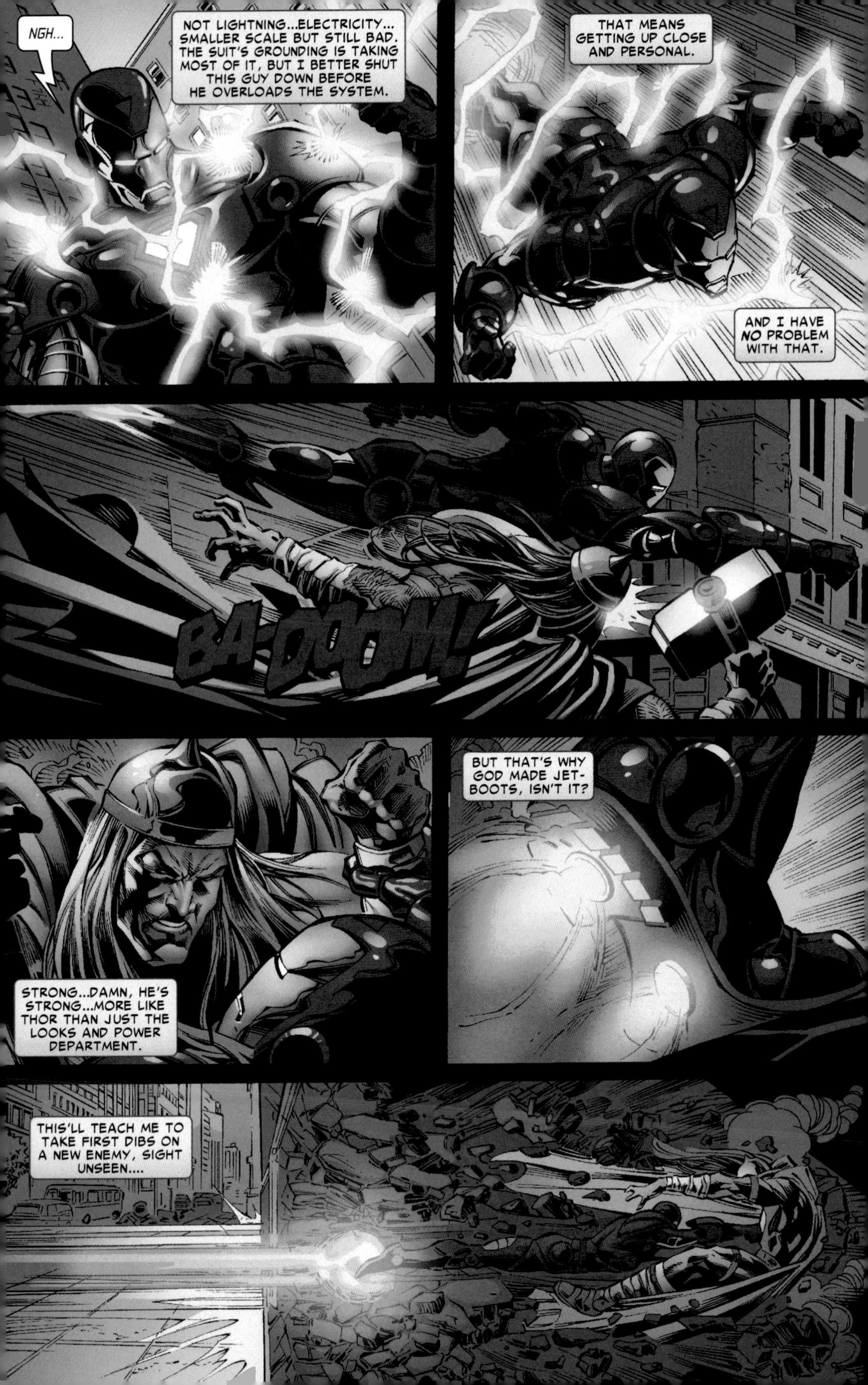
NGH...
NOT LIGHTNING...ELECTRICITY... SMALLER SCALE BUT STILL BAD. THE SUIT'S GROUNDING IS TAKING MOST OF IT, BUT I BETTER SHUT THIS GUY DOWN BEFORE HE OVERLOADS THE SYSTEM.
THAT MEANS GETTING UP CLOSE AND PERSONAL.
AND I HAVE NO PROBLEM WITH THAT.
BA-DOOM!
STRONG...DAMN, HE'S STRONG...MORE LIKE THOR THAN JUST THE LOOKS AND POWER DEPARTMENT.
BUT THAT'S WHY GOD MADE JET-BOOTS, ISN'T IT?
THIS'LL TEACH ME TO TAKE FIRST DIBS ON A NEW ENEMY, SIGHT UNSEEN....

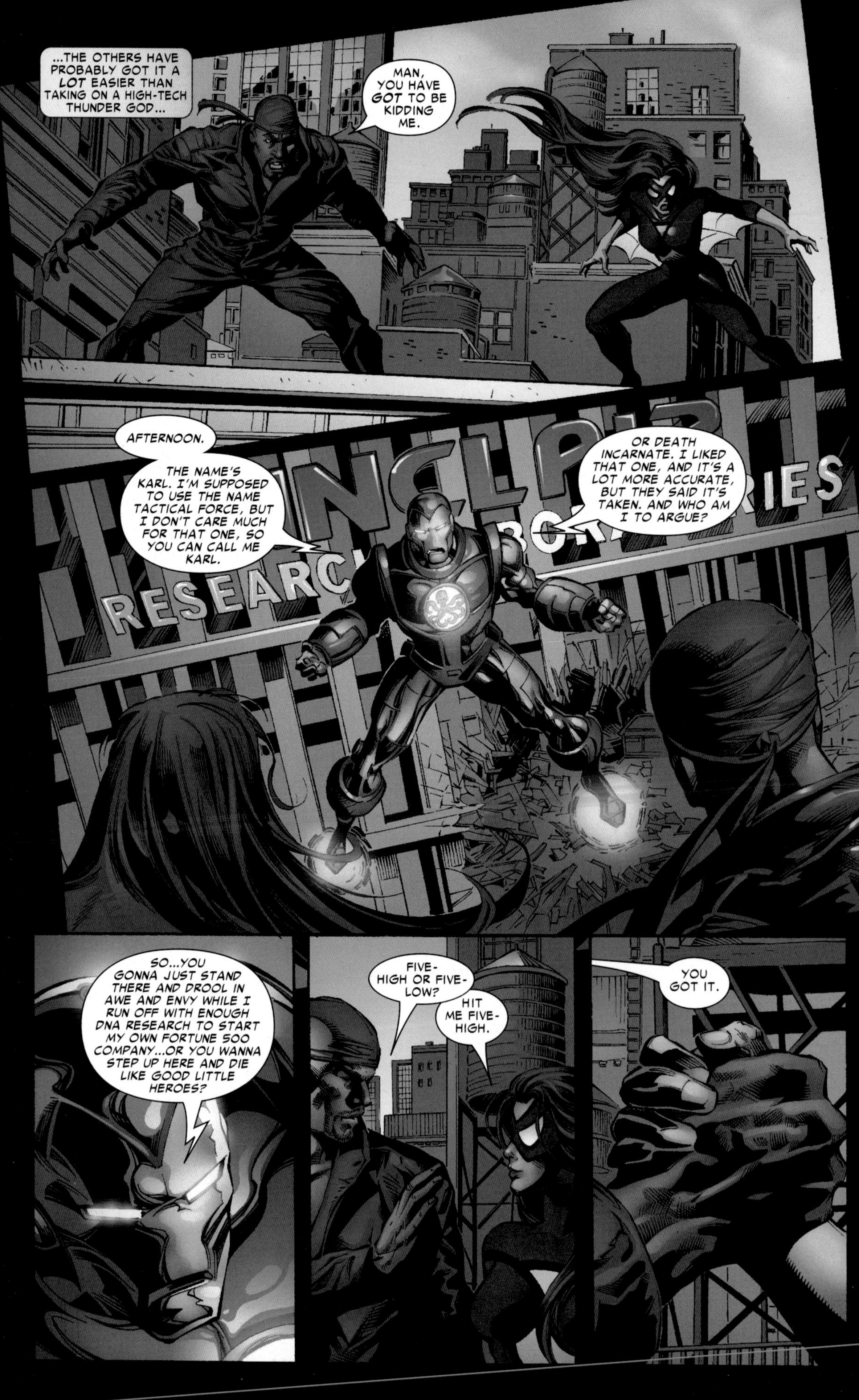
...THE OTHERS HAVE PROBABLY GOT IT A LOT EASIER THAN TAKING ON A HIGH-TECH THUNDER GOD...
MAN, YOU HAVE GOT TO BE KIDDING ME.
AFTERNOON.
THE NAME'S KARL. I'M SUPPOSED TO USE THE NAME TACTICAL FORCE, BUT I DON'T CARE MUCH FOR THAT ONE, SO YOU CAN CALL ME KARL.
OR DEATH INCARNATE. I LIKED THAT ONE, AND IT'S A LOT MORE ACCURATE, BUT THEY SAID IT'S TAKEN. AND WHO AM I TO ARGUE?
SO...YOU GONNA JUST STAND THERE AND DROOL IN AWE AND ENVY WHILE I RUN OFF WITH ENOUGH DNA RESEARCH TO START MY OWN FORTUNE 500 COMPANY...OR YOU WANNA STEP UP HERE AND DIE LIKE GOOD LITTLE HEROES?
FIVE-HIGH OR FIVE-LOW?
HIT ME FIVE-HIGH.
YOU GOT IT.

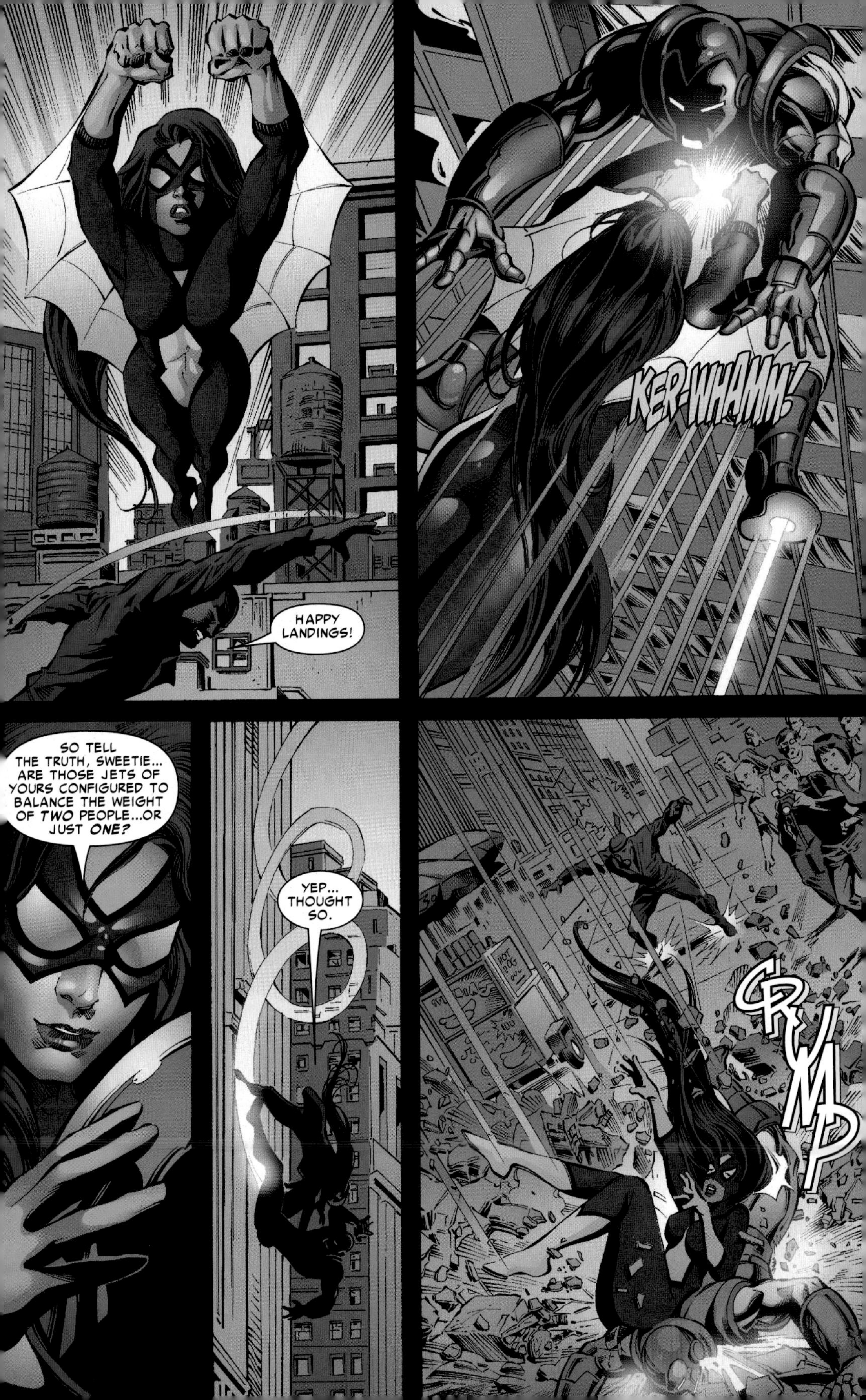
HAPPY LANDINGS!
KER-WHAMM!
SO TELL THE TRUTH, SWEETIE... ARE THOSE JETS OF YOURS CONFIGURED TO BALANCE THE WEIGHT OF TWO PEOPLE...OR JUST ONE?
YEP... THOUGHT SO.
CRUMP

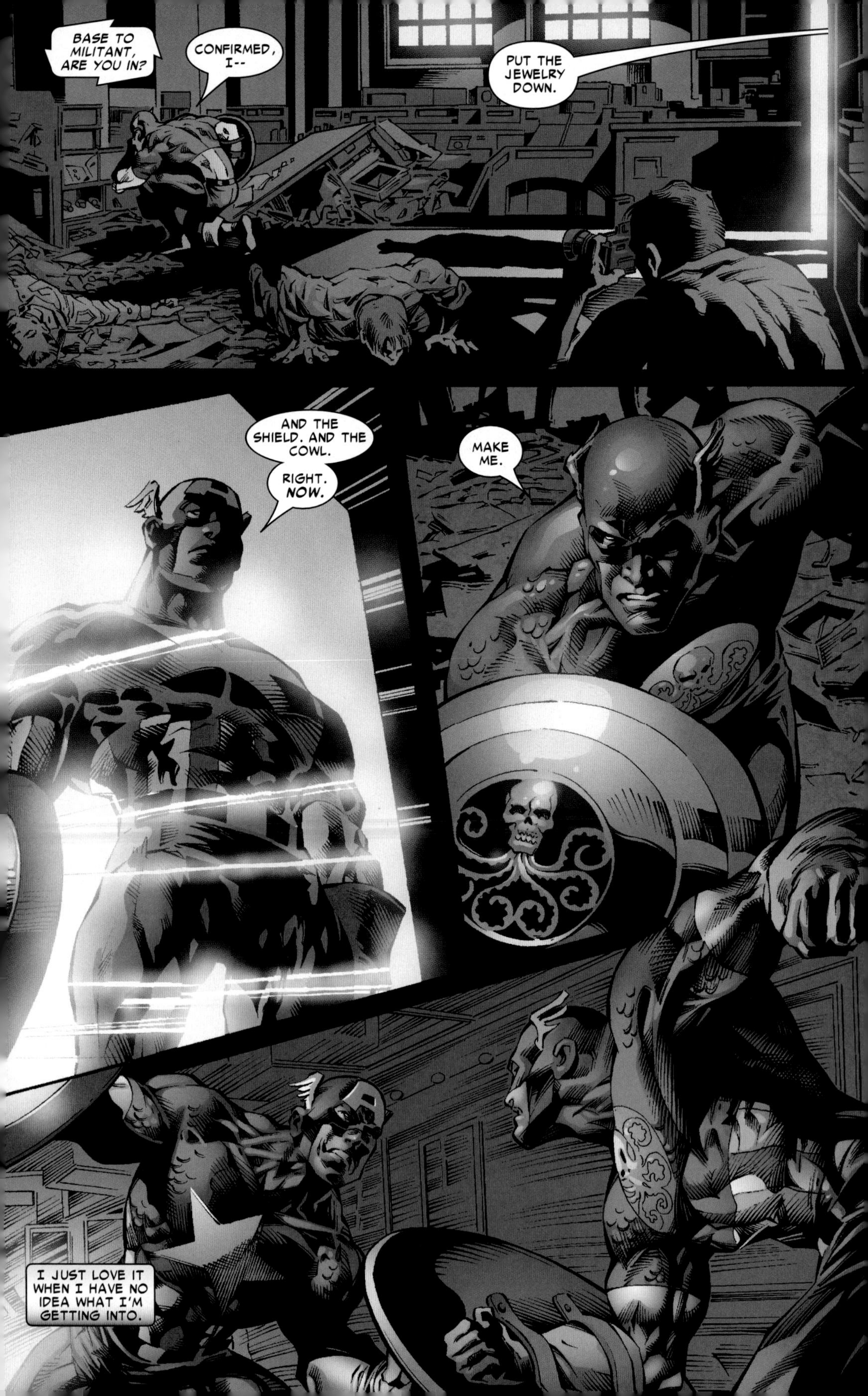
BASE TO MILITANT, ARE YOU IN?
CONFIRMED, I--
PUT THE JEWELRY DOWN.
AND THE SHIELD. AND THE COWL.
RIGHT. NOW.
MAKE ME.
I JUST LOVE IT WHEN I HAVE NO IDEA WHAT I'M GETTING INTO.

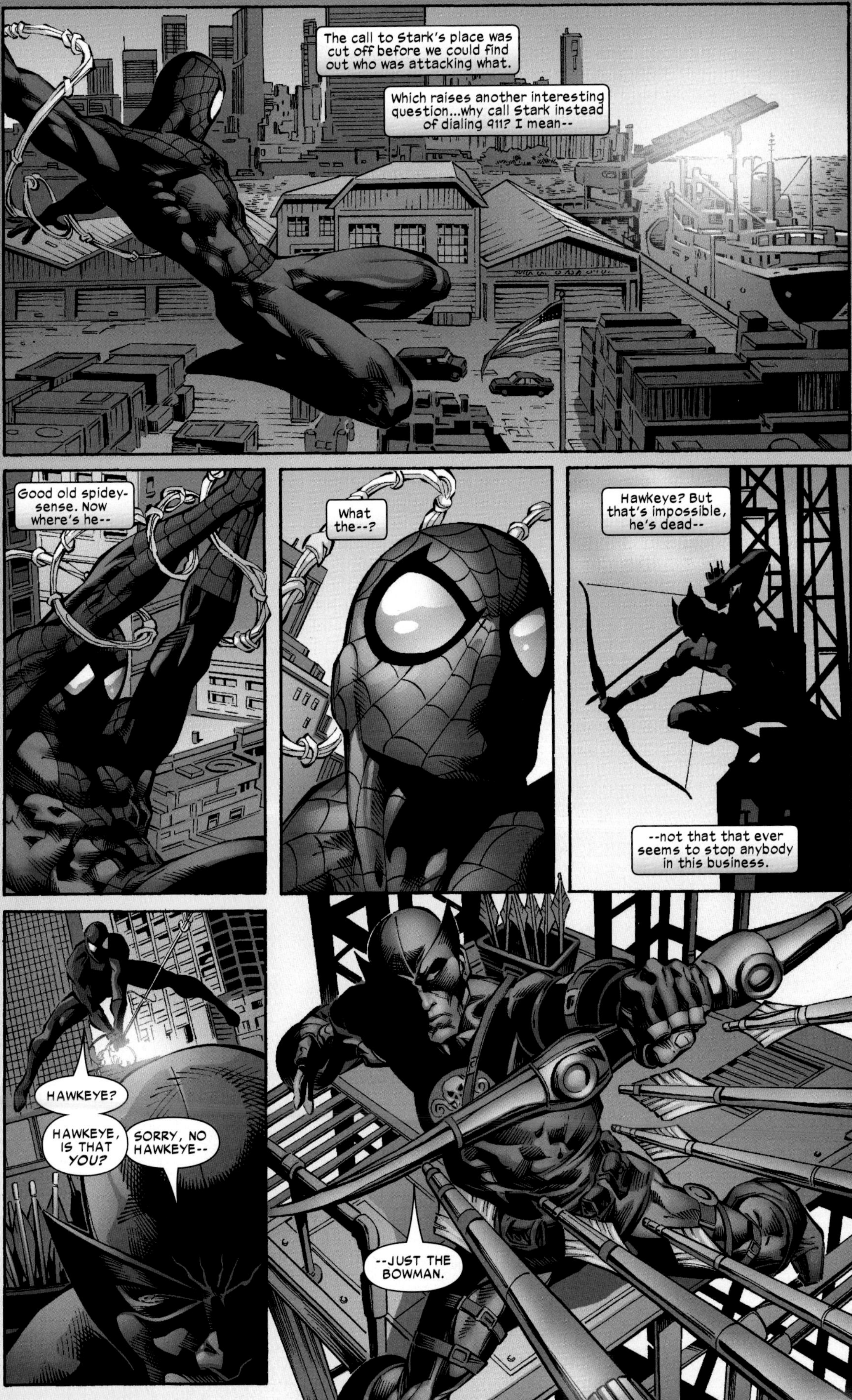

The call to Stark's place was cut off before we could find out who was attacking what.
Which raises another interesting question...why call Stark instead of dialing 911? I mean--
Good old spidey-sense. Now where's he--
What the--?
Hawkeye? But that's impossible, he's dead--
--not that that ever seems to stop anybody in this business.
HAWKEYE?
HAWKEYE, IS THAT *YOU?*
SORRY, NO HAWKEYE--
--JUST THE BOWMAN.

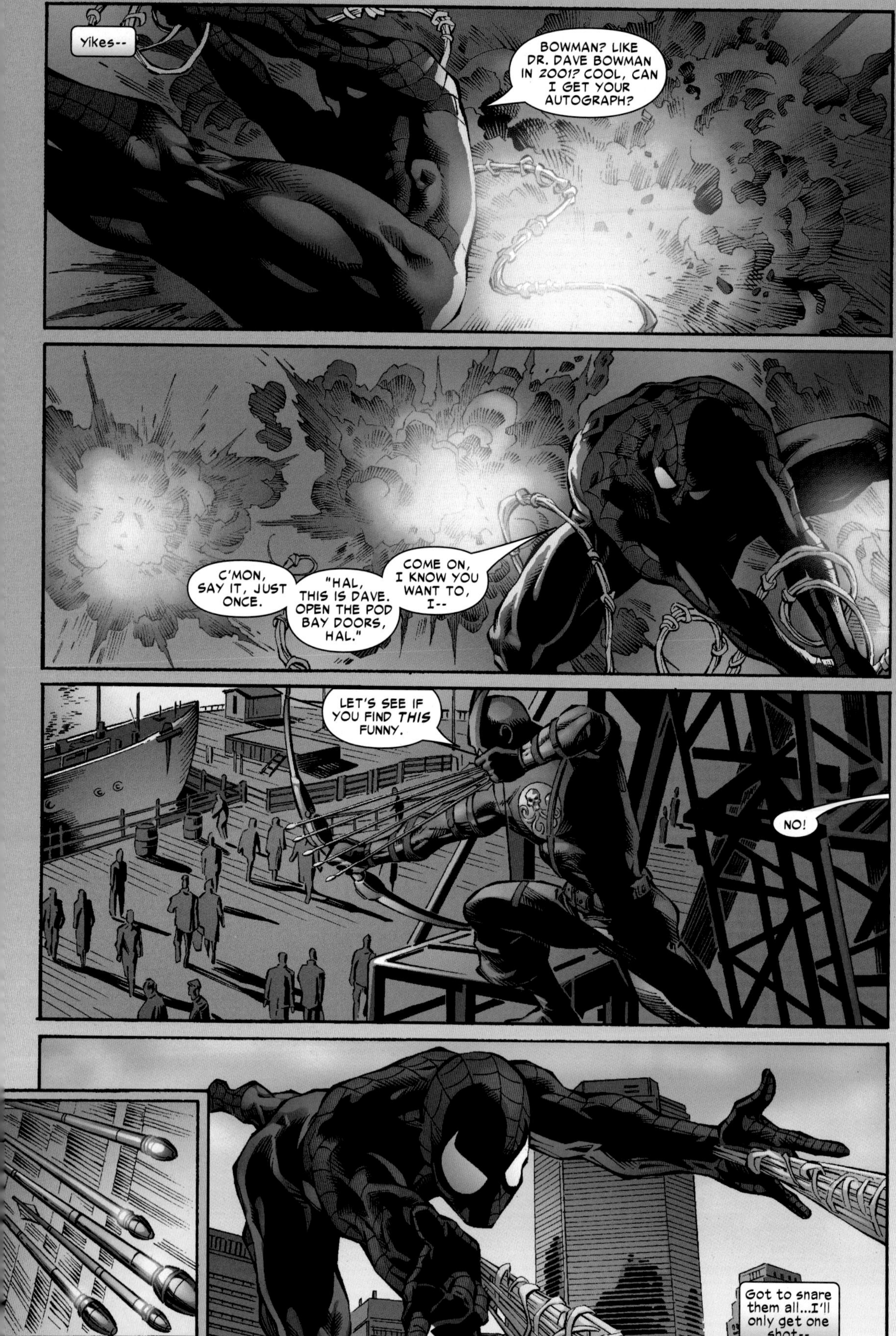
Yikes--
BOWMAN? LIKE DR. DAVE BOWMAN IN *2001*? COOL, CAN I GET YOUR AUTOGRAPH?
C'MON, SAY IT, JUST ONCE.
"HAL, THIS IS DAVE. OPEN THE POD BAY DOORS, HAL."
COME ON, I KNOW YOU WANT TO, I--
LET'S SEE IF YOU FIND *THIS* FUNNY.
NO!
Got to snare them all...I'll only get one shot--

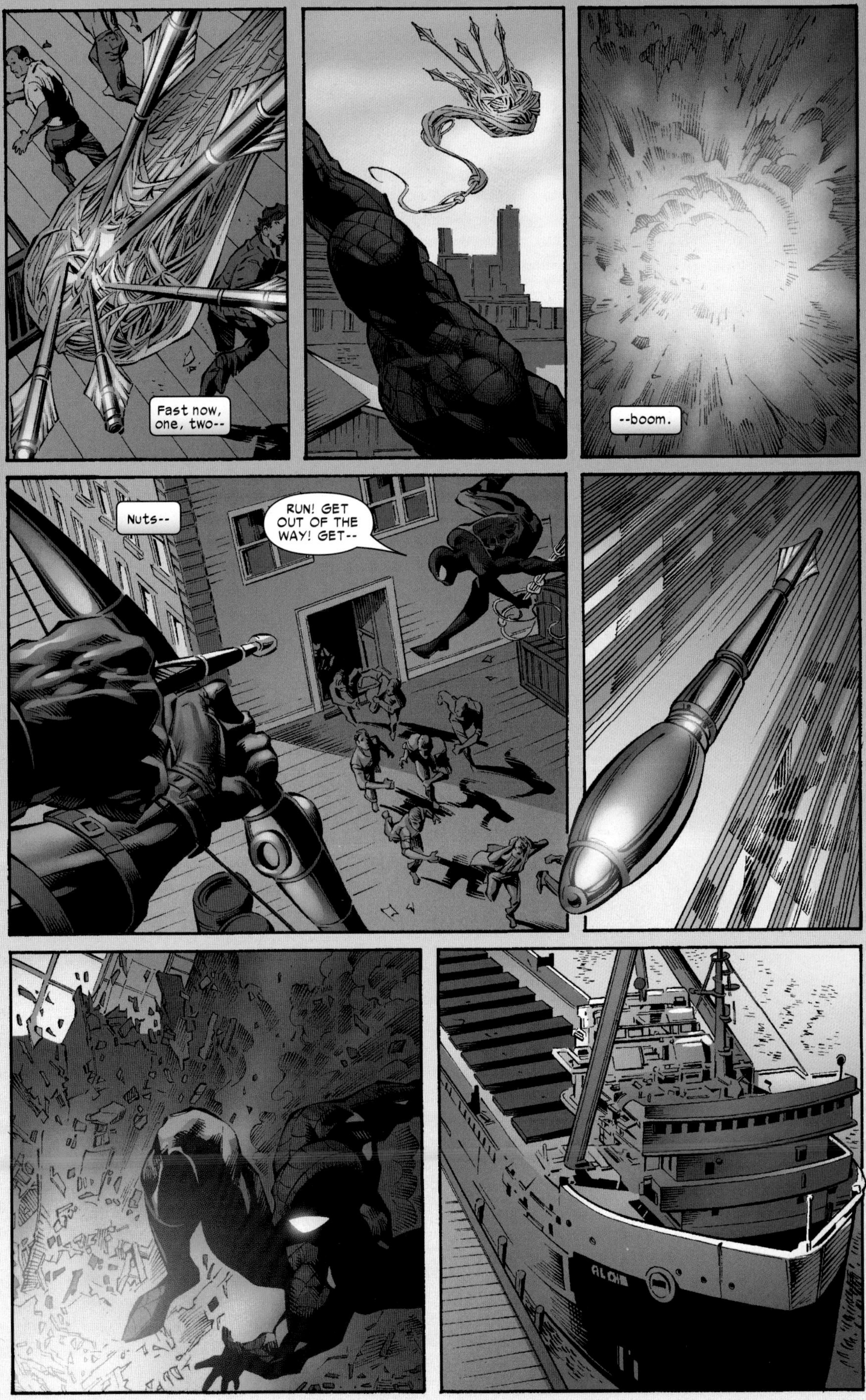
Fast now, one, two--
--boom.
Nuts--
RUN! GET OUT OF THE WAY! GET--

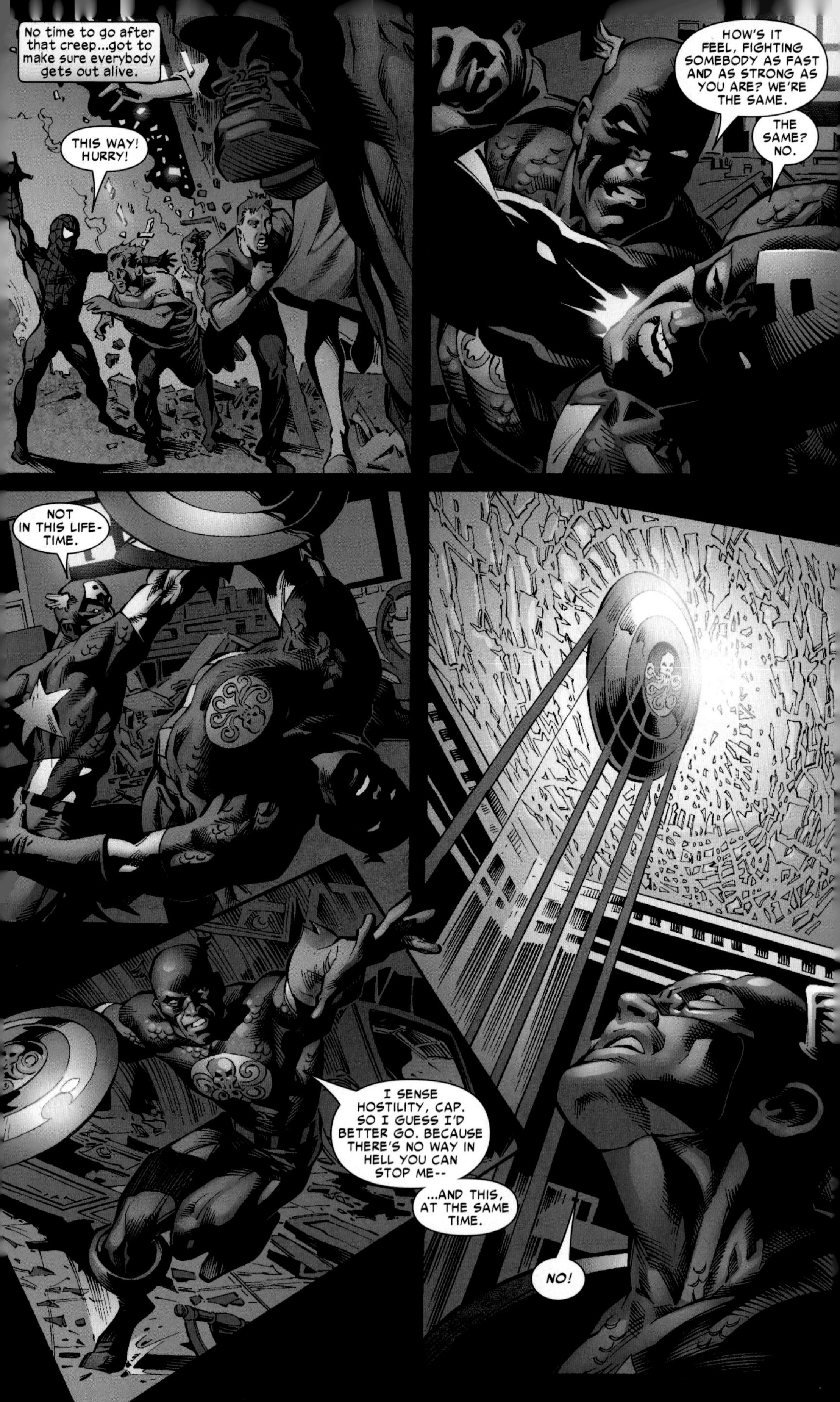
No time to go after that creep...got to make sure everybody gets out alive.
THIS WAY! HURRY!
HOW'S IT FEEL, FIGHTING SOMEBODY AS FAST AND AS STRONG AS YOU ARE? WE'RE THE SAME.
THE SAME? NO.
NOT IN THIS LIFE-TIME.
I SENSE HOSTILITY, CAP. SO I GUESS I'D BETTER GO. BECAUSE THERE'S NO WAY IN HELL YOU CAN STOP ME--
...AND THIS, AT THE SAME TIME.
NO!

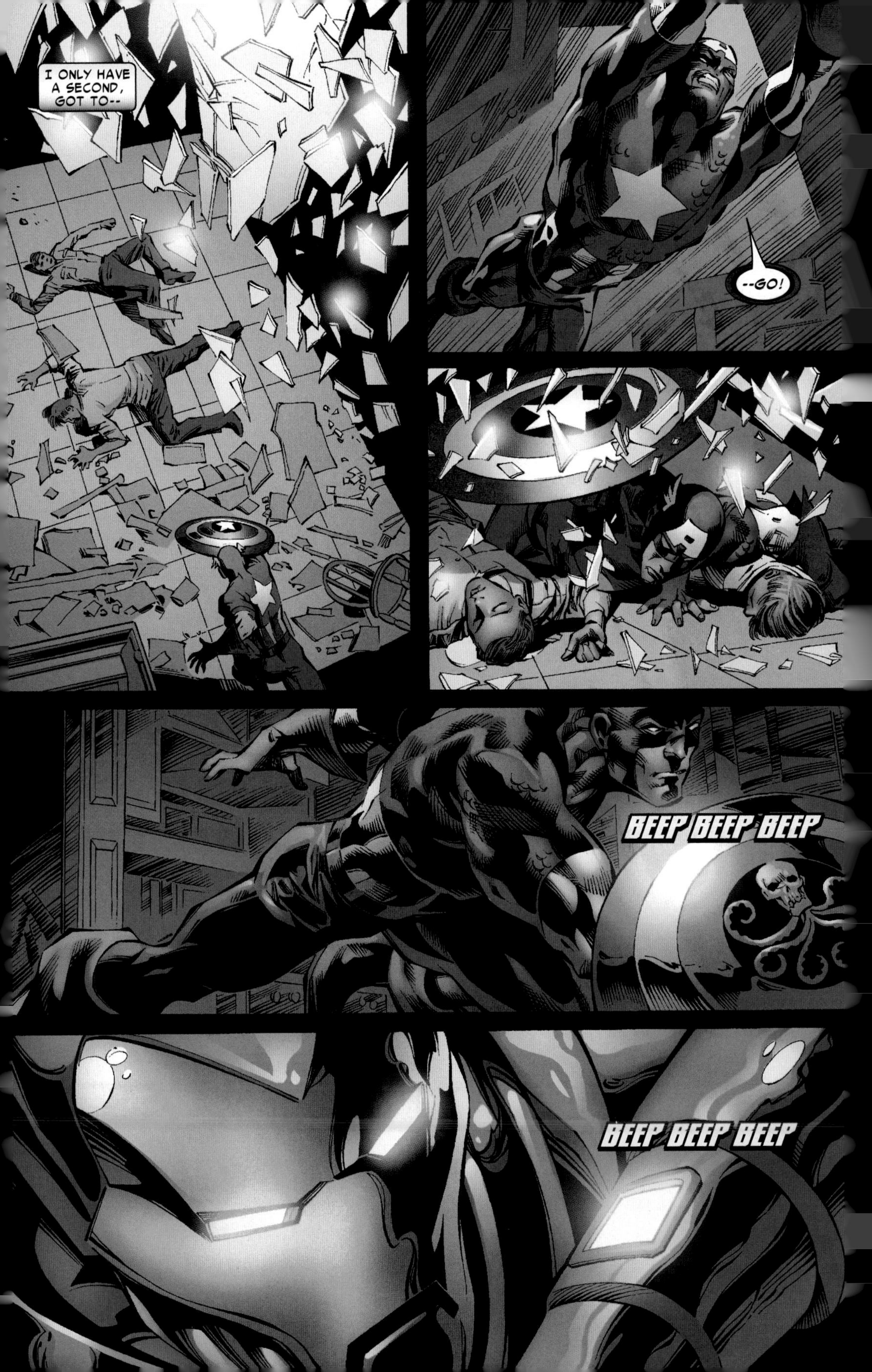
I ONLY HAVE A SECOND, GOT TO--
--GO!
BEEP BEEP BEEP
BEEP BEEP BEEP

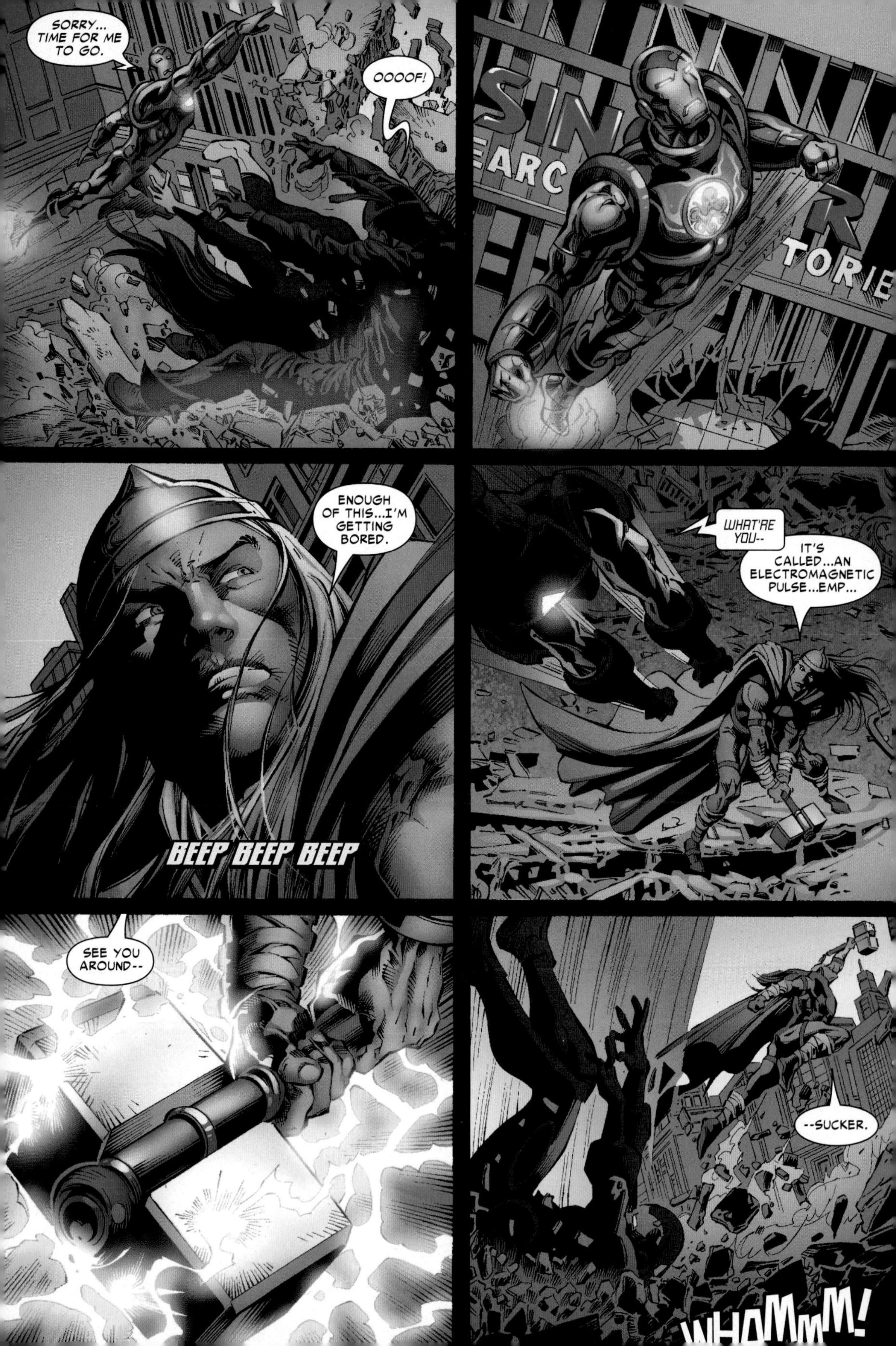
SORRY... TIME FOR ME TO GO.
OOOOF!
SIN
EARC
R
TORIE
ENOUGH OF THIS...I'M GETTING BORED.
BEEP BEEP BEEP
WHAT'RE YOU--
IT'S CALLED...AN ELECTROMAGNETIC PULSE...EMP...
SEE YOU AROUND--
--SUCKER.
WHAMMM!

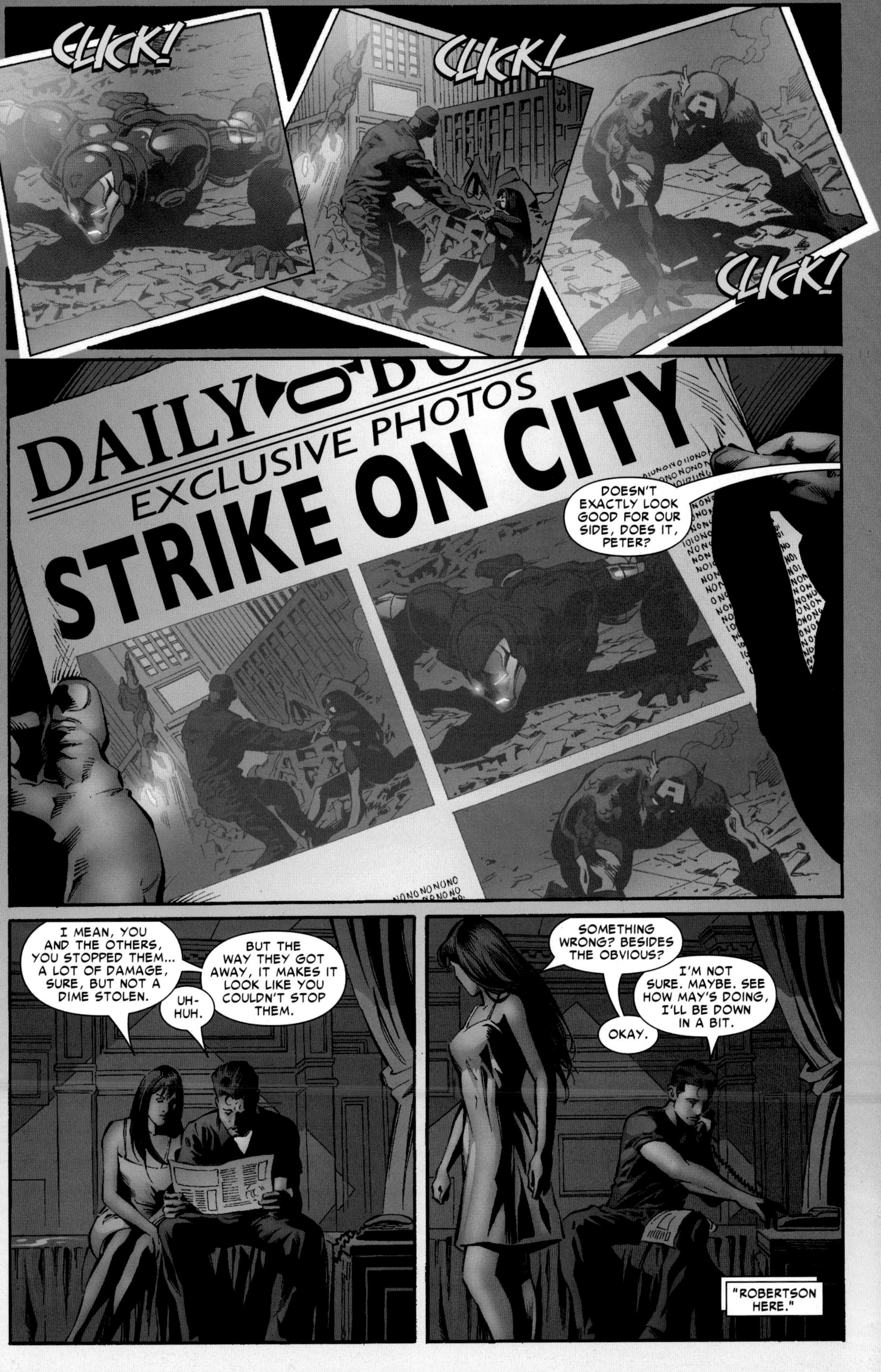
CLICK!
CLICK!
CLICK!
DAILY
EXCLUSIVE PHOTOS
STRIKE ON CITY
DOESN'T EXACTLY LOOK GOOD FOR OUR SIDE, DOES IT, PETER?
I MEAN, YOU AND THE OTHERS, YOU STOPPED THEM... A LOT OF DAMAGE, SURE, BUT NOT A DIME STOLEN.
UH-HUH.
BUT THE WAY THEY GOT AWAY, IT MAKES IT LOOK LIKE YOU COULDN'T STOP THEM.
SOMETHING WRONG? BESIDES THE OBVIOUS?
I'M NOT SURE. MAYBE. SEE HOW MAY'S DOING, I'LL BE DOWN IN A BIT.
OKAY.
"ROBERTSON HERE."

PETE? WHAT CAN I DO FOR YOU?

FAST QUESTION, ROBBIE...HOW DID THE *BUGLE* GET THREE PHOTOGRAPHERS ON THE SCENE OF THOSE ATTACKS SO FAST YESTERDAY?

WELL, I--

C'MON, ROBBIE, THIS IS ME. NOBODY'S THAT LUCKY THREE TIMES IN A ROW AT THE SAME TIME. SO SPILL.

"IT'S...A LONG STORY."

YOU GOTTA LOVE IT, RIGHT? WE RISK OUR LIVES AND WE END UP LOOKING LIKE SAPS. WHAT LUCK, RIGHT?

IT WASN'T LUCK.

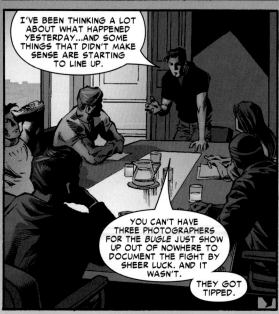

I'VE BEEN THINKING A LOT ABOUT WHAT HAPPENED YESTERDAY...AND SOME THINGS THAT DIDN'T MAKE SENSE ARE STARTING TO LINE UP.

YOU CAN'T HAVE THREE PHOTOGRAPHERS FOR THE *BUGLE* JUST SHOW UP OUT OF NOWHERE TO DOCUMENT THE FIGHT BY SHEER LUCK. AND IT WASN'T.

THEY GOT TIPPED.

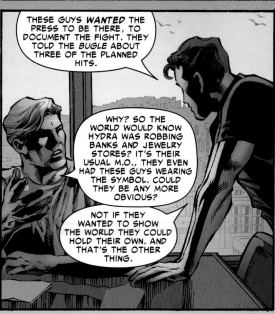

THESE GUYS *WANTED* THE PRESS TO BE THERE, TO DOCUMENT THE FIGHT. THEY TOLD THE *BUGLE* ABOUT THREE OF THE PLANNED HITS.

WHY? SO THE WORLD WOULD KNOW HYDRA WAS ROBBING BANKS AND JEWELRY STORES? IT'S THEIR USUAL M.O., THEY EVEN HAD THESE GUYS WEARING THE SYMBOL. COULD THEY BE ANY MORE OBVIOUS?

NOT IF THEY WANTED TO SHOW THE WORLD THEY COULD HOLD THEIR OWN. AND THAT'S THE OTHER THING.

THEY COULD'VE GRABBED ANY OF THE MONEY OR JEWELS AS THEY LEFT, BUT DIDN'T BOTHER. WHICH SAYS THEY WEREN'T WORRIED ABOUT THE MONEY, AND *THAT* TELLS US TWO THINGS.

FIRST, THAT THEY DON'T *NEED* THE MONEY, AND THAT'S SCARY BY ITSELF.

SECOND...IF THEY WERE AFTER MONEY, WHY HIT THE DOCKS? THERE WEREN'T ANY EXPENSIVE CARGOS COMING IN, NOTHING TO STEAL...THEY JUST BLEW UP THE MAIN BUILDING.

THE *RECORDS* BUILDING, WHERE SHIPS LOG IN THEIR CARGO MANIFESTS.

SO YOU'RE SAYING IT WAS A WORTHLESS ATTACK?

JUST THE OPPOSITE...

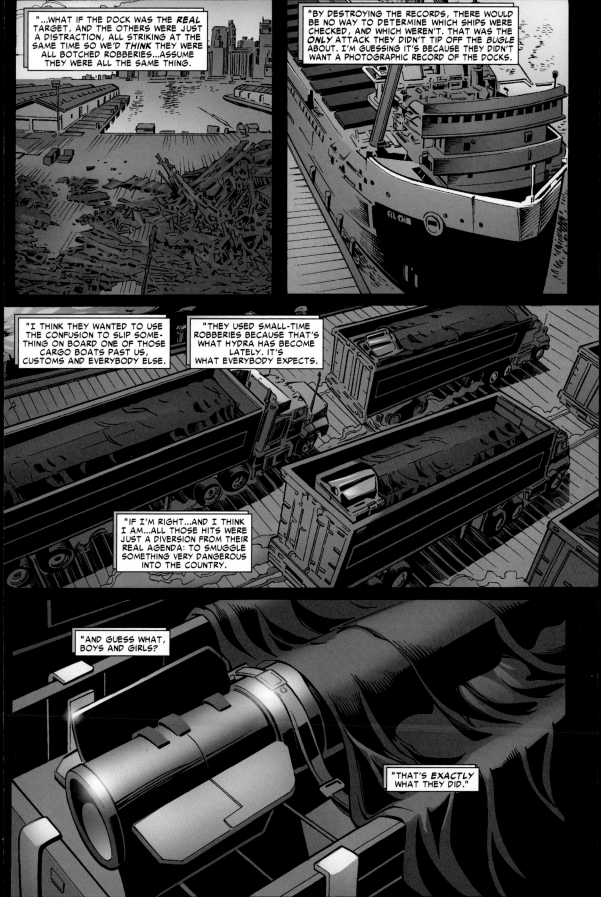

"...WHAT IF THE DOCK WAS THE *REAL* TARGET, AND THE OTHERS WERE JUST A DISTRACTION, ALL STRIKING AT THE SAME TIME SO WE'D *THINK* THEY WERE ALL BOTCHED ROBBERIES...ASSUME THEY WERE ALL THE SAME THING.

"BY DESTROYING THE RECORDS, THERE WOULD BE NO WAY TO DETERMINE WHICH SHIPS WERE CHECKED, AND WHICH WEREN'T. THAT WAS THE *ONLY* ATTACK THEY DIDN'T TIP OFF THE *BUGLE* ABOUT. I'M GUESSING IT'S BECAUSE THEY DIDN'T WANT A PHOTOGRAPHIC RECORD OF THE DOCKS.

"I THINK THEY WANTED TO USE THE CONFUSION TO SLIP SOME-THING ON BOARD ONE OF THOSE CARGO BOATS PAST US, CUSTOMS AND EVERYBODY ELSE.

"THEY USED SMALL-TIME ROBBERIES BECAUSE THAT'S WHAT HYDRA HAS BECOME LATELY. IT'S WHAT EVERYBODY EXPECTS.

"IF I'M RIGHT...AND I THINK I AM...ALL THOSE HITS WERE JUST A DIVERSION FROM THEIR REAL AGENDA: TO SMUGGLE SOMETHING VERY DANGEROUS INTO THE COUNTRY.

"AND GUESS WHAT, BOYS AND GIRLS?

"THAT'S *EXACTLY* WHAT THEY DID."

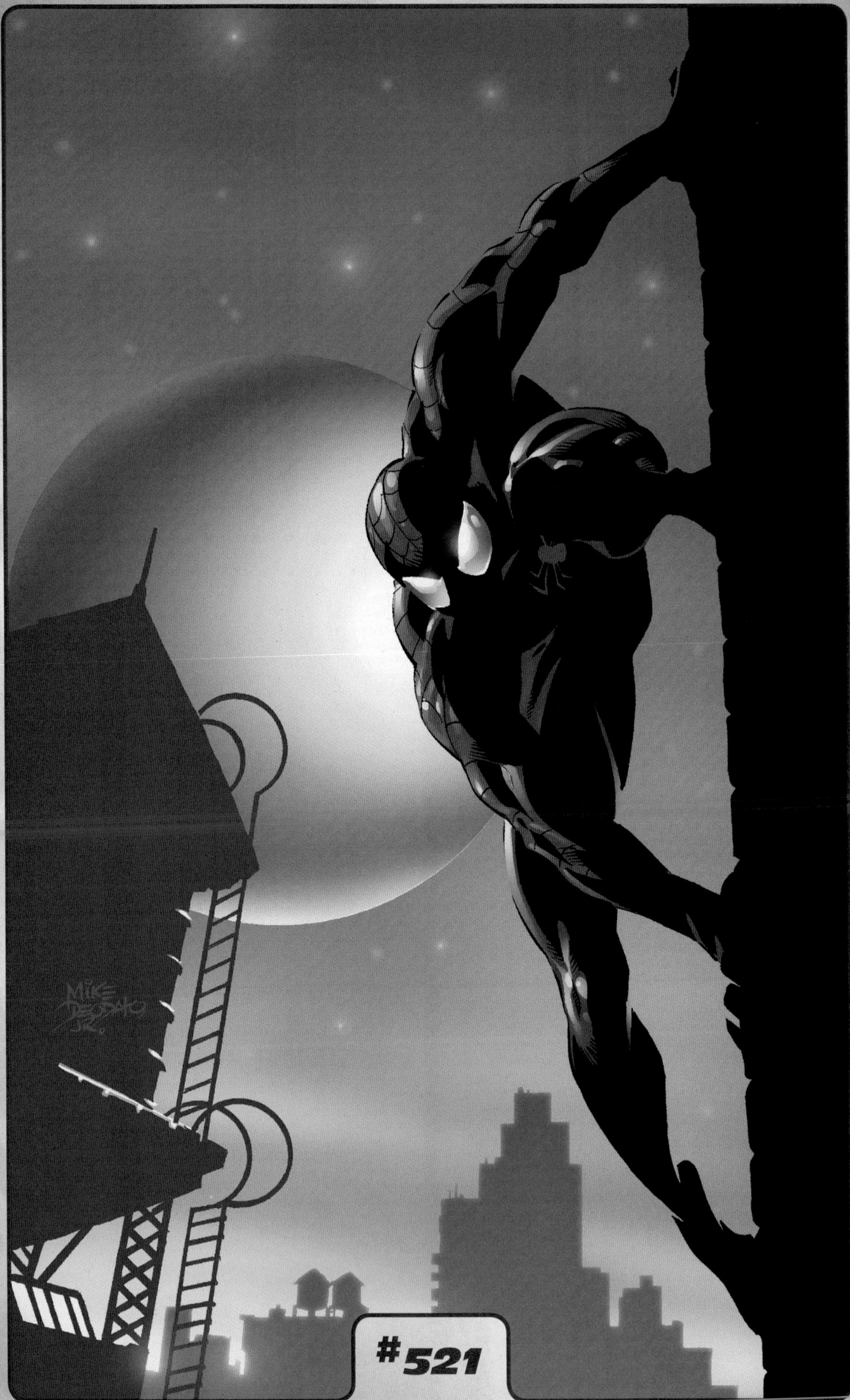
MIKE DEODATO JR.
#521

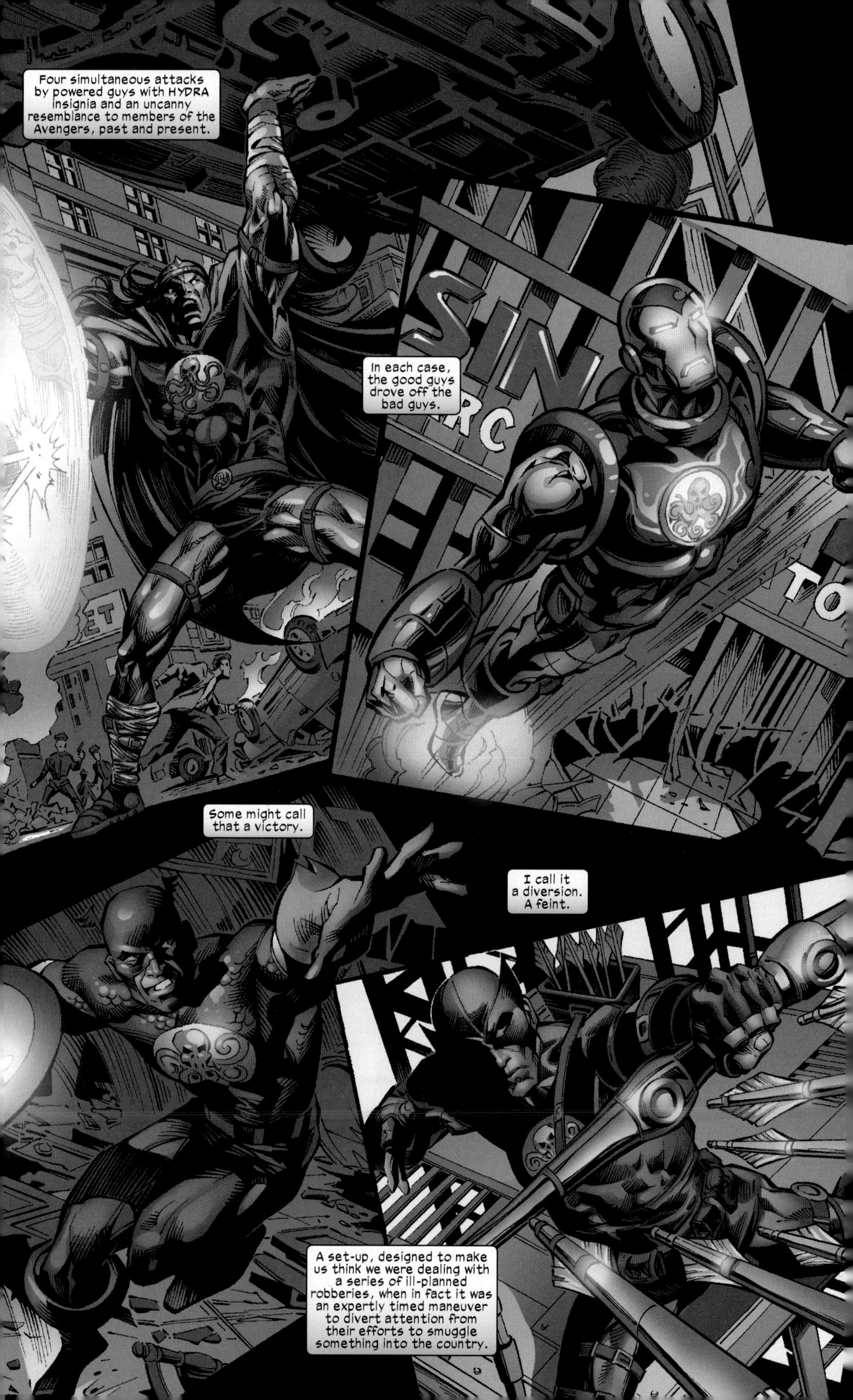

Four simultaneous attacks by powered guys with HYDRA insignia and an uncanny resemblance to members of the Avengers, past and present.
In each case, the good guys drove off the bad guys.
Some might call that a victory.
I call it a diversion. A feint.
A set-up, designed to make us think we were dealing with a series of ill-planned robberies, when in fact it was an expertly timed maneuver to divert attention from their efforts to smuggle something into the country.

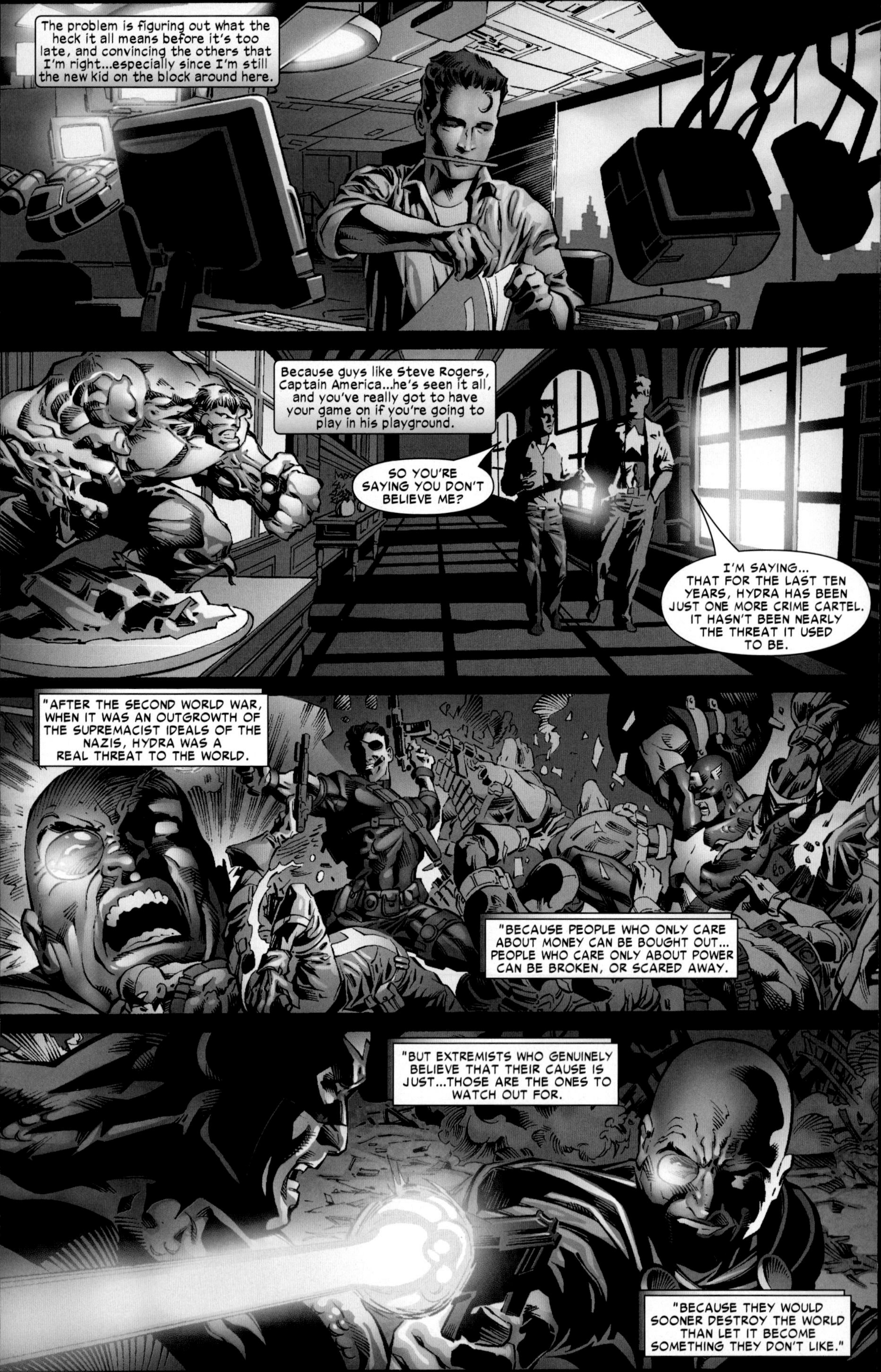
The problem is figuring out what the heck it all means before it's too late, and convincing the others that I'm right...especially since I'm still the new kid on the block around here.
Because guys like Steve Rogers, Captain America...he's seen it all, and you've really got to have your game on if you're going to play in his playground.
SO YOU'RE SAYING YOU DON'T BELIEVE ME?
I'M SAYING... THAT FOR THE LAST TEN YEARS, HYDRA HAS BEEN JUST ONE MORE CRIME CARTEL. IT HASN'T BEEN NEARLY THE THREAT IT USED TO BE.
"AFTER THE SECOND WORLD WAR, WHEN IT WAS AN OUTGROWTH OF THE SUPREMACIST IDEALS OF THE NAZIS, HYDRA WAS A REAL THREAT TO THE WORLD.
"BECAUSE PEOPLE WHO ONLY CARE ABOUT MONEY CAN BE BOUGHT OUT... PEOPLE WHO CARE ONLY ABOUT POWER CAN BE BROKEN, OR SCARED AWAY.
"BUT EXTREMISTS WHO GENUINELY BELIEVE THAT THEIR CAUSE IS JUST...THOSE ARE THE ONES TO WATCH OUT FOR.
"BECAUSE THEY WOULD SOONER DESTROY THE WORLD THAN LET IT BECOME SOMETHING THEY DON'T LIKE."

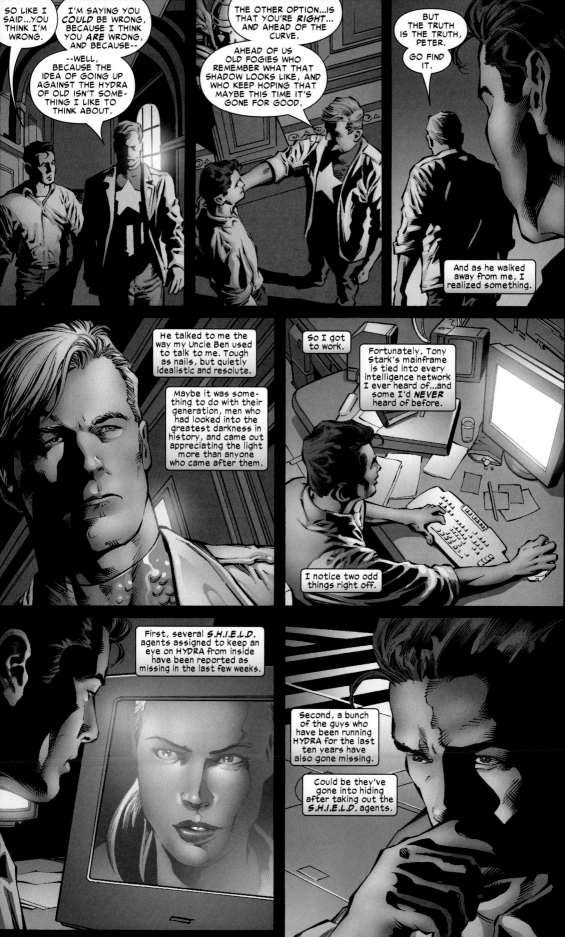

SO LIKE I SAID...YOU THINK I'M WRONG.

I'M SAYING YOU *COULD* BE WRONG, BECAUSE I THINK YOU *ARE* WRONG, AND BECAUSE--

--WELL, BECAUSE THE IDEA OF GOING UP AGAINST THE HYDRA OF OLD ISN'T SOMETHING I LIKE TO THINK ABOUT.

THE OTHER OPTION...IS THAT YOU'RE *RIGHT*...AND AHEAD OF THE CURVE.

AHEAD OF US OLD FOGIES WHO REMEMBER WHAT THAT SHADOW LOOKS LIKE, AND WHO KEEP HOPING THAT MAYBE THIS TIME IT'S GONE FOR GOOD.

BUT THE TRUTH IS THE TRUTH, PETER. GO FIND IT.

And as he walked away from me, I realized something.

He talked to me the way my Uncle Ben used to talk to me. Tough as nails, but quietly idealistic and resolute.

Maybe it was something to do with their generation, men who had looked into the greatest darkness in history, and came out appreciating the light more than anyone who came after them.

So I got to work.

Fortunately, Tony Stark's mainframe is tied into every intelligence network I ever heard of...and some I'd *NEVER* heard of before.

I notice two odd things right off.

First, several *S.H.I.E.L.D.* agents assigned to keep an eye on HYDRA from inside have been reported as missing in the last few weeks.

Second, a bunch of the guys who have been running HYDRA for the last ten years have also gone missing.

Could be they've gone into hiding after taking out the *S.H.I.E.L.D.* agents.

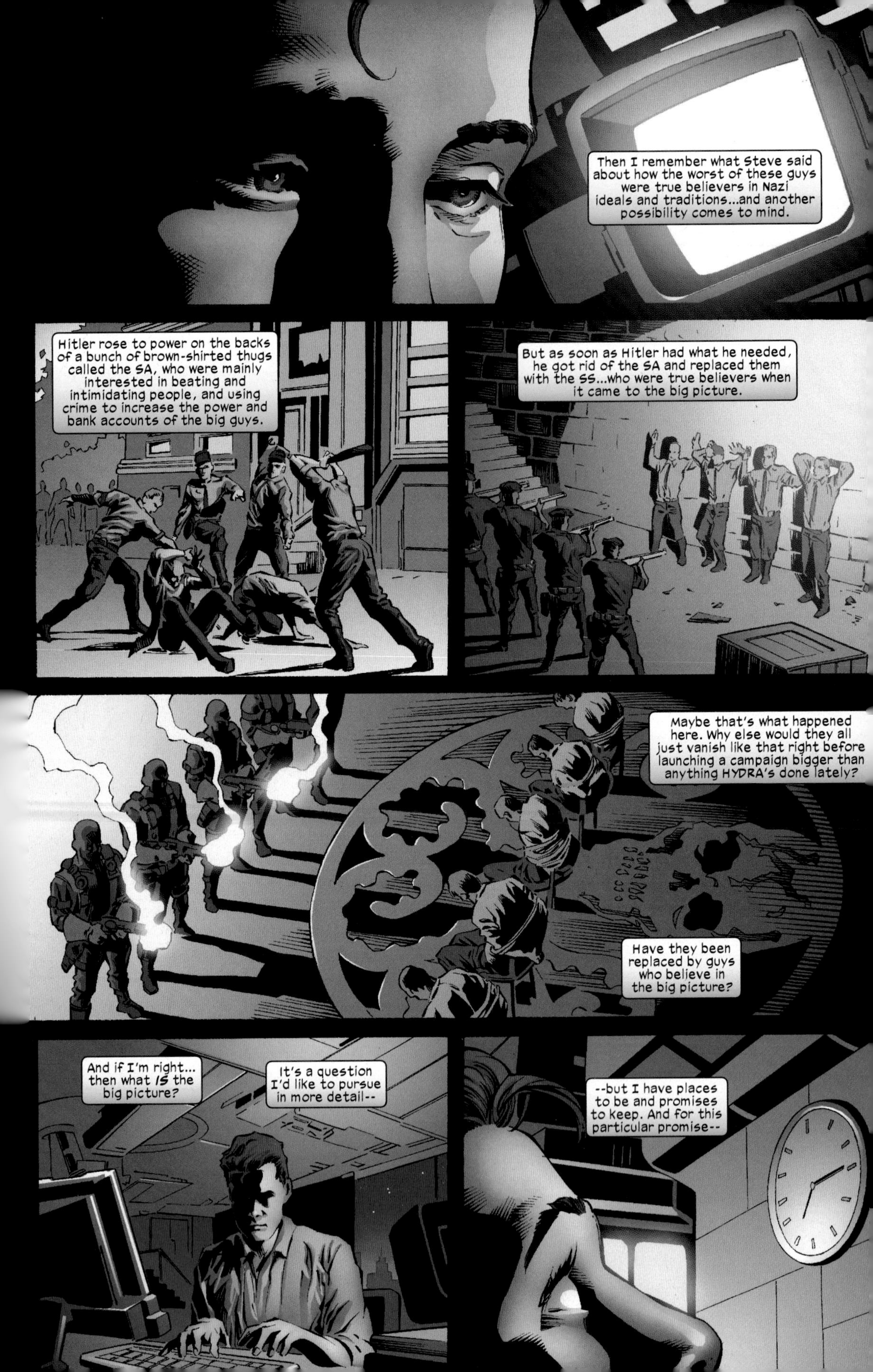
Then I remember what Steve said about how the worst of these guys were true believers in Nazi ideals and traditions...and another possibility comes to mind.
Hitler rose to power on the backs of a bunch of brown-shirted thugs called the SA, who were mainly interested in beating and intimidating people, and using crime to increase the power and bank accounts of the big guys.
But as soon as Hitler had what he needed, he got rid of the SA and replaced them with the SS...who were true believers when it came to the big picture.
Maybe that's what happened here. Why else would they all just vanish like that right before launching a campaign bigger than anything HYDRA's done lately?
Have they been replaced by guys who believe in the big picture?
And if I'm right... then what IS the big picture?
It's a question I'd like to pursue in more detail--
--but I have places to be and promises to keep. And for this particular promise--

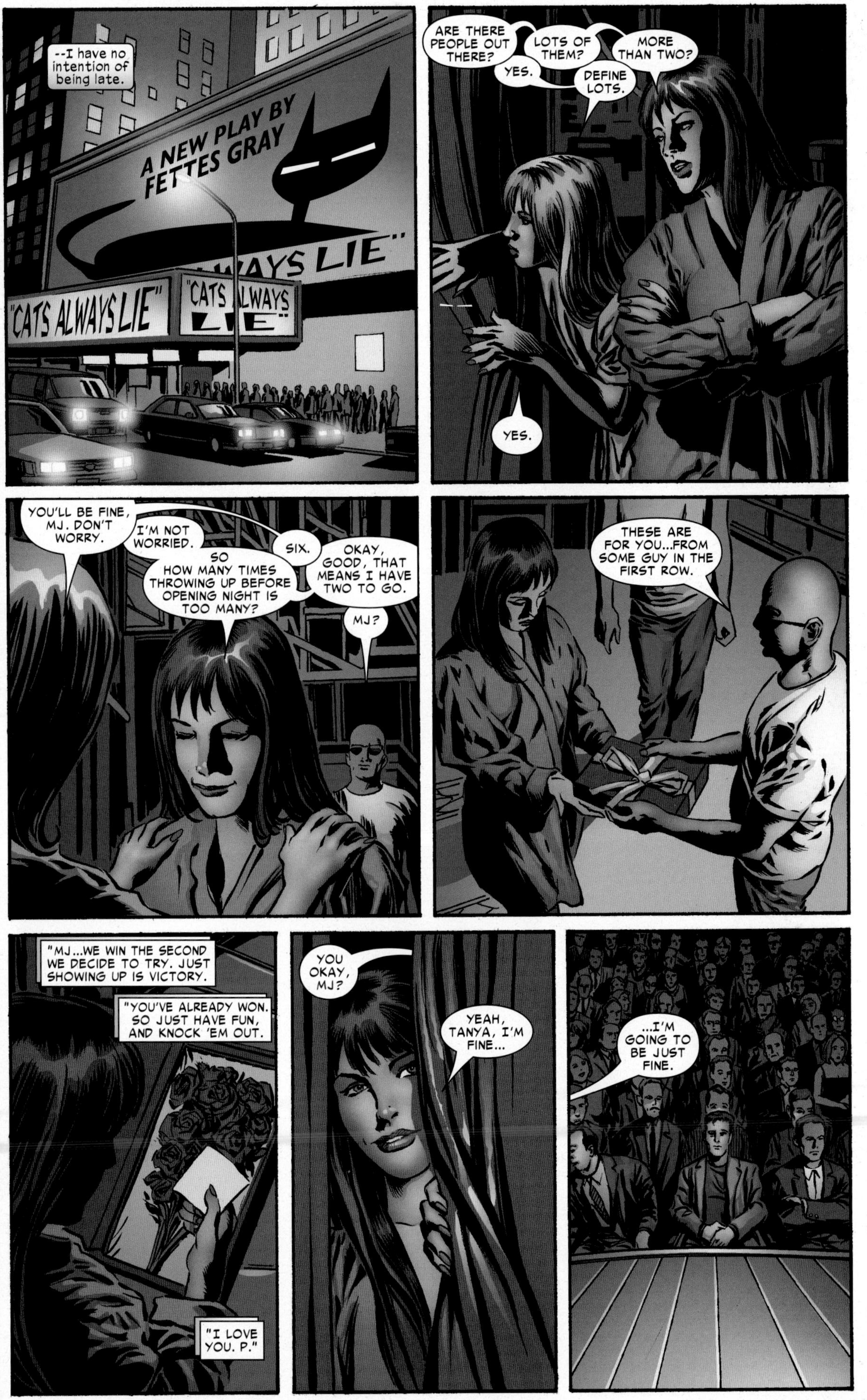
--I have no intention of being late.
A NEW PLAY BY FETTES GRAY
"CATS ALWAYS LIE"
"CATS ALWAYS LIE"
ARE THERE PEOPLE OUT THERE?
YES.
LOTS OF THEM?
YES.
MORE THAN TWO?
DEFINE LOTS.
YOU'LL BE FINE, MJ. DON'T WORRY.
I'M NOT WORRIED.
SO HOW MANY TIMES THROWING UP BEFORE OPENING NIGHT IS TOO MANY?
SIX.
OKAY, GOOD, THAT MEANS I HAVE TWO TO GO.
MJ?
THESE ARE FOR YOU...FROM SOME GUY IN THE FIRST ROW.
"MJ...WE WIN THE SECOND WE DECIDE TO TRY. JUST SHOWING UP IS VICTORY.
"YOU'VE ALREADY WON. SO JUST HAVE FUN, AND KNOCK 'EM OUT.
"I LOVE YOU. P."
YOU OKAY, MJ?
YEAH, TANYA, I'M FINE...
...I'M GOING TO BE JUST FINE.

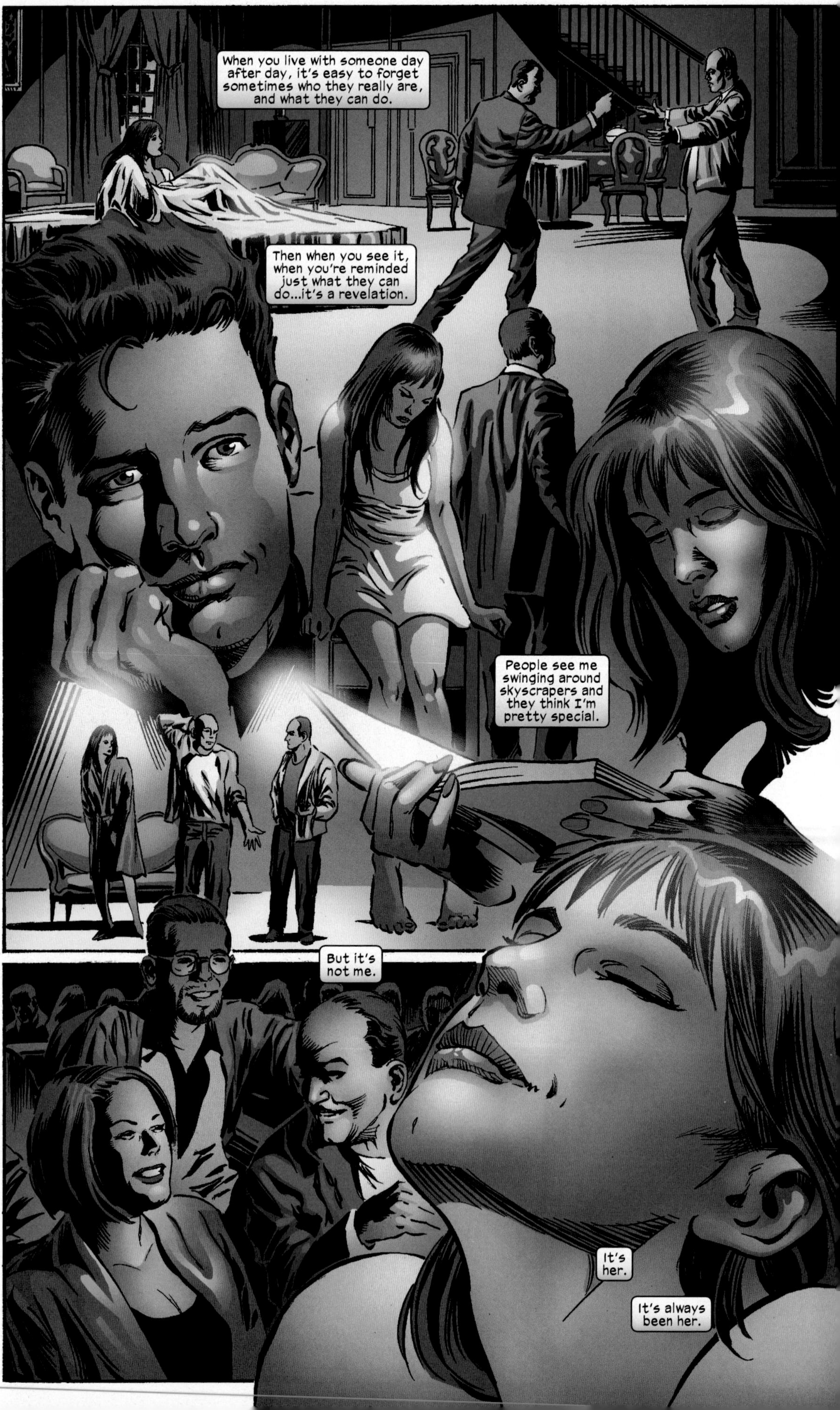
When you live with someone day after day, it's easy to forget sometimes who they really are, and what they can do.
Then when you see it, when you're reminded just what they can do...it's a revelation.
People see me swinging around skyscrapers and they think I'm pretty special.
But it's not me.
It's her.
It's always been her.

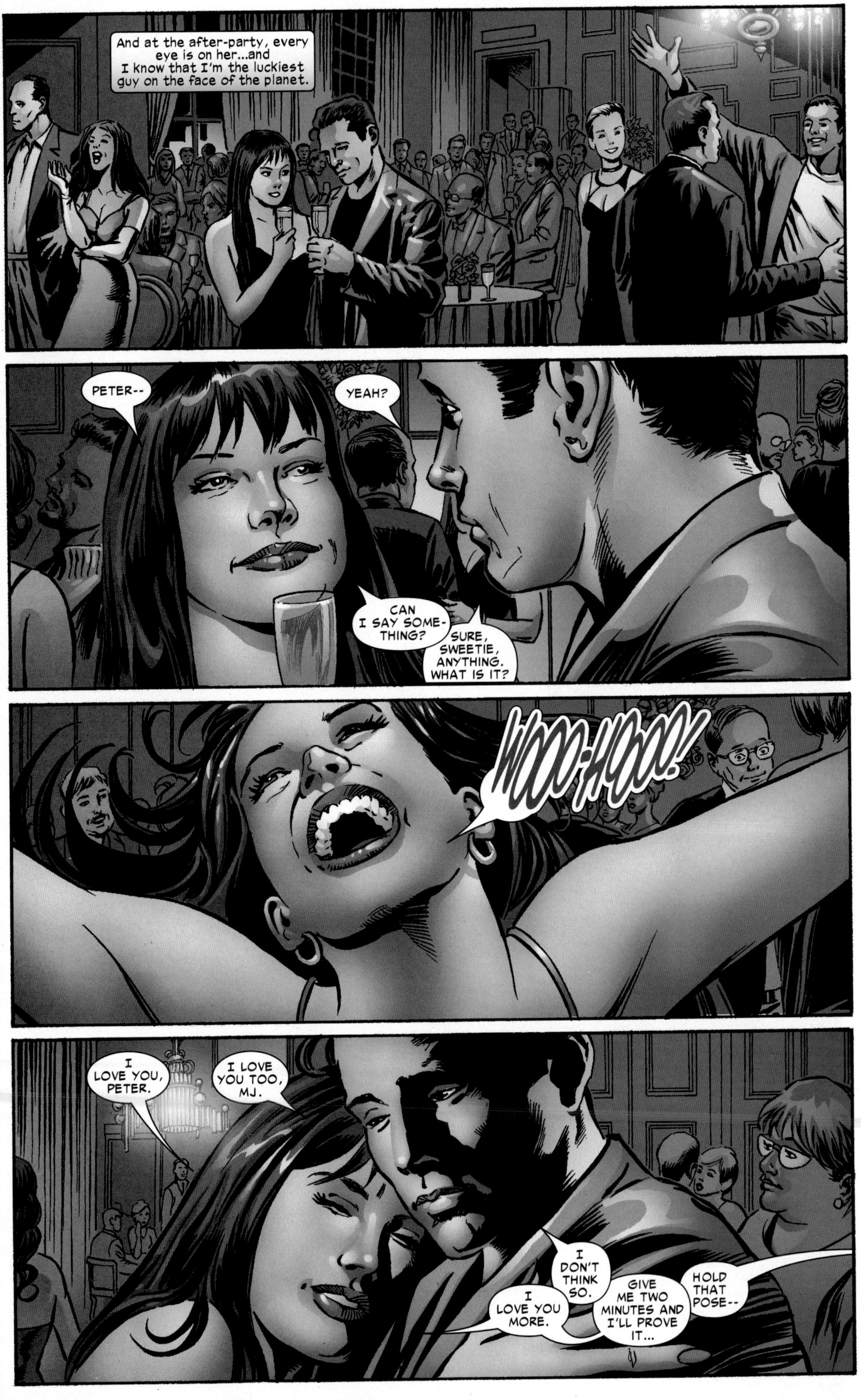

And at the after-party, every eye is on her...and I know that I'm the luckiest guy on the face of the planet.
PETER--
YEAH?
CAN I SAY SOME-THING?
SURE, SWEETIE, ANYTHING. WHAT IS IT?
WOOO-HOOO!
I LOVE YOU, PETER.
I LOVE YOU TOO, MJ.
I LOVE YOU MORE.
I DON'T THINK SO.
GIVE ME TWO MINUTES AND I'LL PROVE IT...
HOLD THAT POSE--

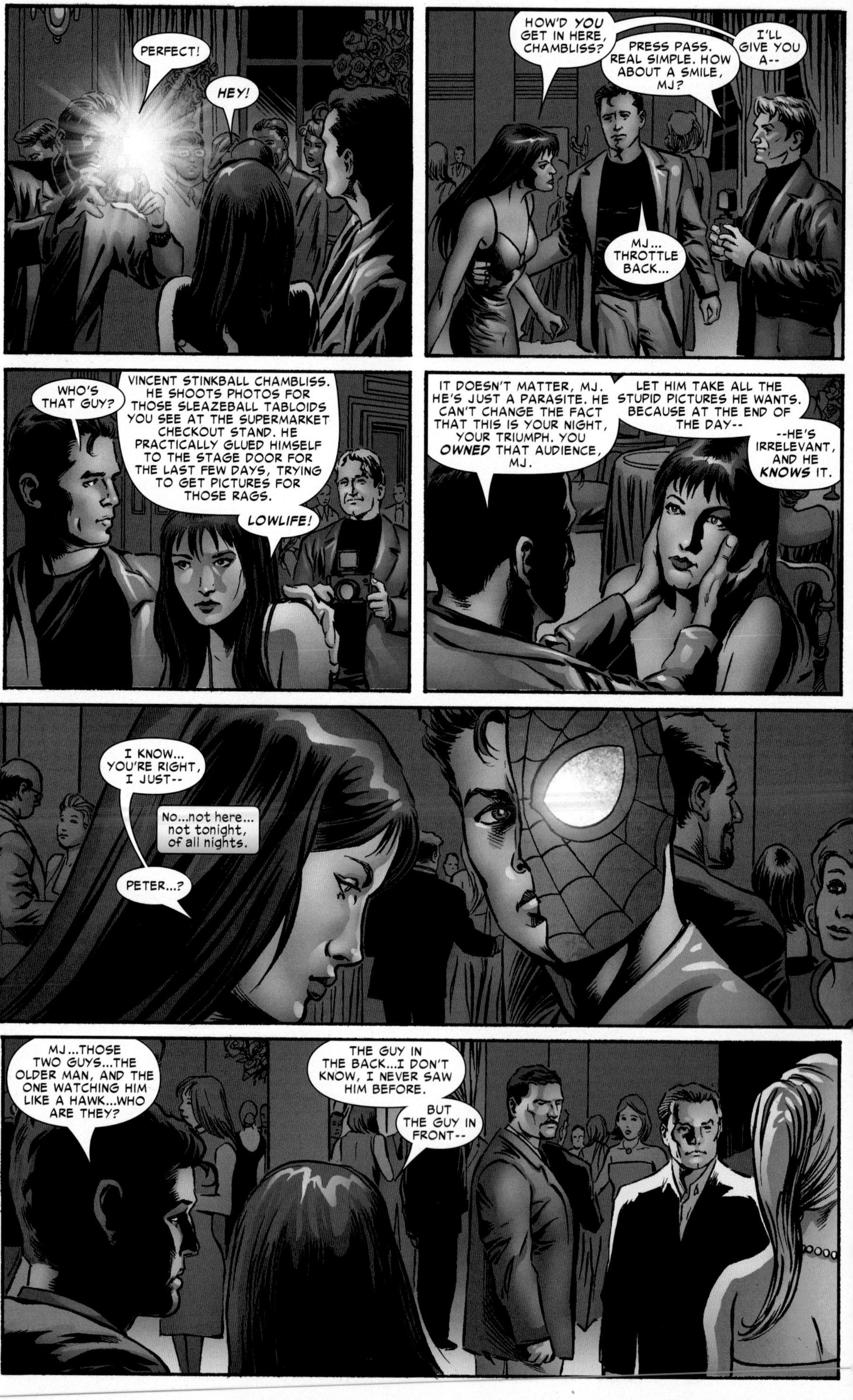

PERFECT!
HEY!
HOW'D YOU GET IN HERE, CHAMBLISS?
PRESS PASS. REAL SIMPLE. HOW ABOUT A SMILE, MJ?
I'LL GIVE YOU A--
MJ... THROTTLE BACK...
WHO'S THAT GUY?
VINCENT STINKBALL CHAMBLISS. HE SHOOTS PHOTOS FOR THOSE SLEAZEBALL TABLOIDS YOU SEE AT THE SUPERMARKET CHECKOUT STAND. HE PRACTICALLY GLUED HIMSELF TO THE STAGE DOOR FOR THE LAST FEW DAYS, TRYING TO GET PICTURES FOR THOSE RAGS.
LOWLIFE!
IT DOESN'T MATTER, MJ. HE'S JUST A PARASITE. HE CAN'T CHANGE THE FACT THAT THIS IS YOUR NIGHT, YOUR TRIUMPH. YOU OWNED THAT AUDIENCE, MJ.
LET HIM TAKE ALL THE STUPID PICTURES HE WANTS. BECAUSE AT THE END OF THE DAY--
--HE'S IRRELEVANT, AND HE KNOWS IT.
I KNOW... YOU'RE RIGHT, I JUST--
No...not here... not tonight, of all nights.
PETER...?
MJ...THOSE TWO GUYS...THE OLDER MAN, AND THE ONE WATCHING HIM LIKE A HAWK...WHO ARE THEY?
THE GUY IN THE BACK...I DON'T KNOW, I NEVER SAW HIM BEFORE.
BUT THE GUY IN FRONT--

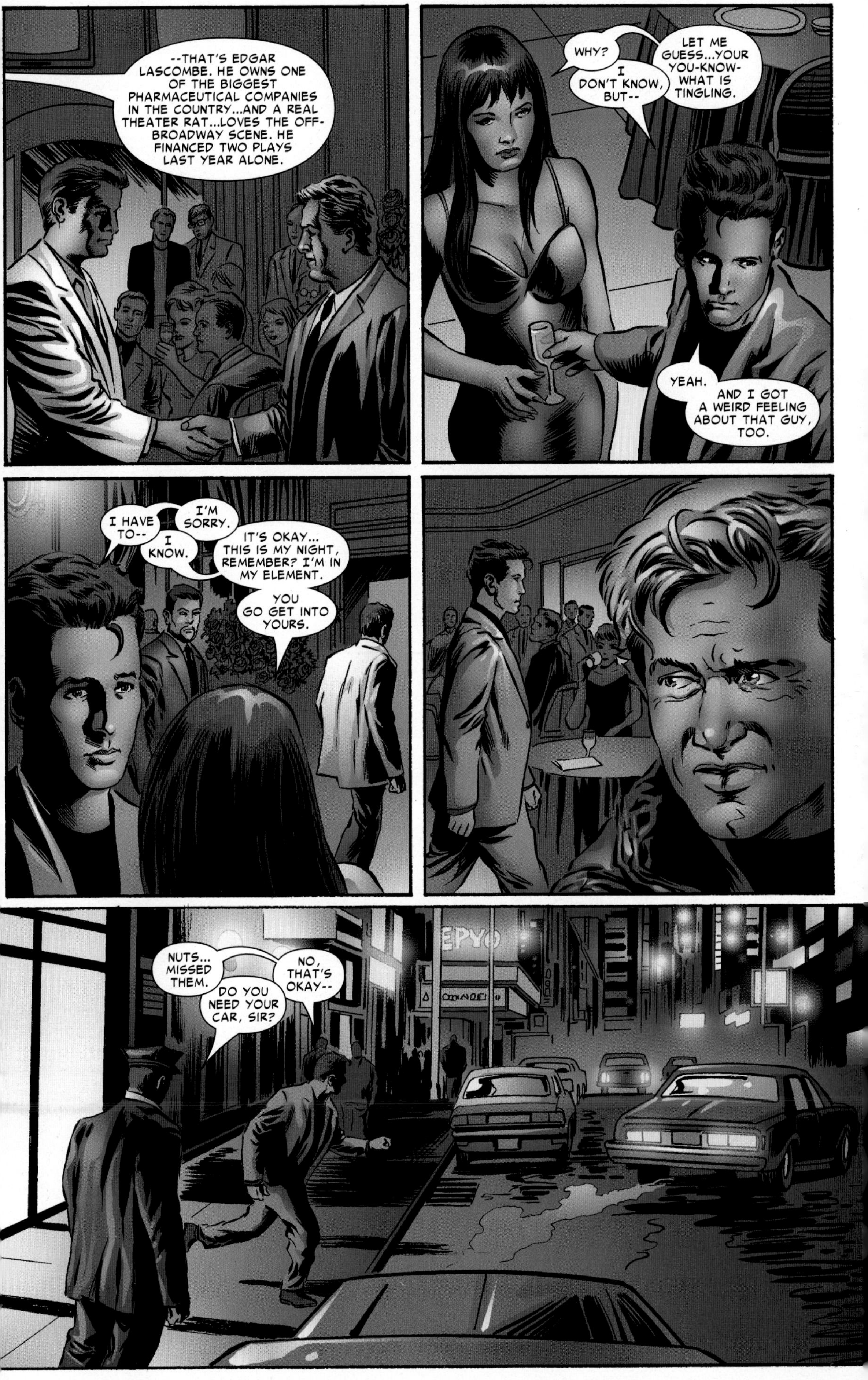
--THAT'S EDGAR LASCOMBE. HE OWNS ONE OF THE BIGGEST PHARMACEUTICAL COMPANIES IN THE COUNTRY...AND A REAL THEATER RAT...LOVES THE OFF-BROADWAY SCENE. HE FINANCED TWO PLAYS LAST YEAR ALONE.
LET ME GUESS...YOUR YOU-KNOW-WHAT IS TINGLING.
WHY?
I DON'T KNOW, BUT--
YEAH.
AND I GOT A WEIRD FEELING ABOUT THAT GUY, TOO.
I HAVE TO--
I'M SORRY.
I KNOW.
IT'S OKAY... THIS IS MY NIGHT, REMEMBER? I'M IN MY ELEMENT.
YOU GO GET INTO YOURS.
NUTS... MISSED THEM.
DO YOU NEED YOUR CAR, SIR?
NO, THAT'S OKAY--

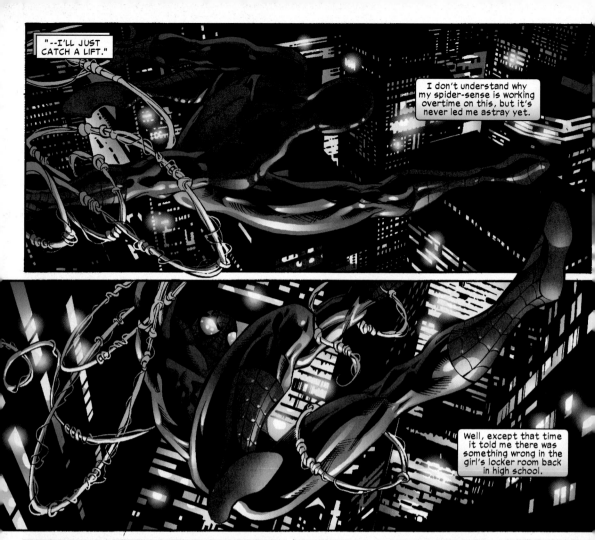

"--I'LL JUST CATCH A LIFT."

I don't understand why my spider-sense is working overtime on this, but it's never led me astray yet.

Well, except that time it told me there was something wrong in the girl's locker room back in high school.

At least, that's how I chose to *INTERPRET* it, anyway.

End of the line, let's see where this goes.

Okay, bad sign number one on display.

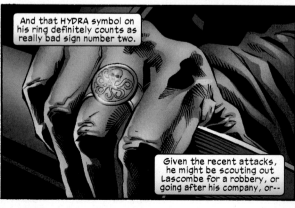

And that *HYDRA* symbol on his ring definitely counts as really bad sign number two.

Given the recent attacks, he might be scouting out Lascombe for a robbery, or going after his company, or--

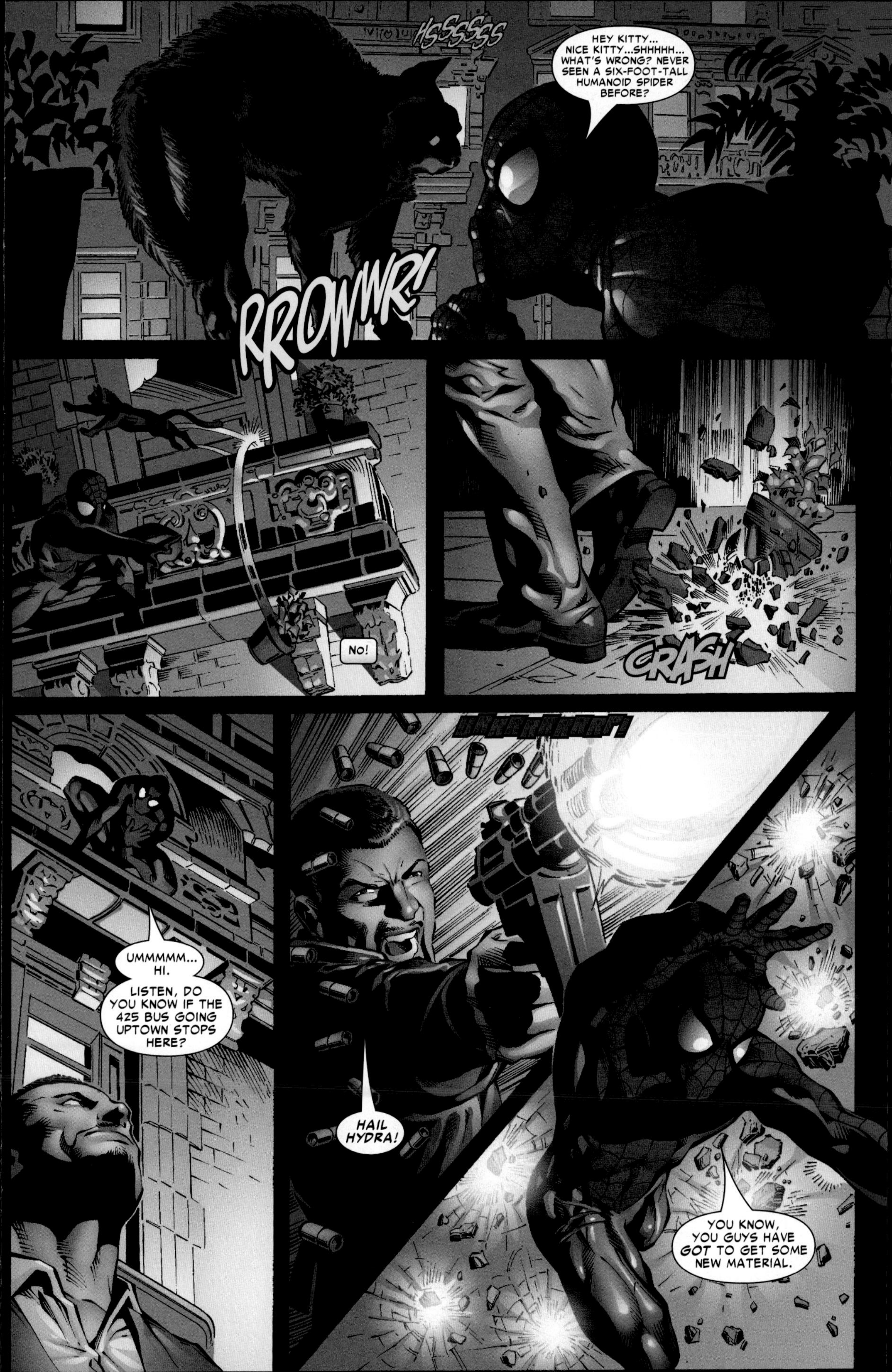
HSSSSSS
HEY KITTY... NICE KITTY...SHHHHH... WHAT'S WRONG? NEVER SEEN A SIX-FOOT-TALL HUMANOID SPIDER BEFORE?
RROWWR!
NO!
CRASH
UMMMMM... HI.
LISTEN, DO YOU KNOW IF THE 425 BUS GOING UPTOWN STOPS HERE?
HAIL HYDRA!
YOU KNOW, YOU GUYS HAVE GOT TO GET SOME NEW MATERIAL.

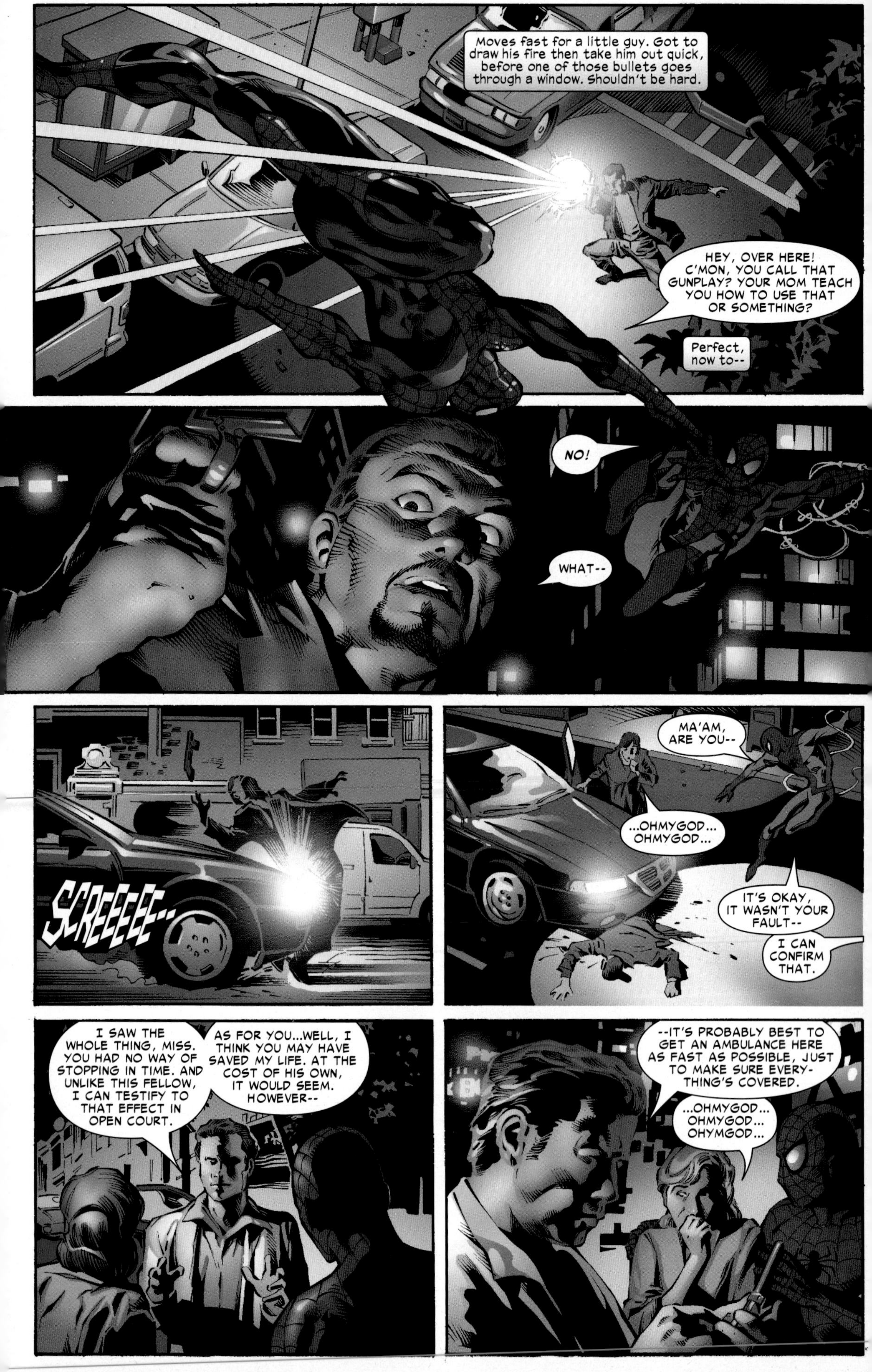
Moves fast for a little guy. Got to draw his fire then take him out quick, before one of those bullets goes through a window. Shouldn't be hard.
HEY, OVER HERE! C'MON, YOU CALL THAT GUNPLAY? YOUR MOM TEACH YOU HOW TO USE THAT OR SOMETHING?
Perfect, now to--
NO!
WHAT--
SCREEEEE--
MA'AM, ARE YOU--
...OHMYGOD... OHMYGOD...
IT'S OKAY, IT WASN'T YOUR FAULT--
I CAN CONFIRM THAT.
I SAW THE WHOLE THING, MISS. YOU HAD NO WAY OF STOPPING IN TIME. AND UNLIKE THIS FELLOW, I CAN TESTIFY TO THAT EFFECT IN OPEN COURT.
AS FOR YOU...WELL, I THINK YOU MAY HAVE SAVED MY LIFE. AT THE COST OF HIS OWN, IT WOULD SEEM. HOWEVER--
--IT'S PROBABLY BEST TO GET AN AMBULANCE HERE AS FAST AS POSSIBLE, JUST TO MAKE SURE EVERY-THING'S COVERED.
...OHMYGOD... OHMYGOD... OHYMGOD...

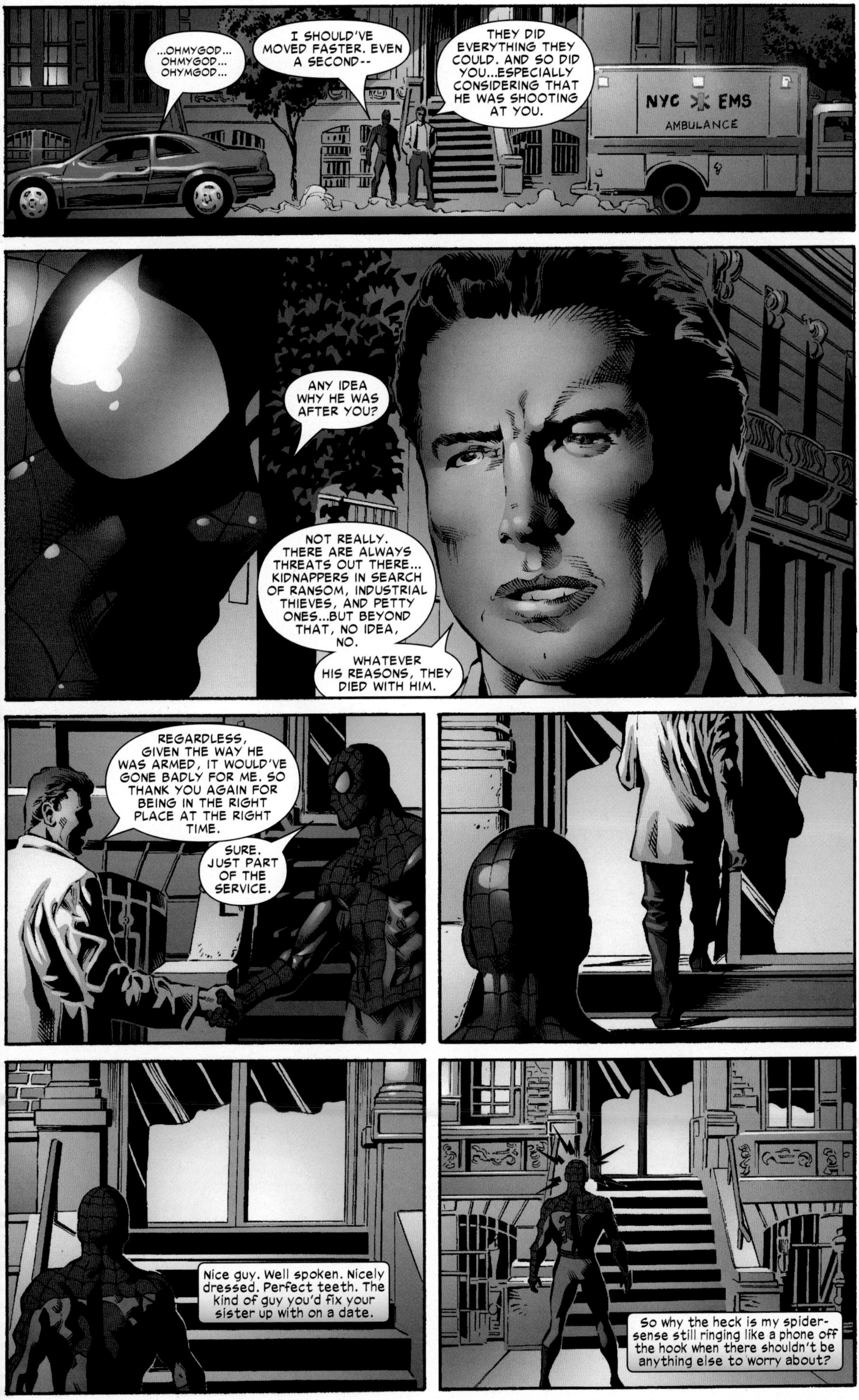
...OHMYGOD... OHMYGOD... OHYMGOD...
I SHOULD'VE MOVED FASTER. EVEN A SECOND--
THEY DID EVERYTHING THEY COULD. AND SO DID YOU...ESPECIALLY CONSIDERING THAT HE WAS SHOOTING AT YOU.
NYC EMS
AMBULANCE
ANY IDEA WHY HE WAS AFTER YOU?
NOT REALLY. THERE ARE ALWAYS THREATS OUT THERE... KIDNAPPERS IN SEARCH OF RANSOM, INDUSTRIAL THIEVES, AND PETTY ONES...BUT BEYOND THAT, NO IDEA, NO.
WHATEVER HIS REASONS, THEY DIED WITH HIM.
REGARDLESS, GIVEN THE WAY HE WAS ARMED, IT WOULD'VE GONE BADLY FOR ME. SO THANK YOU AGAIN FOR BEING IN THE RIGHT PLACE AT THE RIGHT TIME.
SURE. JUST PART OF THE SERVICE.
Nice guy. Well spoken. Nicely dressed. Perfect teeth. The kind of guy you'd fix your sister up with on a date.
So why the heck is my spider-sense still ringing like a phone off the hook when there shouldn't be anything else to worry about?

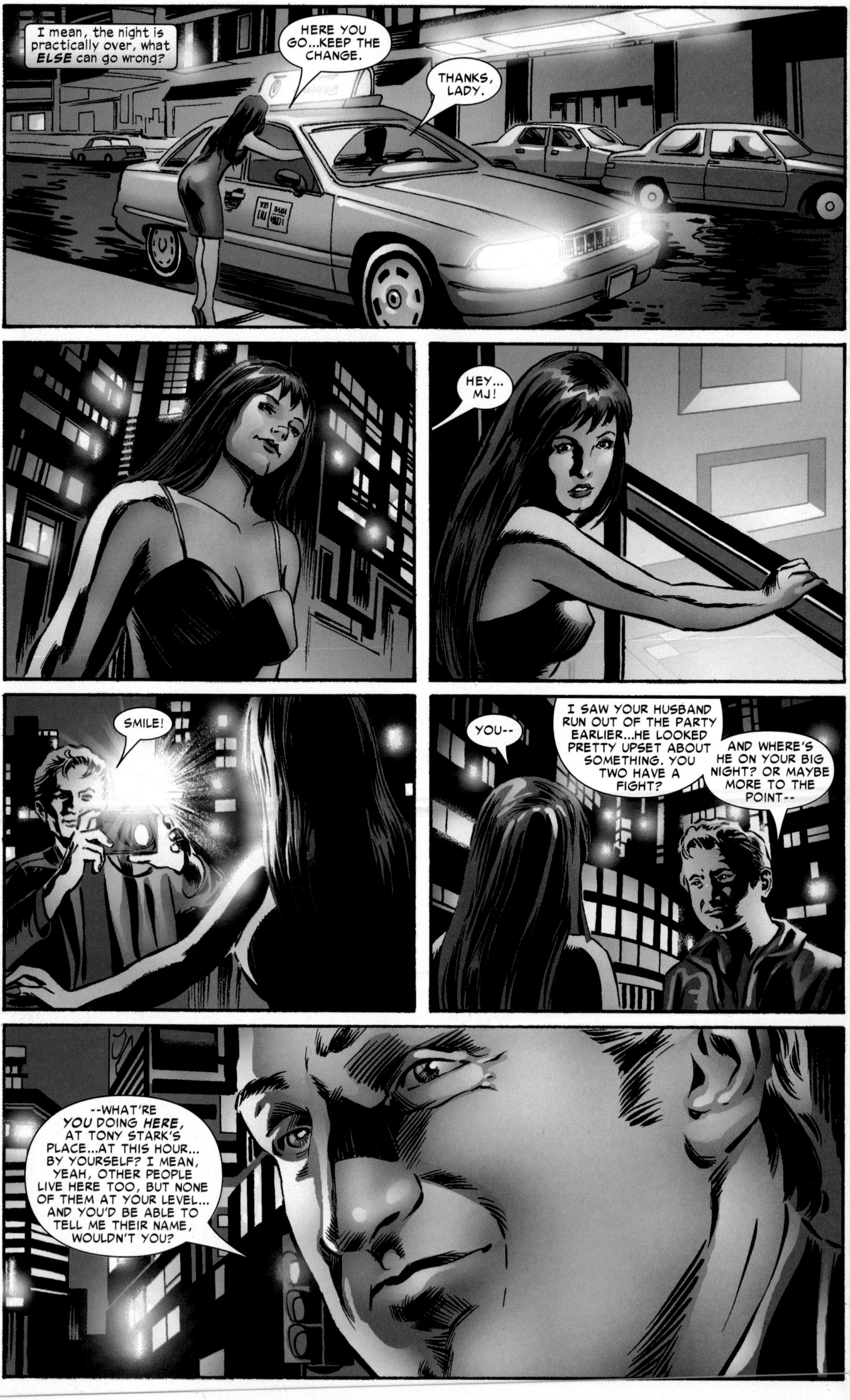
I mean, the night is practically over, what *ELSE* can go wrong?
HERE YOU GO...KEEP THE CHANGE.
THANKS, LADY.
HEY... MJ!
SMILE!
YOU--
I SAW YOUR HUSBAND RUN OUT OF THE PARTY EARLIER...HE LOOKED PRETTY UPSET ABOUT SOMETHING. YOU TWO HAVE A FIGHT?
AND WHERE'S HE ON YOUR BIG NIGHT? OR MAYBE MORE TO THE POINT--
--WHAT'RE *YOU* DOING *HERE,* AT TONY STARK'S PLACE...AT THIS HOUR... BY YOURSELF? I MEAN, YEAH, OTHER PEOPLE LIVE HERE TOO, BUT NONE OF THEM AT YOUR LEVEL... AND YOU'D BE ABLE TO TELL ME THEIR NAME, WOULDN'T YOU?

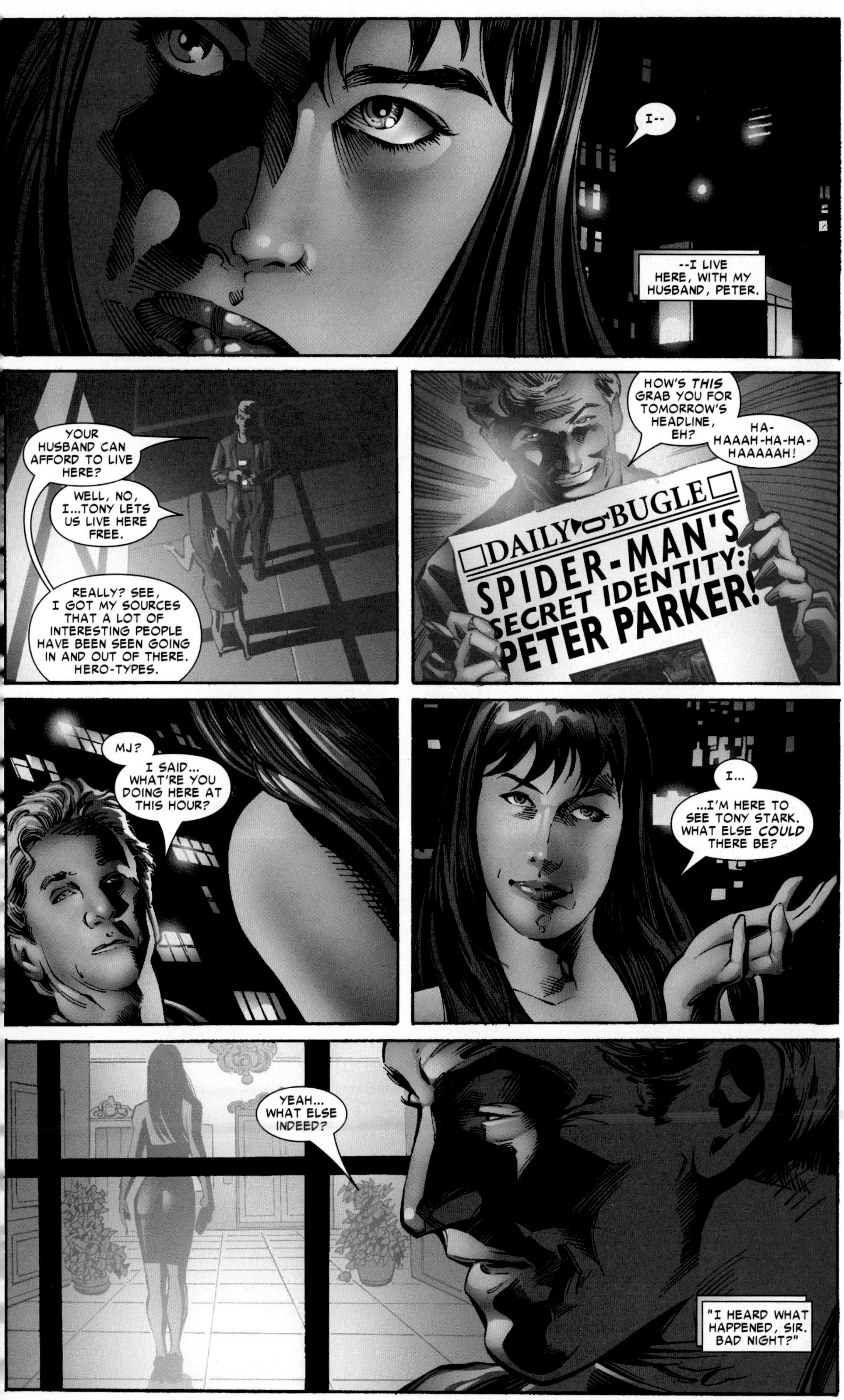
I--
--I LIVE HERE, WITH MY HUSBAND, PETER.
YOUR HUSBAND CAN AFFORD TO LIVE HERE?
WELL, NO, I...TONY LETS US LIVE HERE FREE.
REALLY? SEE, I GOT MY SOURCES THAT A LOT OF INTERESTING PEOPLE HAVE BEEN SEEN GOING IN AND OUT OF THERE. HERO-TYPES.
HOW'S THIS GRAB YOU FOR TOMORROW'S HEADLINE, EH?
HA-HAAAH-HA-HA-HAAAAAH!
DAILY BUGLE
SPIDER-MAN'S SECRET IDENTITY: PETER PARKER!
MJ?
I SAID... WHAT'RE YOU DOING HERE AT THIS HOUR?
I...
...I'M HERE TO SEE TONY STARK. WHAT ELSE COULD THERE BE?
YEAH... WHAT ELSE INDEED?
"I HEARD WHAT HAPPENED, SIR. BAD NIGHT?"

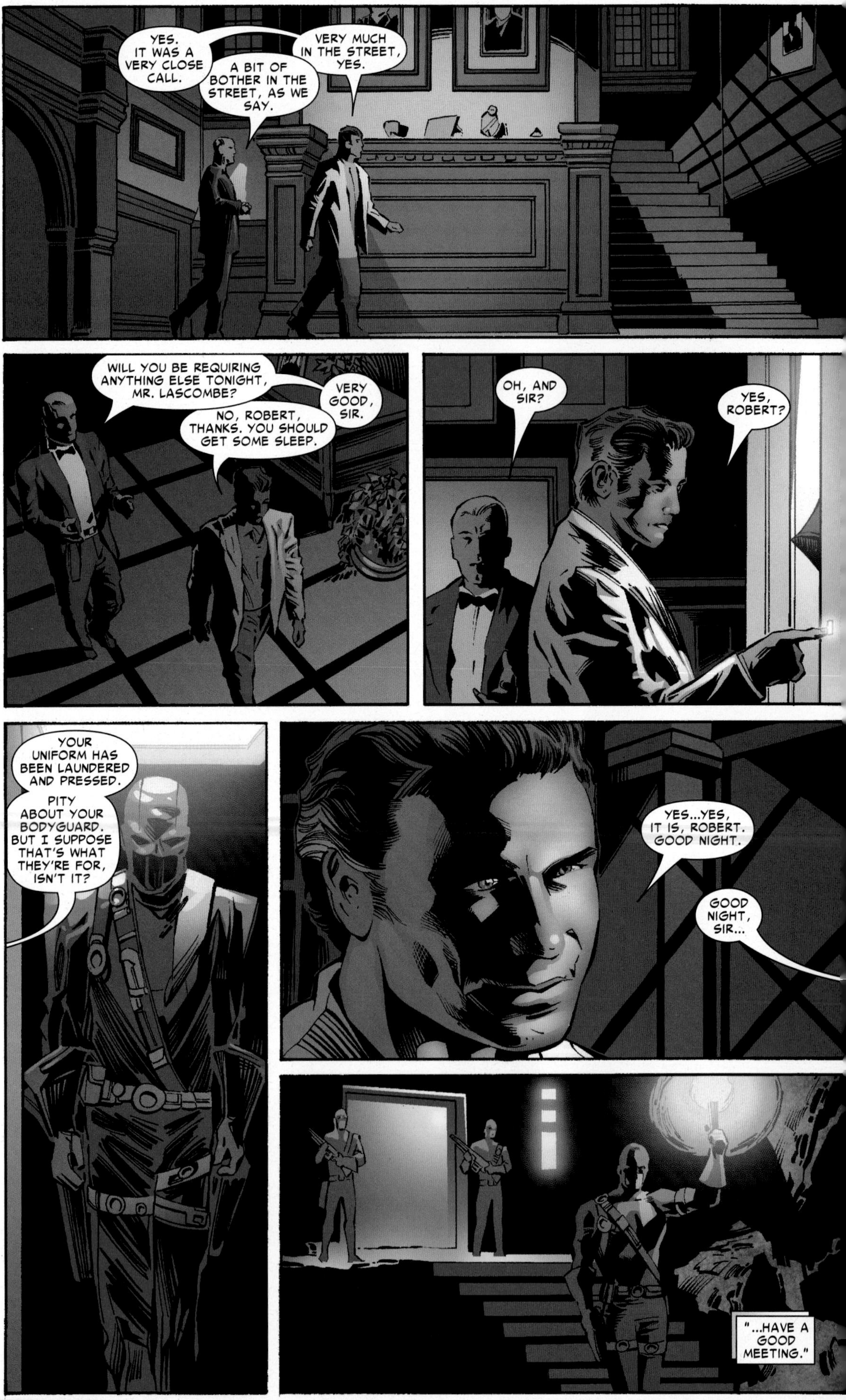
YES. IT WAS A VERY CLOSE CALL.
A BIT OF BOTHER IN THE STREET, AS WE SAY.
VERY MUCH IN THE STREET, YES.
WILL YOU BE REQUIRING ANYTHING ELSE TONIGHT, MR. LASCOMBE?
NO, ROBERT, THANKS. YOU SHOULD GET SOME SLEEP.
VERY GOOD, SIR.
OH, AND SIR?
YES, ROBERT?
YOUR UNIFORM HAS BEEN LAUNDERED AND PRESSED.
PITY ABOUT YOUR BODYGUARD. BUT I SUPPOSE THAT'S WHAT THEY'RE FOR, ISN'T IT?
YES...YES, IT IS, ROBERT. GOOD NIGHT.
GOOD NIGHT, SIR...
"...HAVE A GOOD MEETING."

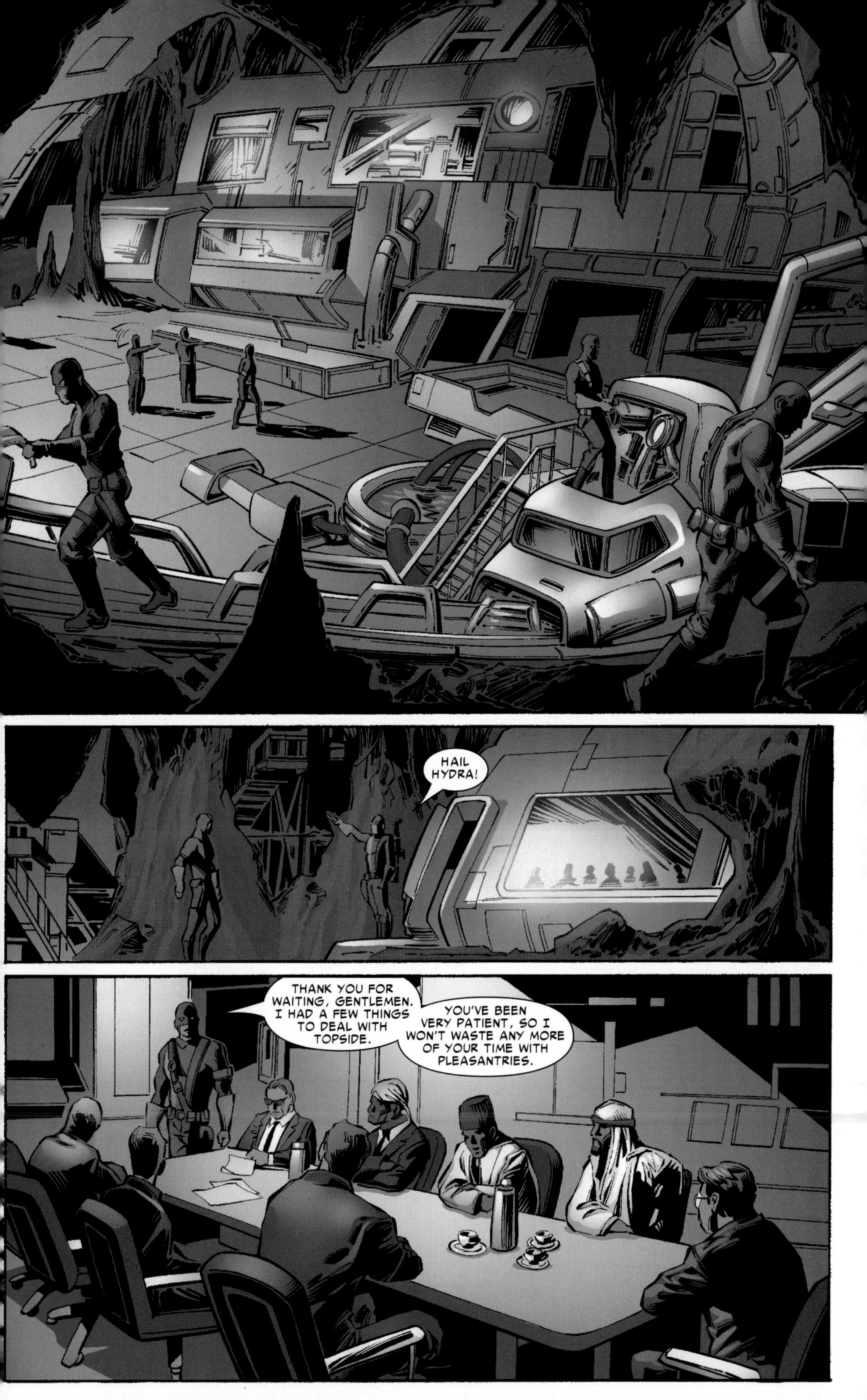
HAIL HYDRA!
THANK YOU FOR WAITING, GENTLEMEN. I HAD A FEW THINGS TO DEAL WITH TOPSIDE.
YOU'VE BEEN VERY PATIENT, SO I WON'T WASTE ANY MORE OF YOUR TIME WITH PLEASANTRIES.

EACH OF YOU REPRESENTS A FOREIGN INTEREST WHO WISHES TO SEE IF HYDRA'S BITE CAN NOW MATCH OUR BARK. WE HAVE NOT ASKED FOR MONEY OR SUPPORT FROM ANY OF YOU...ONLY YOUR RESPECT, AND A SEAT AT THE TABLE AS PLAYERS ON THE INTERNATIONAL STAGE.

YOU'VE ALL BEEN FIGHTING A WAR OF ATTRITION AGAINST THE WEST. A LITTLE VICTORY HERE, A STALEMATE THERE... WE ARE TRYING A DIFFERENT WAY. WE ARE GOING TO ANSWER A SEEMINGLY IMPOSSIBLE QUESTION.

AND THAT QUESTION IS THIS:

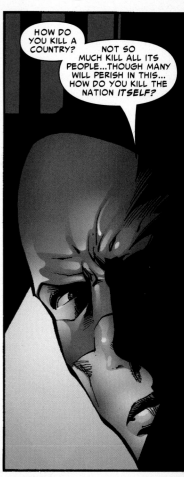

HOW DO YOU KILL A COUNTRY?

NOT SO MUCH KILL ALL ITS PEOPLE...THOUGH MANY WILL PERISH IN THIS... HOW DO YOU KILL THE NATION *ITSELF*?

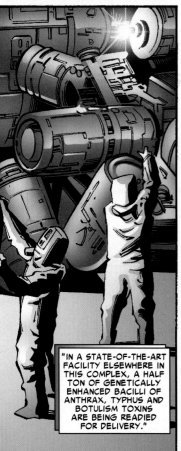

"IN A STATE-OF-THE-ART FACILITY ELSEWHERE IN THIS COMPLEX, A HALF TON OF GENETICALLY ENHANCED BACILLI OF ANTHRAX, TYPHUS AND BOTULISM TOXINS ARE BEING READIED FOR DELIVERY."

OTHERS MIGHT CHOOSE TO USE THIS TO STRIKE AT A CITY...AND THEY WOULD SUCCEED IN KILLING EVERYONE IN THAT CITY. BUT *ONLY* THOSE PEOPLE.

AFTERWARD, AS WE HAVE SEEN, THE REST OF THE NATION WOULD RISE UP AND STRIKE DOWN THOSE RESPONSIBLE. THE NATION WOULD REMAIN.

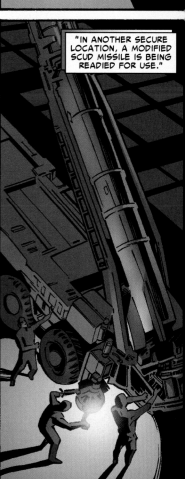

"IN ANOTHER SECURE LOCATION, A MODIFIED SCUD MISSILE IS BEING READIED FOR USE."

OTHERS WOULD LOAD UP SUCH A MISSILE WITH EXPLOSIVES, TO STRIKE AN IMPORTANT TARGET. BUT WE ARE DOING SOMETHING VERY, VERY DIFFERENT.

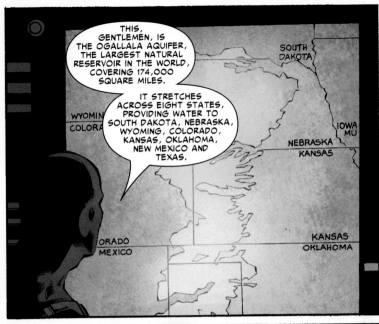

THIS, GENTLEMEN, IS THE OGALLALA AQUIFER, THE LARGEST NATURAL RESERVOIR IN THE WORLD, COVERING 174,000 SQUARE MILES.

IT STRETCHES ACROSS EIGHT STATES, PROVIDING WATER TO SOUTH DAKOTA, NEBRASKA, WYOMING, COLORADO, KANSAS, OKLAHOMA, NEW MEXICO AND TEXAS.

SOUTH DAKOTA

WYOMING
COLORA

IOWA
MU

NEBRASKA

KANSAS

ORADO
MEXICO

KANSAS
OKLAHOMA

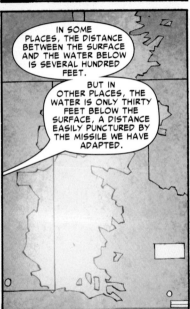

IN SOME PLACES, THE DISTANCE BETWEEN THE SURFACE AND THE WATER BELOW IS SEVERAL HUNDRED FEET.

BUT IN OTHER PLACES, THE WATER IS ONLY THIRTY FEET BELOW THE SURFACE, A DISTANCE EASILY PUNCTURED BY THE MISSILE WE HAVE ADAPTED.

HALF A TON OF ANTHRAX, TYPHUS AND BOTULISM TOXINS DEPOSITED INTO THE OGALLALA AQUIFER WILL RENDER IT MASSIVELY POISONOUS TO ALL PLANT, ANIMAL AND HUMAN LIFE.

IT WILL BE UNFIT FOR DRINKING OR GROWING CROPS. EVERY LAKE AND RIVER THAT FEEDS FROM THE AQUIFER WILL BECOME TOXIC, KILLING EVERYTHING THAT DRINKS OR SWIMS IN THEM.

MILLIONS WILL PERISH IN THE FIRST 48 HOURS, BEFORE THE GOVERNMENT REALIZES WHAT HAS HAPPENED.

THE ENTIRE AMERICAN MIDWEST WILL BECOME A DEATHBED...AND A DUSTBOWL. CROPS DESTROYED FOR THE NEXT TWENTY YEARS. FISH AND LIVESTOCK WIPED OUT. AND THE TENS OF MILLIONS NOT KILLED BY THE TOXINS WILL HAVE TO FLEE OR DIE.

IT WILL BE A MADHOUSE.

THE NATION WILL STARVE, BORDERS WILL BE OVERRUN, AND THE ECONOMY WILL COLLAPSE. EIGHT STATES WILL BE UNLIVEABLE, CAUSING MILLIONS OF PANICKED PEOPLE TO FLOOD INTO OTHER STATES. THE NATION WILL BE IN CHAOS: PARALYZED, UNGOVERNABLE, AND UNABLE TO STRIKE BACK.

THAT, GENTLEMEN, IS HOW YOU KILL A COUNTRY. AND THAT IS EXACTLY WHAT IS GOING TO HAPPEN IN JUST A FEW DAYS TIME.

ANY QUESTIONS?

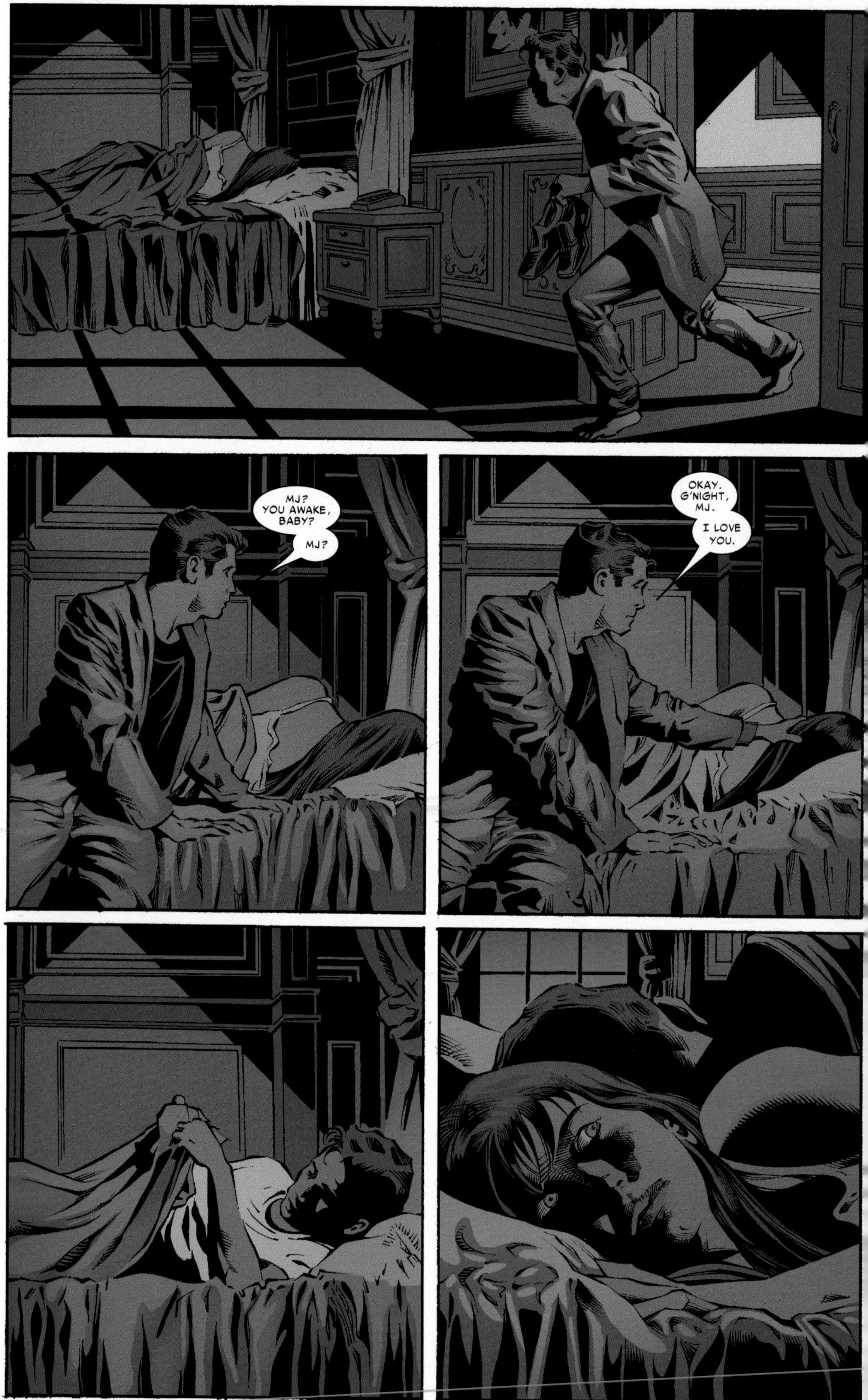
MJ? YOU AWAKE, BABY?
MJ?
OKAY. G'NIGHT, MJ.
I LOVE YOU.

LOOKING FOR THIS, SWEET-CHEEKS?

I...IS THAT--

YEP.

MUST'VE BEEN ONE HECK OF A NIGHT, ALL RIGHT.

NONONONONONONONONONONO
NONONONONONONONONONONO
NONONONONONONONONONONO
NONONONONONONONONONONO
NONONONONONONONONONONO

THE NEW ANNOUN
NONO NONONONO

PAGIN
all na

NONONONONO
NONONONONONO
NONONONONONO

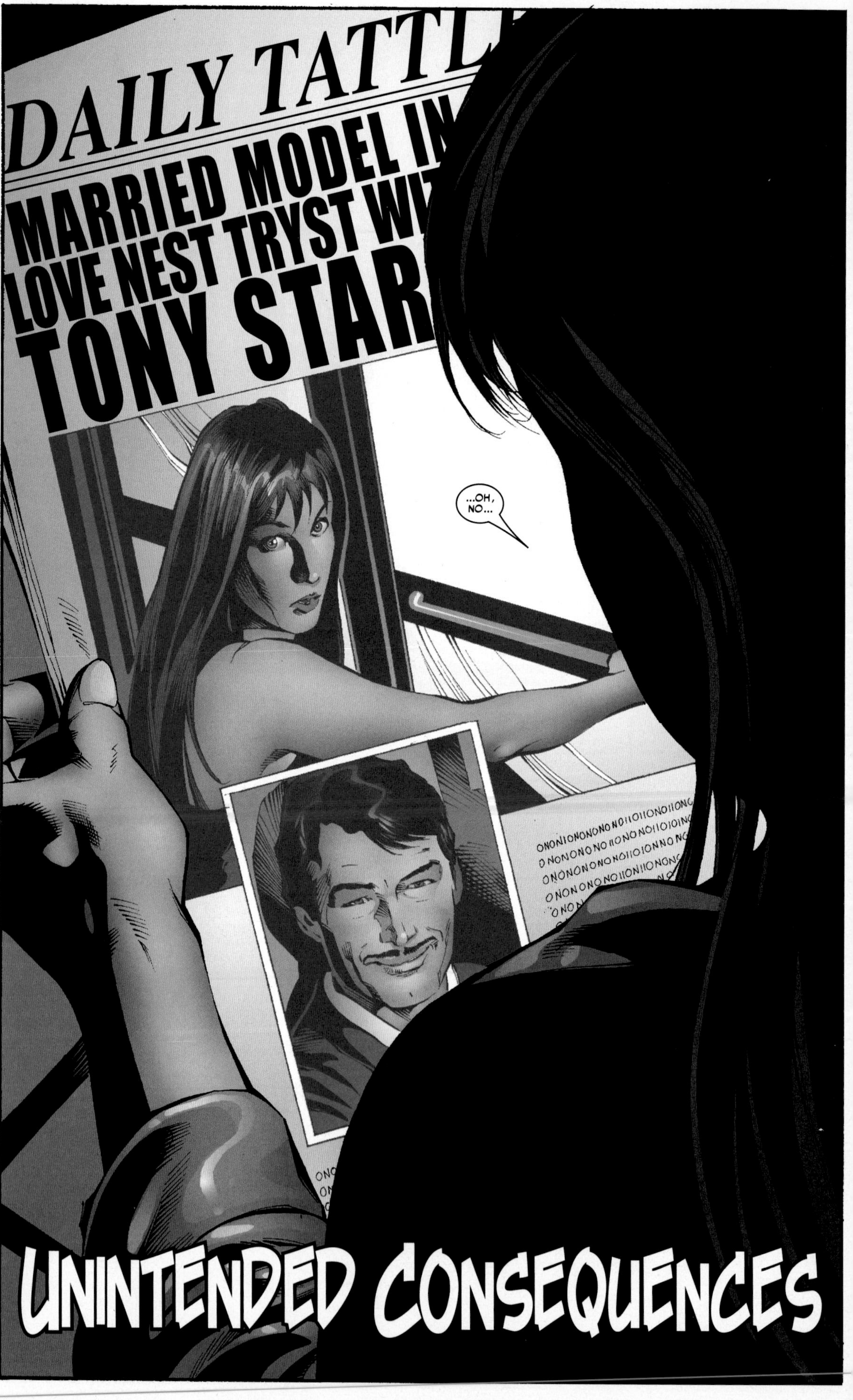
DAILY TATTL
MARRIED MODEL IN
LOVE NEST TRYST WI
TONY STAR
...OH, NO...
UNINTENDED CONSEQUENCES

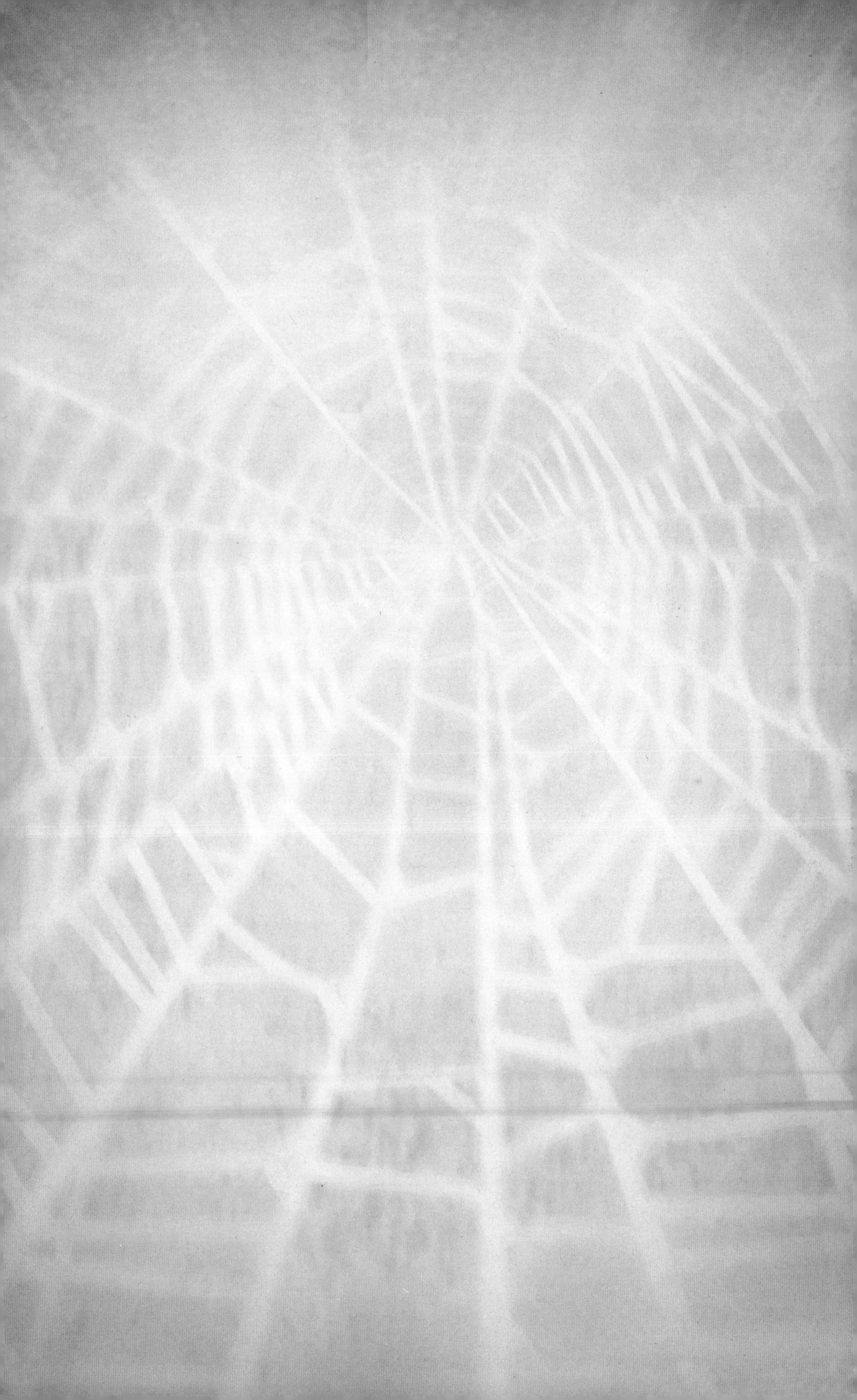

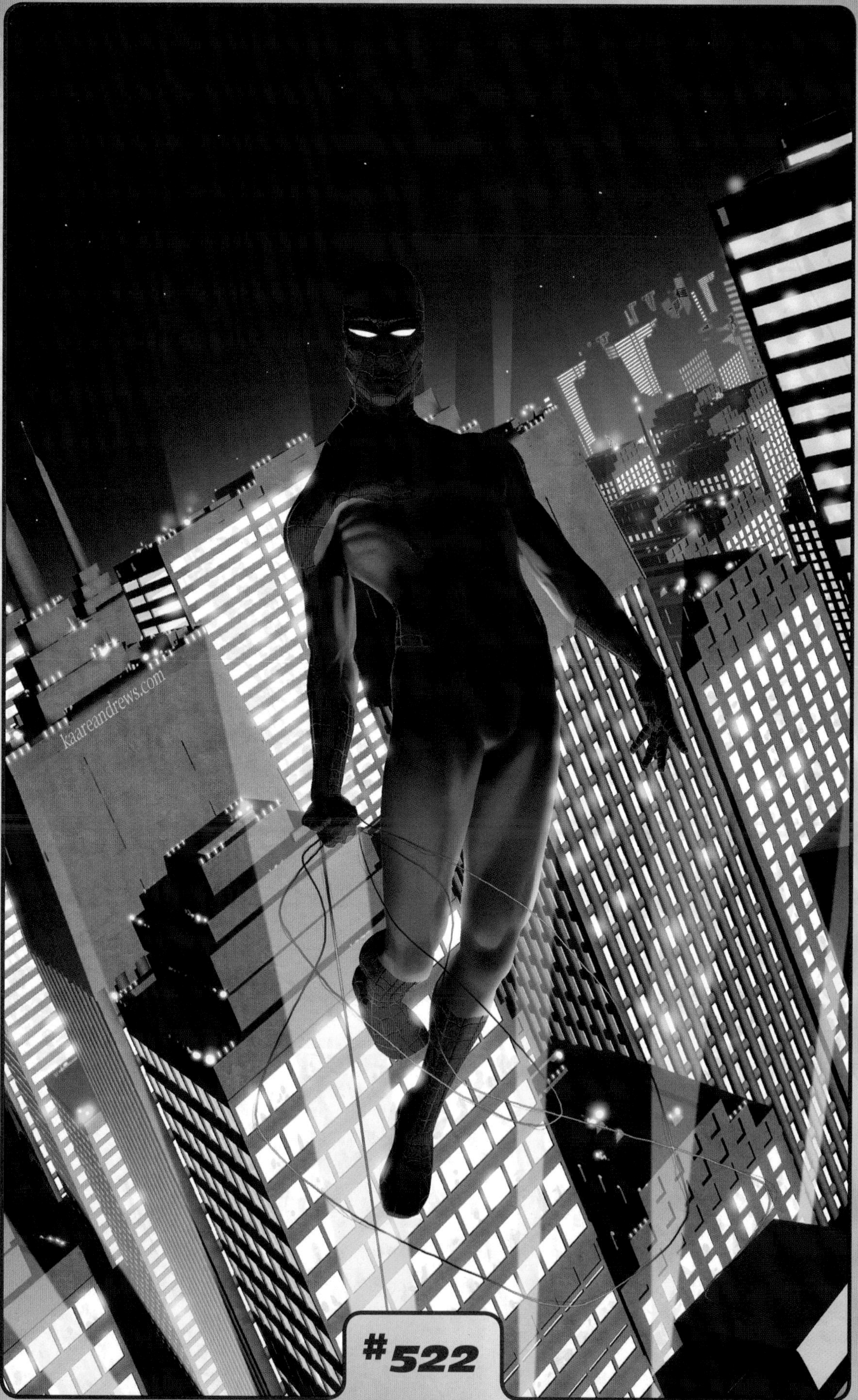
kaareandrews.com
#522

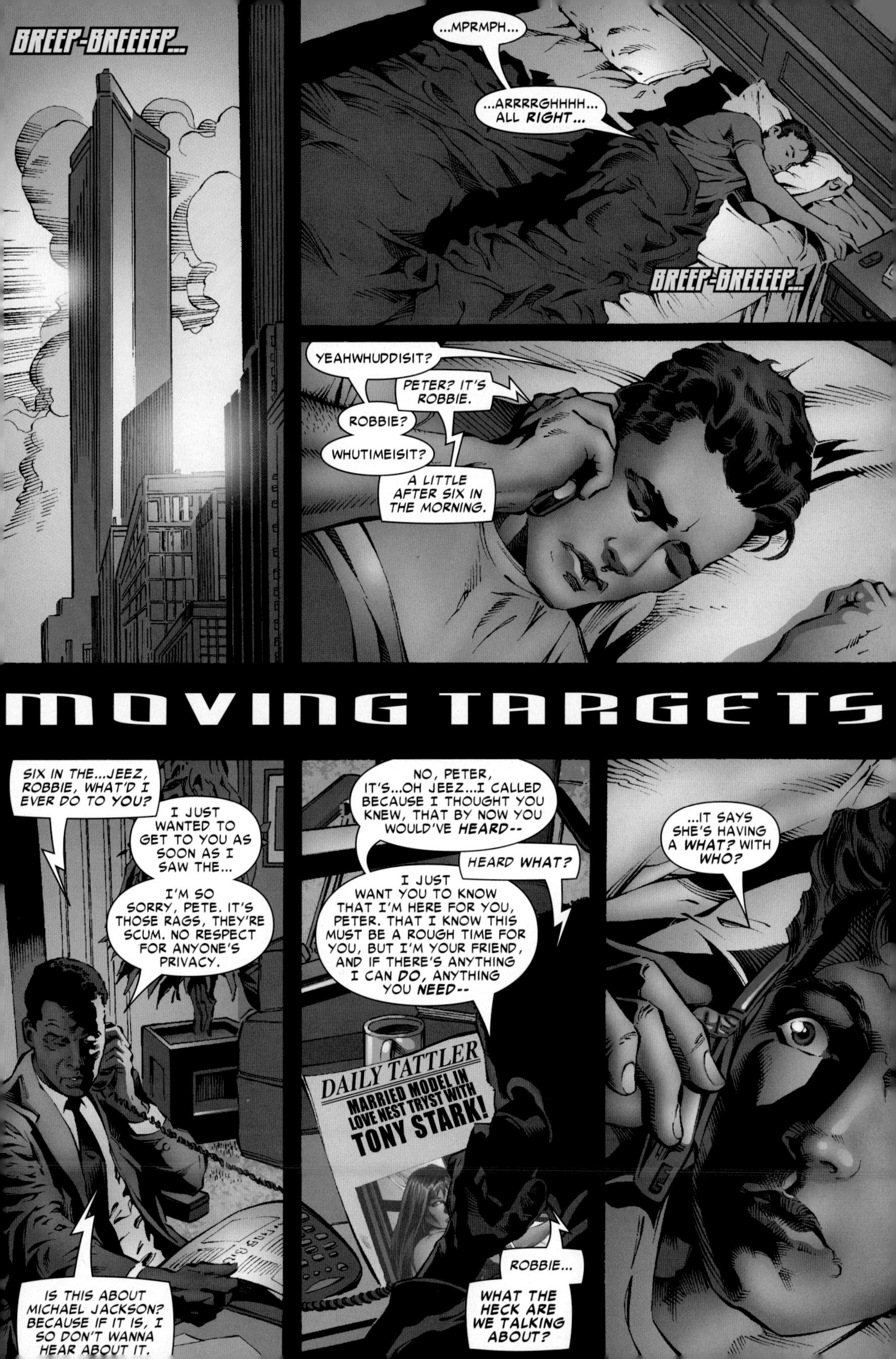
BREEP-BREEEEP...
...MPRMPH...
...ARRRRGHHHH... ALL RIGHT...
BREEP-BREEEEP...
YEAHWHUDDISIT?
PETER? IT'S ROBBIE.
ROBBIE?
WHUTIMEISIT?
A LITTLE AFTER SIX IN THE MORNING.
MOVING TARGETS
SIX IN THE...JEEZ, ROBBIE, WHAT'D I EVER DO TO YOU?
I JUST WANTED TO GET TO YOU AS SOON AS I SAW THE...
I'M SO SORRY, PETE. IT'S THOSE RAGS, THEY'RE SCUM. NO RESPECT FOR ANYONE'S PRIVACY.
IS THIS ABOUT MICHAEL JACKSON? BECAUSE IF IT IS, I SO DON'T WANNA HEAR ABOUT IT.
NO, PETER, IT'S...OH JEEZ...I CALLED BECAUSE I THOUGHT YOU KNEW, THAT BY NOW YOU WOULD'VE HEARD--
HEARD WHAT?
I JUST WANT YOU TO KNOW THAT I'M HERE FOR YOU, PETER. THAT I KNOW THIS MUST BE A ROUGH TIME FOR YOU, BUT I'M YOUR FRIEND, AND IF THERE'S ANYTHING I CAN DO, ANYTHING YOU NEED--
DAILY TATTLER
MARRIED MODEL IN LOVE NEST TRYST WITH TONY STARK!
ROBBIE...
WHAT THE HECK ARE WE TALKING ABOUT?
...IT SAYS SHE'S HAVING A WHAT? WITH WHO?

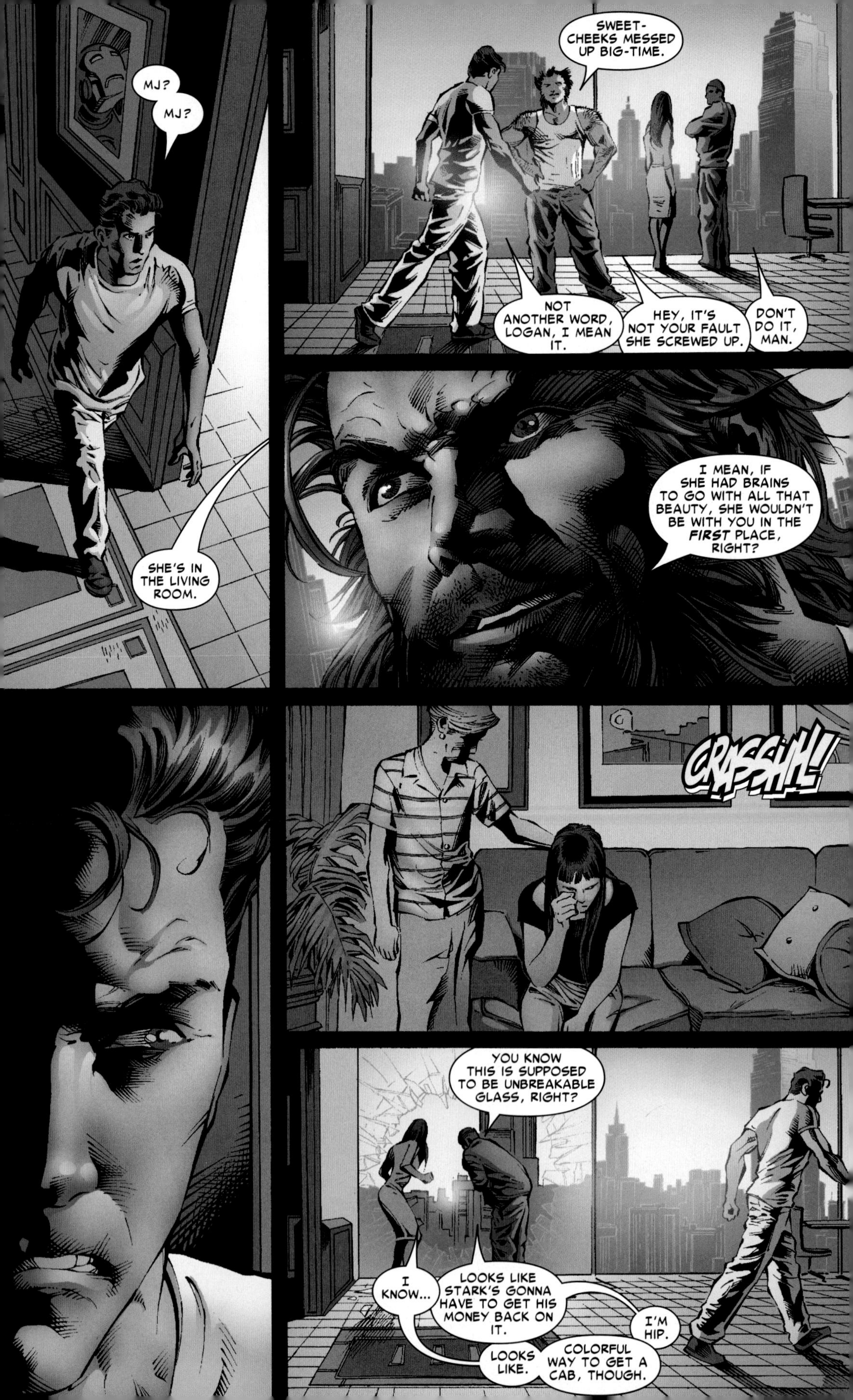
MJ?
MJ?
SHE'S IN THE LIVING ROOM.
SWEET-CHEEKS MESSED UP BIG-TIME.
NOT ANOTHER WORD, LOGAN, I MEAN IT.
HEY, IT'S NOT YOUR FAULT SHE SCREWED UP.
DON'T DO IT, MAN.
I MEAN, IF SHE HAD BRAINS TO GO WITH ALL THAT BEAUTY, SHE WOULDN'T BE WITH YOU IN THE FIRST PLACE, RIGHT?
CRASSHH!
YOU KNOW THIS IS SUPPOSED TO BE UNBREAKABLE GLASS, RIGHT?
I KNOW...
LOOKS LIKE STARK'S GONNA HAVE TO GET HIS MONEY BACK ON IT.
I'M HIP.
LOOKS LIKE.
COLORFUL WAY TO GET A CAB, THOUGH.

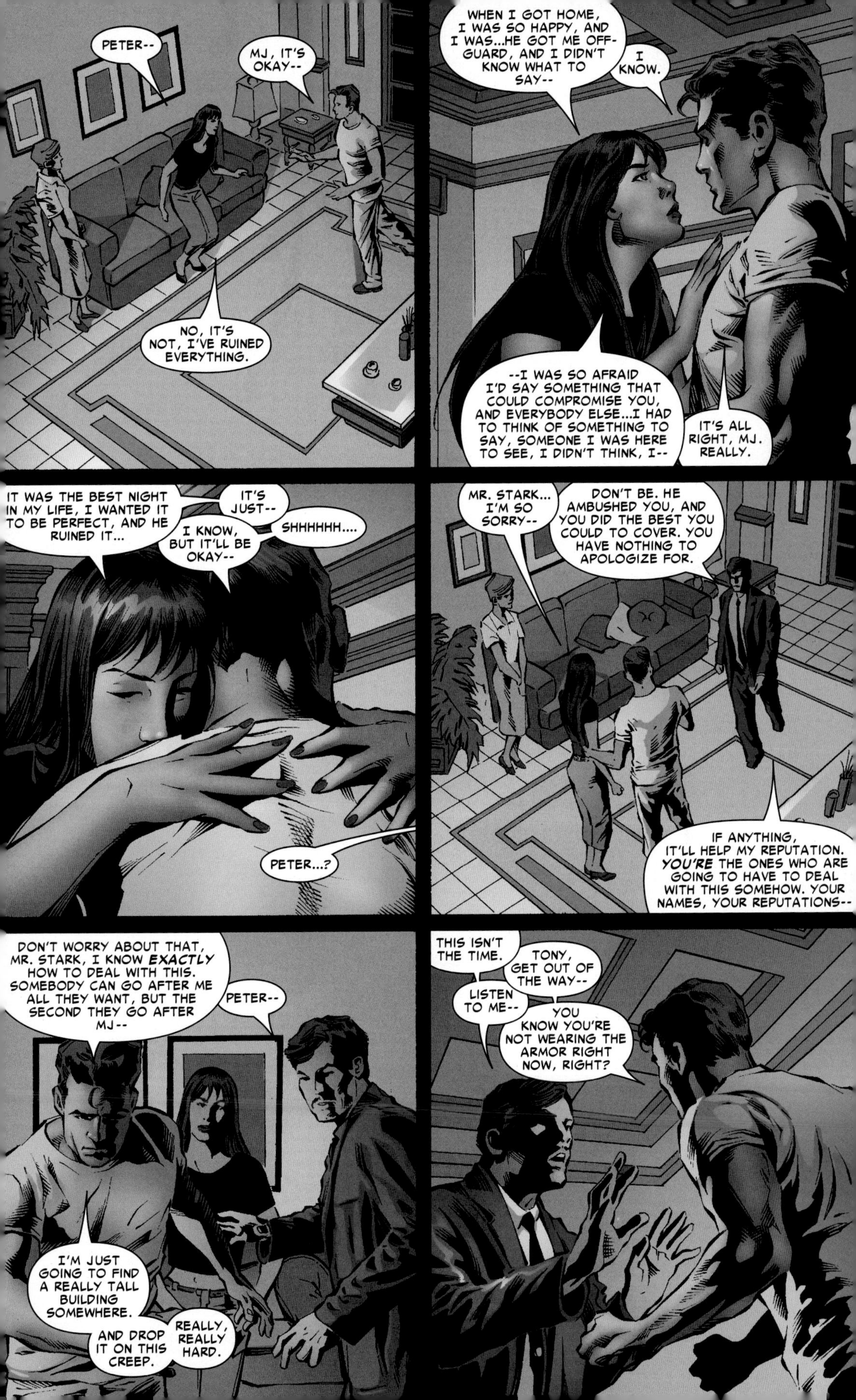
PETER--
MJ, IT'S OKAY--
NO, IT'S NOT, I'VE RUINED EVERYTHING.
WHEN I GOT HOME, I WAS SO HAPPY, AND I WAS...HE GOT ME OFF-GUARD, AND I DIDN'T KNOW WHAT TO SAY--
I KNOW.
--I WAS SO AFRAID I'D SAY SOMETHING THAT COULD COMPROMISE YOU, AND EVERYBODY ELSE...I HAD TO THINK OF SOMETHING TO SAY, SOMEONE I WAS HERE TO SEE, I DIDN'T THINK, I--
IT'S ALL RIGHT, MJ. REALLY.
IT WAS THE BEST NIGHT IN MY LIFE, I WANTED IT TO BE PERFECT, AND HE RUINED IT...
IT'S JUST--
I KNOW, BUT IT'LL BE OKAY--
SHHHHHH....
PETER...?
MR. STARK... I'M SO SORRY--
DON'T BE. HE AMBUSHED YOU, AND YOU DID THE BEST YOU COULD TO COVER. YOU HAVE NOTHING TO APOLOGIZE FOR.
IF ANYTHING, IT'LL HELP MY REPUTATION. *YOU'RE* THE ONES WHO ARE GOING TO HAVE TO DEAL WITH THIS SOMEHOW. YOUR NAMES, YOUR REPUTATIONS--
DON'T WORRY ABOUT THAT, MR. STARK, I KNOW *EXACTLY* HOW TO DEAL WITH THIS. SOMEBODY CAN GO AFTER ME ALL THEY WANT, BUT THE SECOND THEY GO AFTER MJ--
PETER--
I'M JUST GOING TO FIND A REALLY TALL BUILDING SOMEWHERE.
AND DROP IT ON THIS CREEP.
REALLY, REALLY HARD.
THIS ISN'T THE TIME.
TONY, GET OUT OF THE WAY--
LISTEN TO ME--
YOU KNOW YOU'RE NOT WEARING THE ARMOR RIGHT NOW, RIGHT?

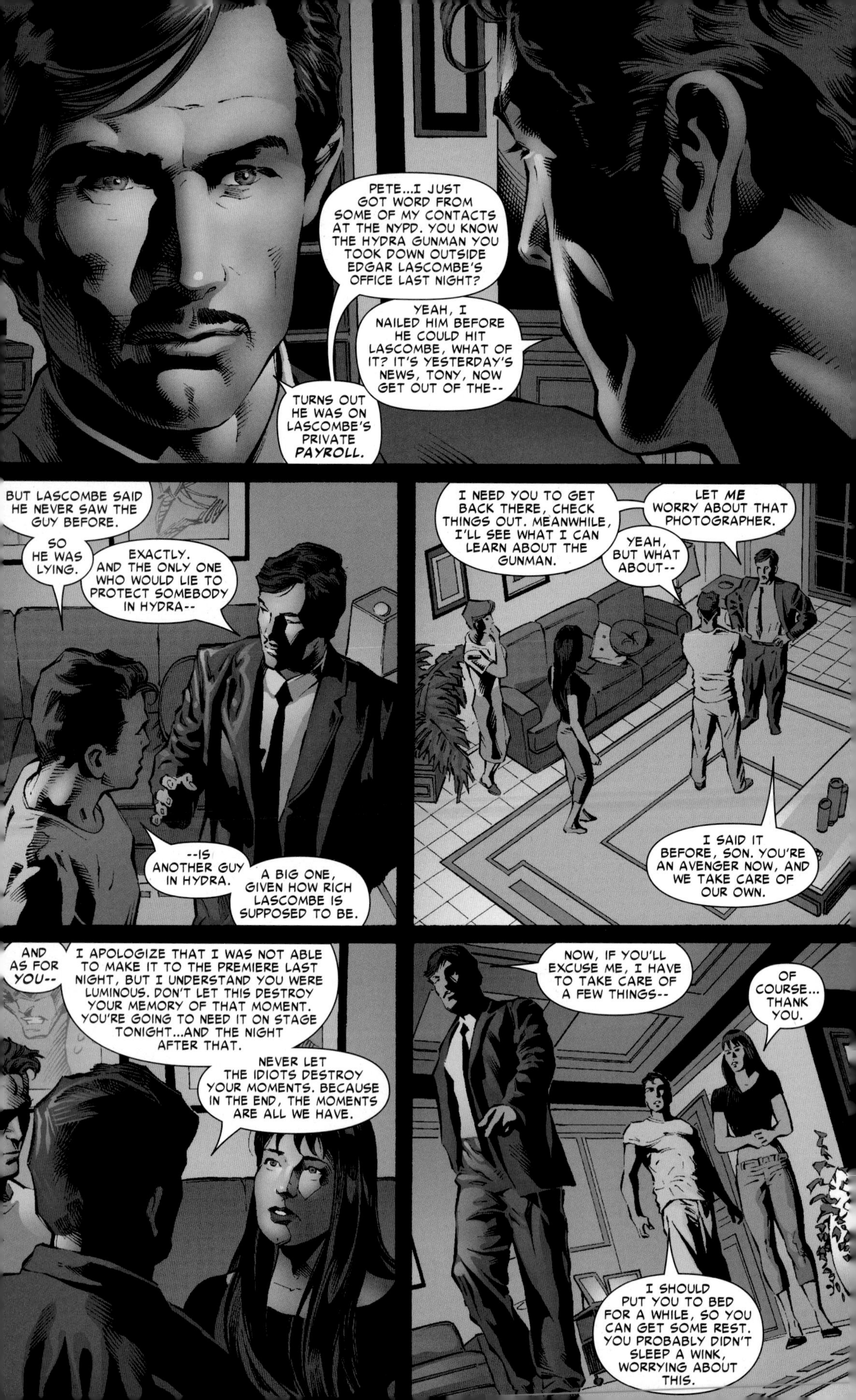
PETE...I JUST GOT WORD FROM SOME OF MY CONTACTS AT THE NYPD. YOU KNOW THE HYDRA GUNMAN YOU TOOK DOWN OUTSIDE EDGAR LASCOMBE'S OFFICE LAST NIGHT?
YEAH, I NAILED HIM BEFORE HE COULD HIT LASCOMBE, WHAT OF IT? IT'S YESTERDAY'S NEWS, TONY, NOW GET OUT OF THE--
TURNS OUT HE WAS ON LASCOMBE'S PRIVATE *PAYROLL.*
BUT LASCOMBE SAID HE NEVER SAW THE GUY BEFORE.
SO HE WAS LYING.
EXACTLY. AND THE ONLY ONE WHO WOULD LIE TO PROTECT SOMEBODY IN HYDRA--
--IS ANOTHER GUY IN HYDRA.
A BIG ONE, GIVEN HOW RICH LASCOMBE IS SUPPOSED TO BE.
I NEED YOU TO GET BACK THERE, CHECK THINGS OUT. MEANWHILE, I'LL SEE WHAT I CAN LEARN ABOUT THE GUNMAN.
YEAH, BUT WHAT ABOUT--
LET *ME* WORRY ABOUT THAT PHOTOGRAPHER.
I SAID IT BEFORE, SON. YOU'RE AN AVENGER NOW, AND WE TAKE CARE OF OUR OWN.
AND AS FOR *YOU*--
I APOLOGIZE THAT I WAS NOT ABLE TO MAKE IT TO THE PREMIERE LAST NIGHT, BUT I UNDERSTAND YOU WERE LUMINOUS. DON'T LET THIS DESTROY YOUR MEMORY OF THAT MOMENT. YOU'RE GOING TO NEED IT ON STAGE TONIGHT...AND THE NIGHT AFTER THAT.
NEVER LET THE IDIOTS DESTROY YOUR MOMENTS. BECAUSE IN THE END, THE MOMENTS ARE ALL WE HAVE.
NOW, IF YOU'LL EXCUSE ME, I HAVE TO TAKE CARE OF A FEW THINGS--
OF COURSE... THANK YOU.
I SHOULD PUT YOU TO BED FOR A WHILE, SO YOU CAN GET SOME REST. YOU PROBABLY DIDN'T SLEEP A WINK, WORRYING ABOUT THIS.

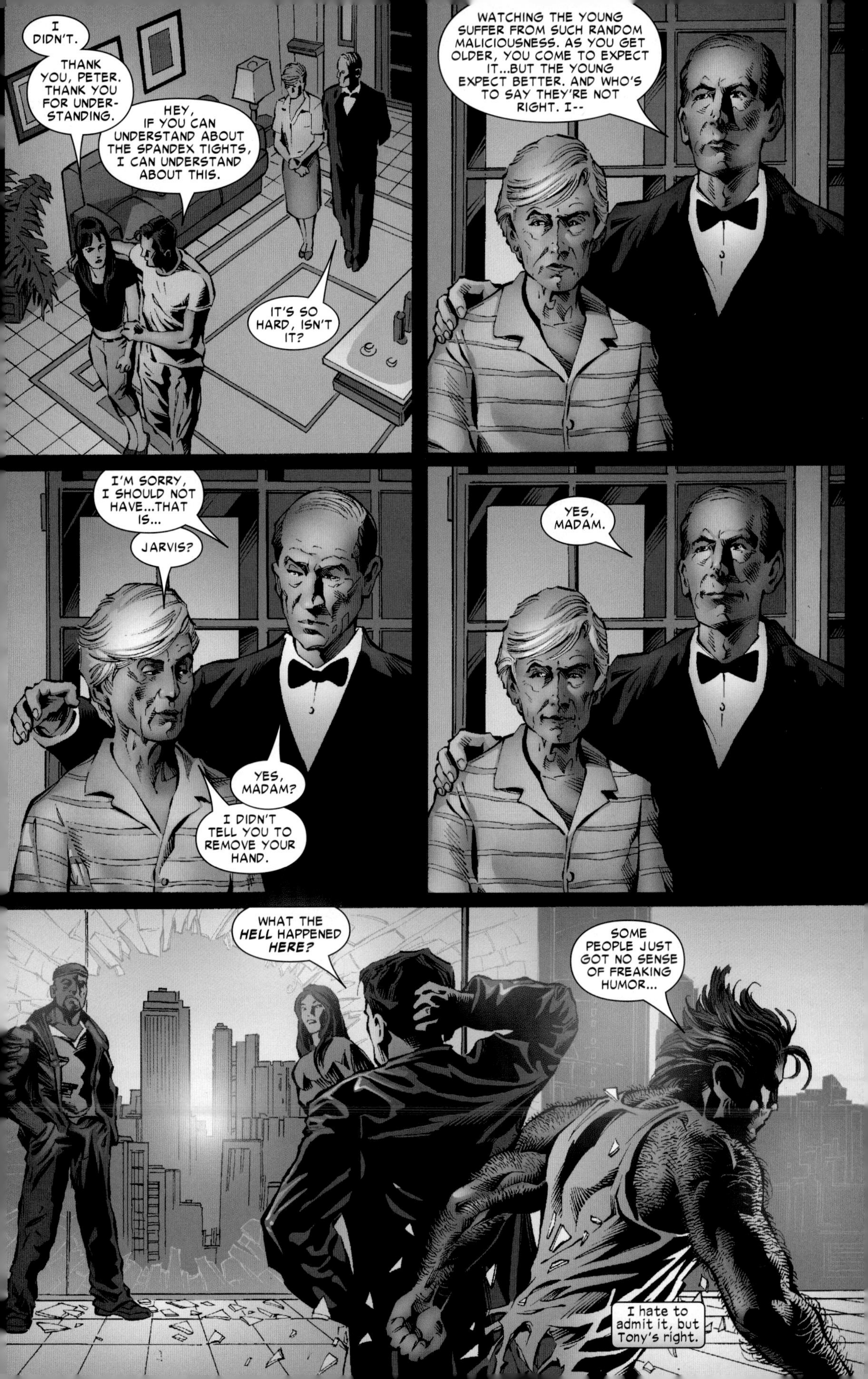
I DIDN'T.
THANK YOU, PETER. THANK YOU FOR UNDER-STANDING.
HEY, IF YOU CAN UNDERSTAND ABOUT THE SPANDEX TIGHTS, I CAN UNDERSTAND ABOUT THIS.
IT'S SO HARD, ISN'T IT?
WATCHING THE YOUNG SUFFER FROM SUCH RANDOM MALICIOUSNESS. AS YOU GET OLDER, YOU COME TO EXPECT IT...BUT THE YOUNG EXPECT BETTER. AND WHO'S TO SAY THEY'RE NOT RIGHT. I--
I'M SORRY, I SHOULD NOT HAVE...THAT IS...
JARVIS?
YES, MADAM?
I DIDN'T TELL YOU TO REMOVE YOUR HAND.
YES, MADAM.
WHAT THE HELL HAPPENED HERE?
SOME PEOPLE JUST GOT NO SENSE OF FREAKING HUMOR...
I hate to admit it, but Tony's right.

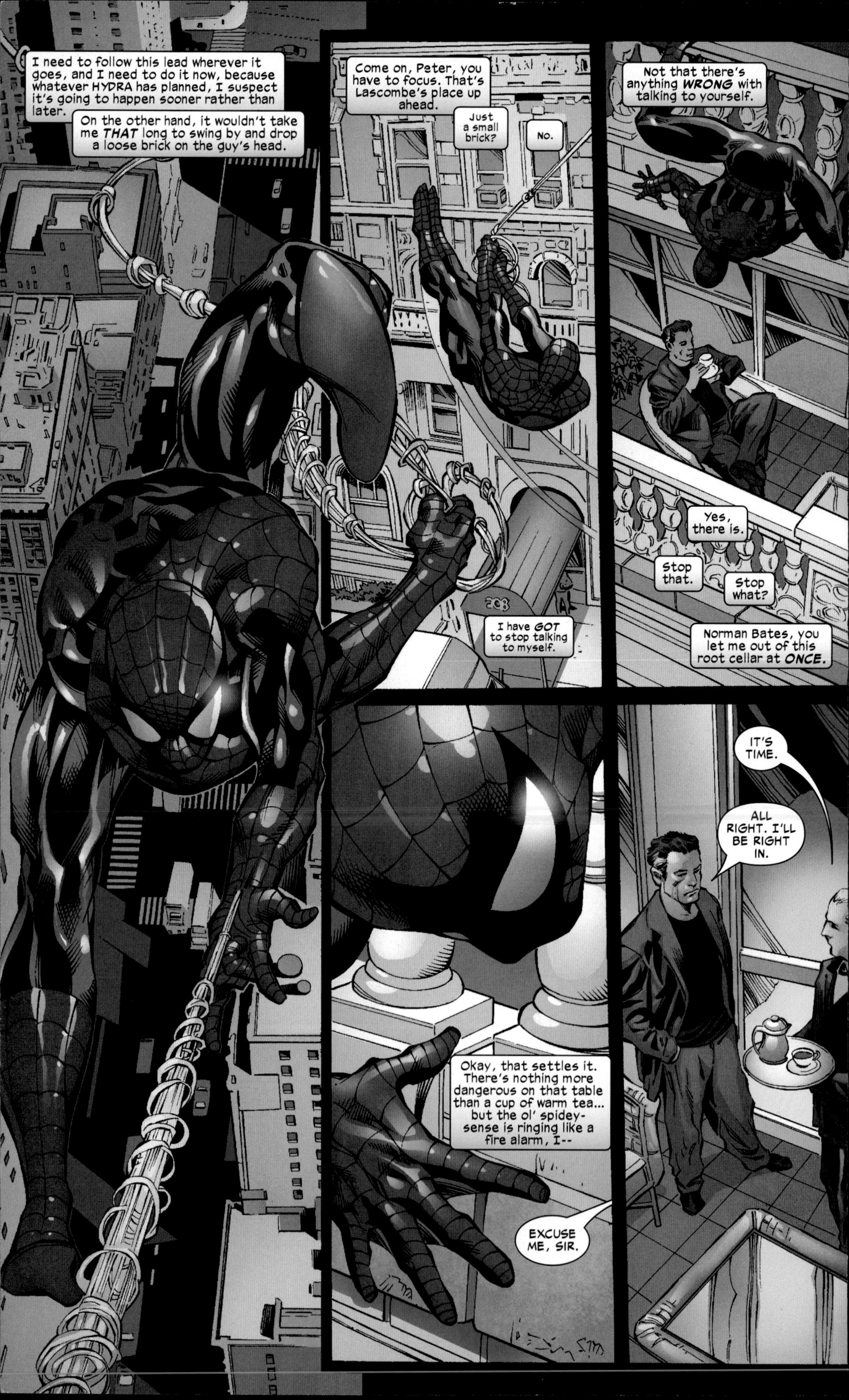
I need to follow this lead wherever it goes, and I need to do it now, because whatever HYDRA has planned, I suspect it's going to happen sooner rather than later.
On the other hand, it wouldn't take me THAT long to swing by and drop a loose brick on the guy's head.
Come on, Peter, you have to focus. That's Lascombe's place up ahead.
Just a small brick?
No.
I have GOT to stop talking to myself.
Not that there's anything WRONG with talking to yourself.
Yes, there is.
Stop that.
Stop what?
Norman Bates, you let me out of this root cellar at ONCE.
Okay, that settles it. There's nothing more dangerous on that table than a cup of warm tea... but the ol' spidey-sense is ringing like a fire alarm, I--
EXCUSE ME, SIR.
IT'S TIME.
ALL RIGHT. I'LL BE RIGHT IN.

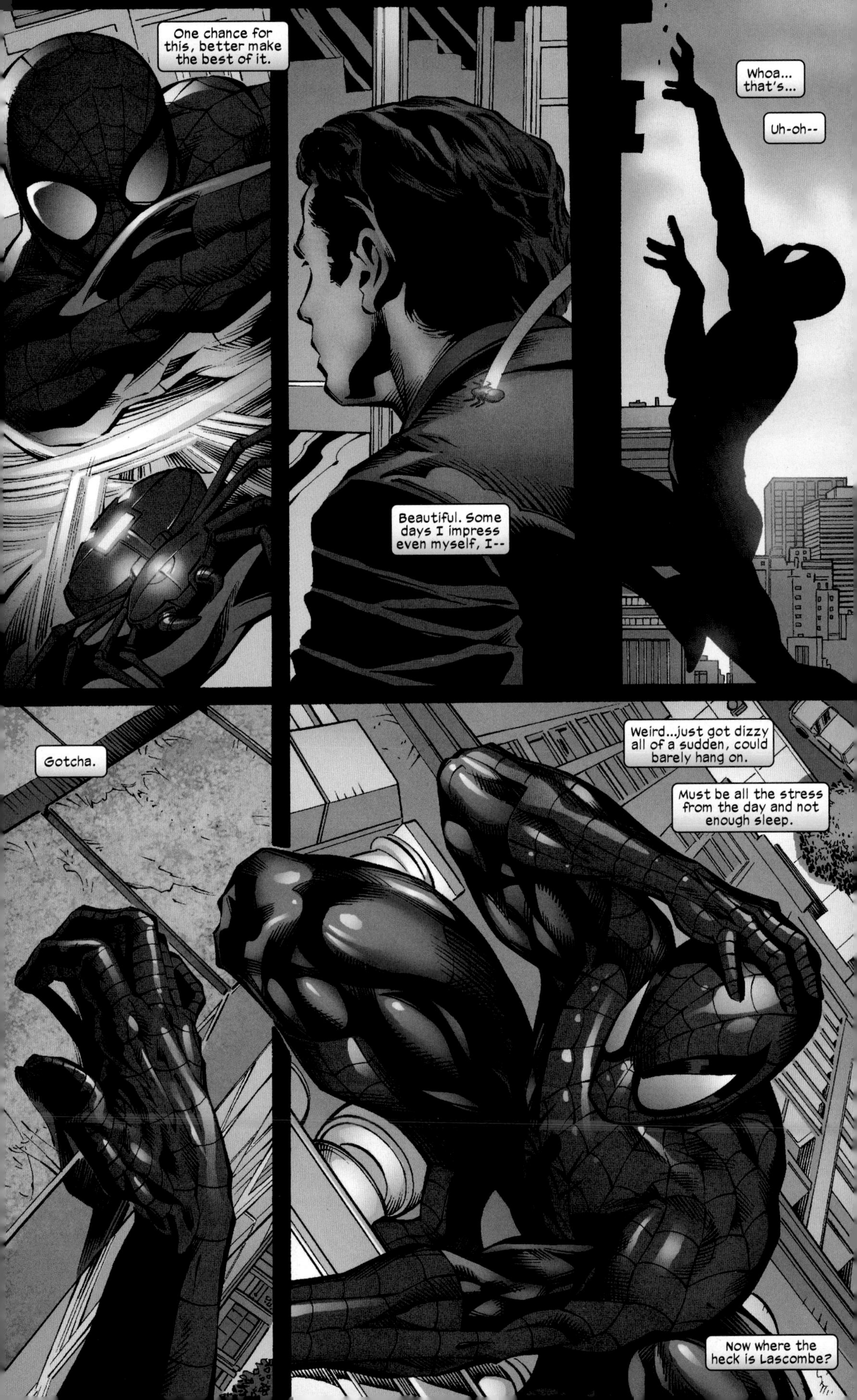
One chance for this, better make the best of it.
Beautiful. Some days I impress even myself, I--
Whoa... that's...
Uh-oh--
Gotcha.
Weird...just got dizzy all of a sudden, could barely hang on.
Must be all the stress from the day and not enough sleep.
Now where the heck is Lascombe?

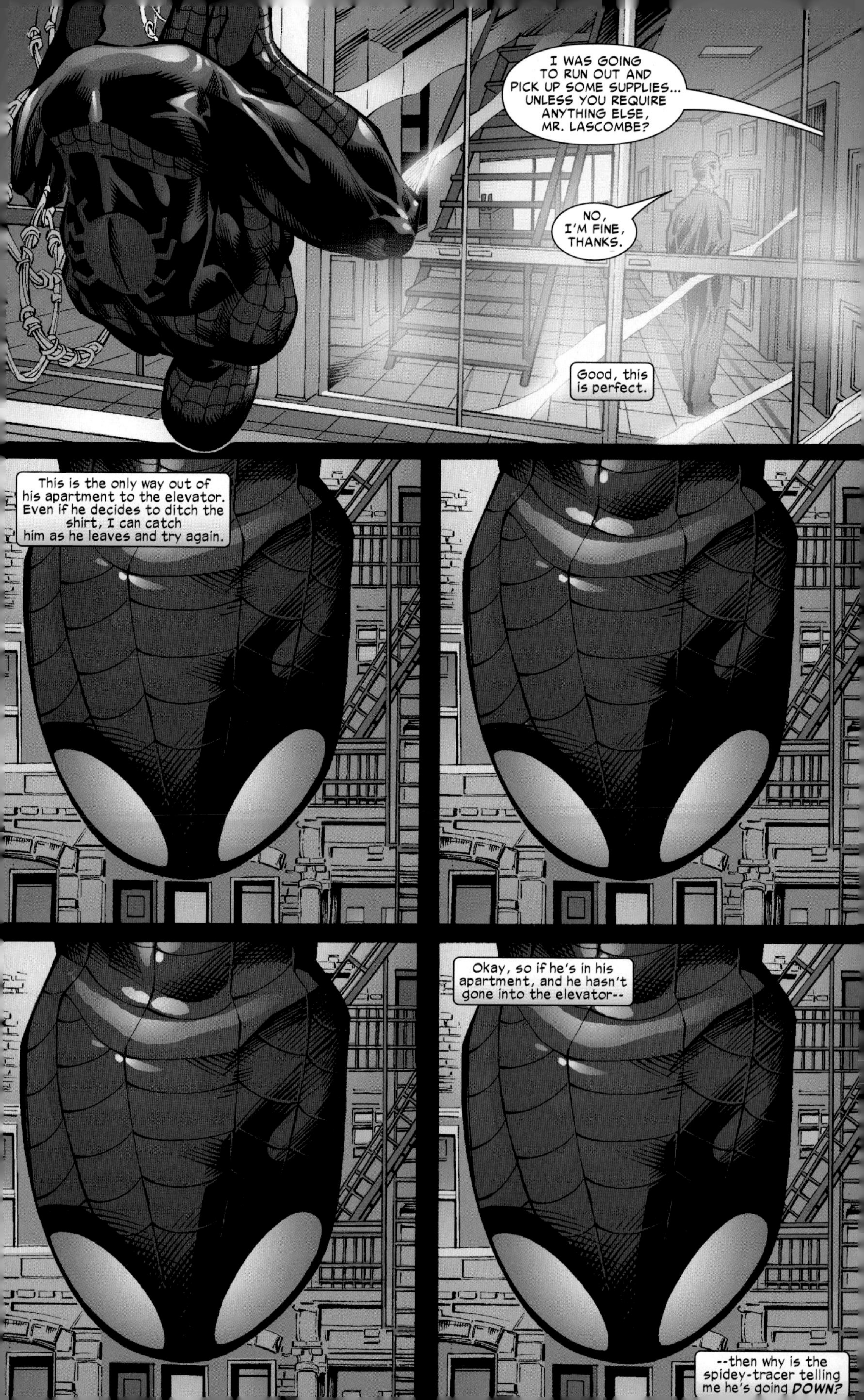
I WAS GOING TO RUN OUT AND PICK UP SOME SUPPLIES... UNLESS YOU REQUIRE ANYTHING ELSE, MR. LASCOMBE?
NO, I'M FINE, THANKS.
Good, this is perfect.
This is the only way out of his apartment to the elevator. Even if he decides to ditch the shirt, I can catch him as he leaves and try again.
Okay, so if he's in his apartment, and he hasn't gone into the elevator--
--then why is the spidey-tracer telling me he's going DOWN?

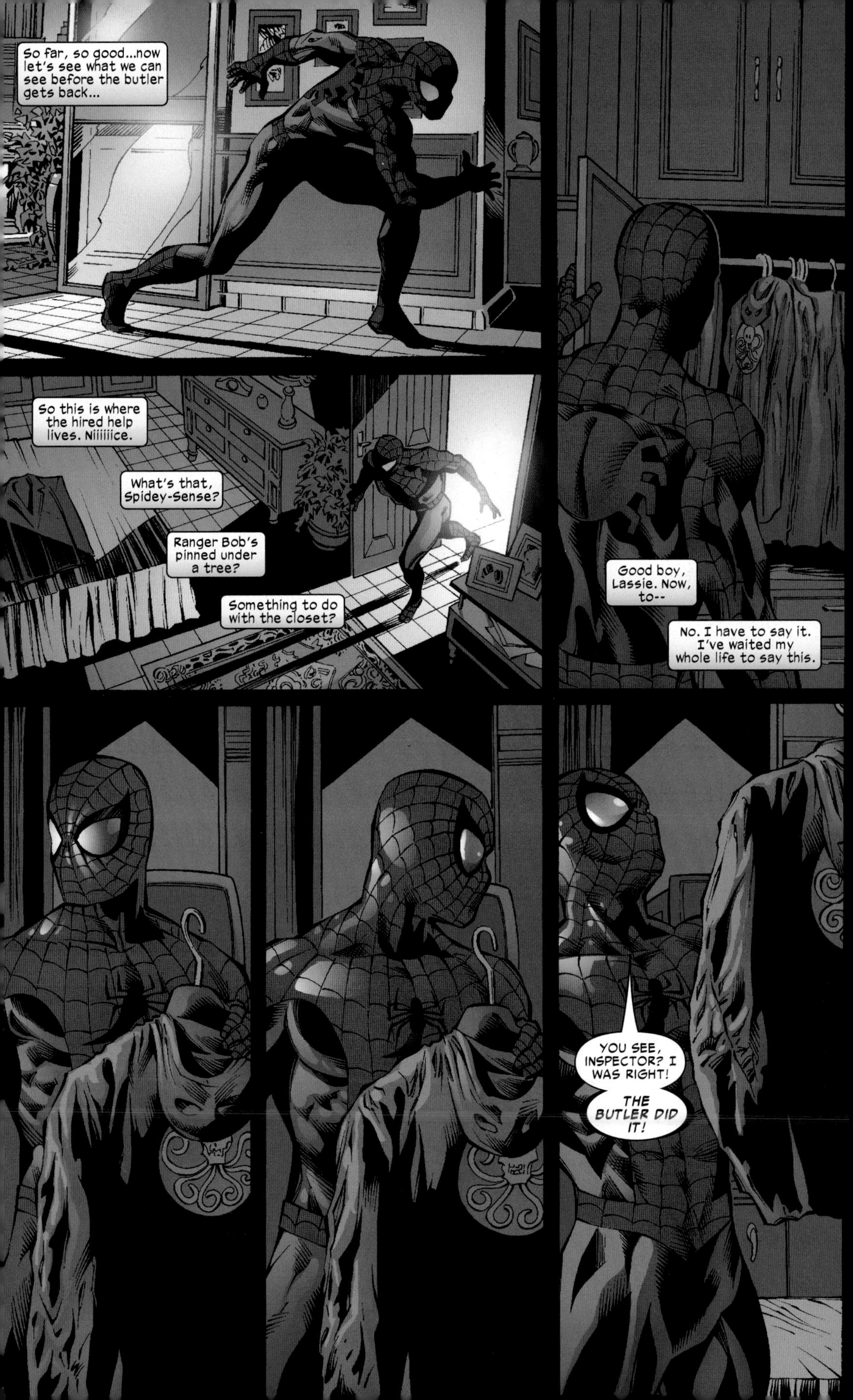
So far, so good...now let's see what we can see before the butler gets back...
So this is where the hired help lives. Niiiiiice.
What's that, Spidey-Sense?
Ranger Bob's pinned under a tree?
Something to do with the closet?
Good boy, Lassie. Now, to--
No. I have to say it. I've waited my whole life to say this.
YOU SEE, INSPECTOR? I WAS RIGHT!
THE BUTLER DID IT!

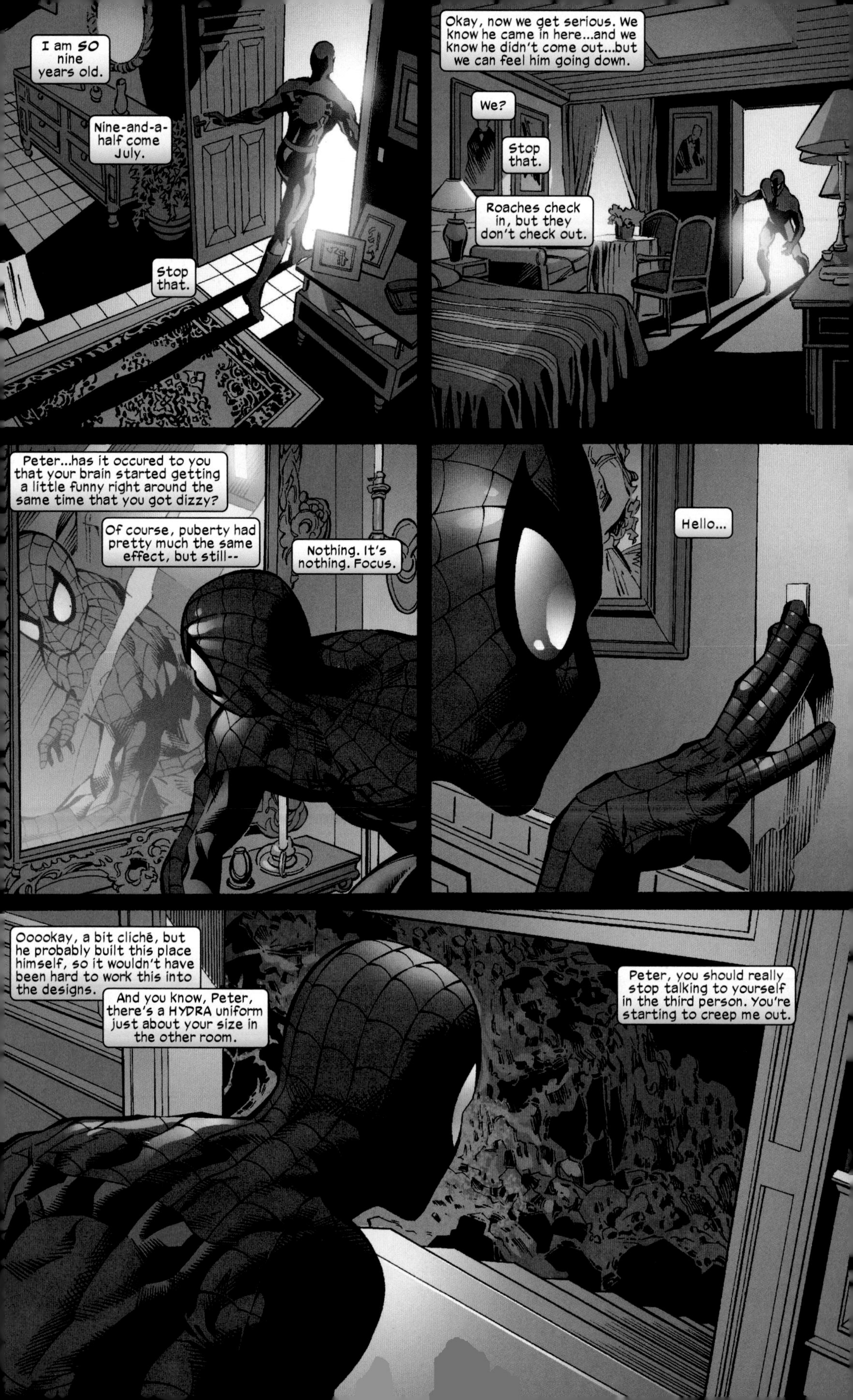
I am SO nine years old.
Nine-and-a-half come July.
Stop that.
Okay, now we get serious. We know he came in here...and we know he didn't come out...but we can feel him going down.
We?
Stop that.
Roaches check in, but they don't check out.
Peter...has it occured to you that your brain started getting a little funny right around the same time that you got dizzy?
Of course, puberty had pretty much the same effect, but still--
Nothing. It's nothing. Focus.
Hello...
Ooookay, a bit cliché, but he probably built this place himself, so it wouldn't have been hard to work this into the designs.
And you know, Peter, there's a HYDRA uniform just about your size in the other room.
Peter, you should really stop talking to yourself in the third person. You're starting to creep me out.

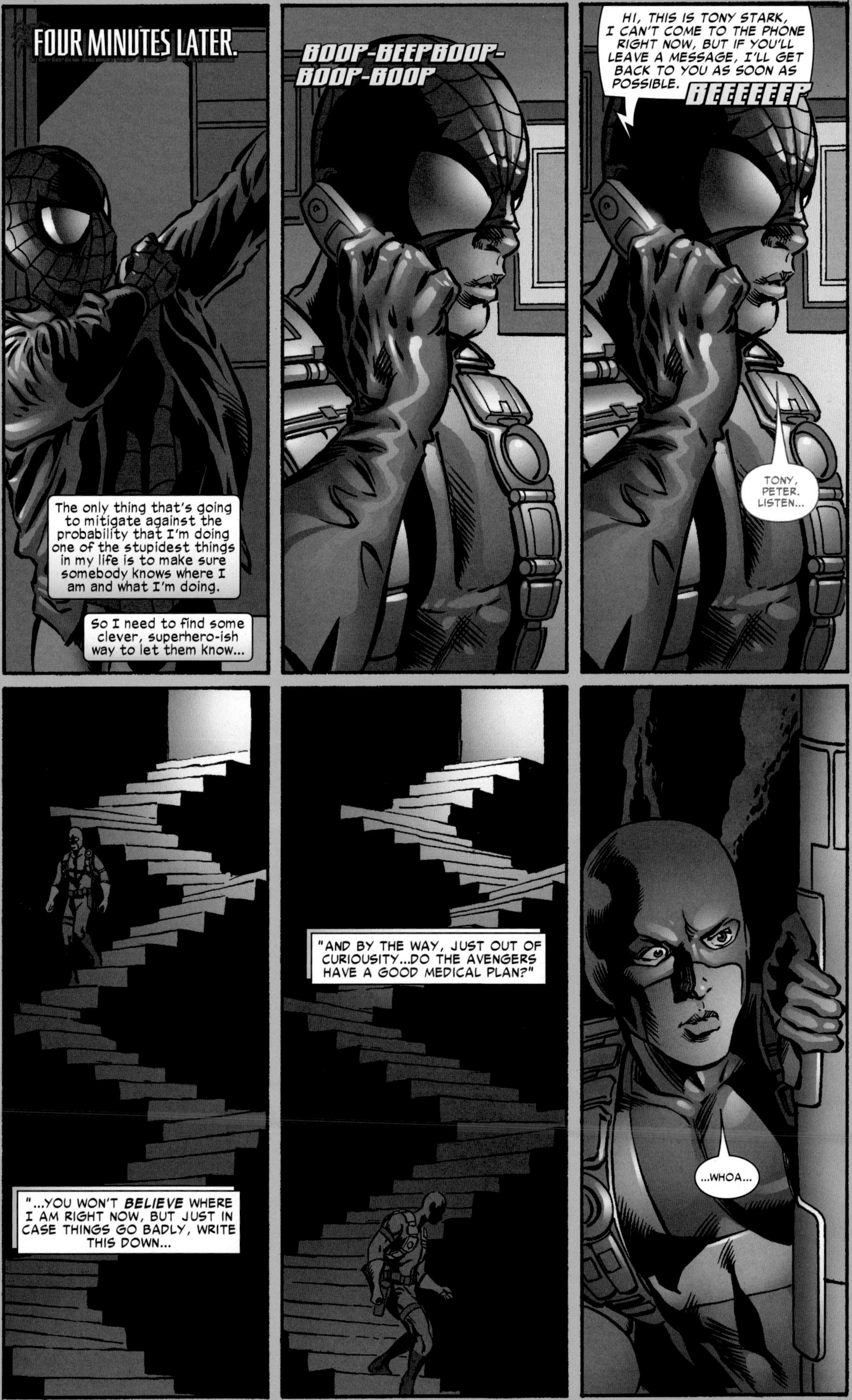
FOUR MINUTES LATER.
The only thing that's going to mitigate against the probability that I'm doing one of the stupidest things in my life is to make sure somebody knows where I am and what I'm doing.
So I need to find some clever, superhero-ish way to let them know...
BOOP-BEEPBOOP-BOOP-BOOP
HI, THIS IS TONY STARK, I CAN'T COME TO THE PHONE RIGHT NOW, BUT IF YOU'LL LEAVE A MESSAGE, I'LL GET BACK TO YOU AS SOON AS POSSIBLE.
BEEEEEEP
TONY, PETER. LISTEN...
"...YOU WON'T BELIEVE WHERE I AM RIGHT NOW, BUT JUST IN CASE THINGS GO BADLY, WRITE THIS DOWN...
"AND BY THE WAY, JUST OUT OF CURIOUSITY...DO THE AVENGERS HAVE A GOOD MEDICAL PLAN?"
...WHOA...

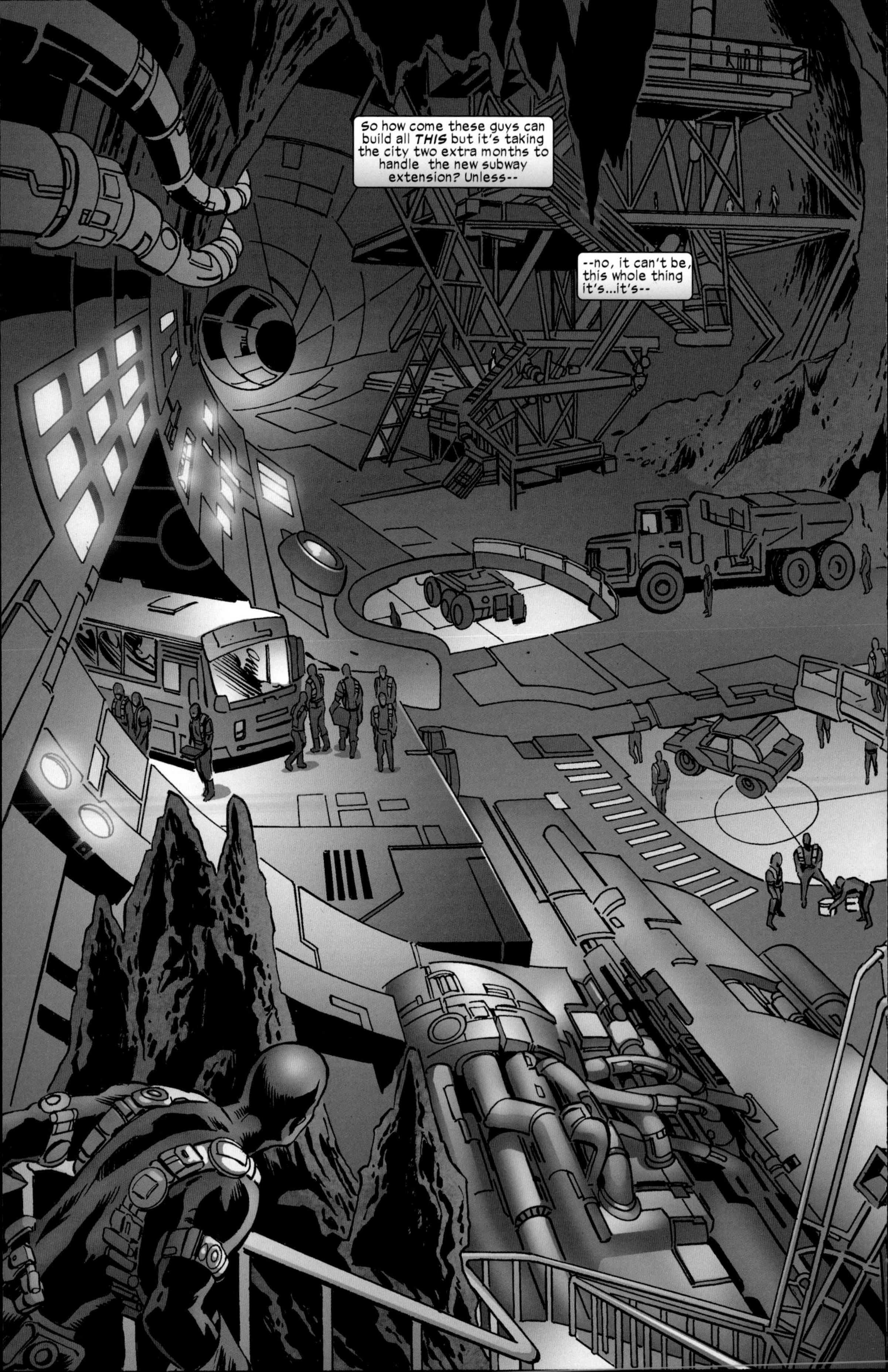
So how come these guys can build all THIS but it's taking the city two extra months to handle the new subway extension? Unless--
--no, it can't be, this whole thing it's...it's--

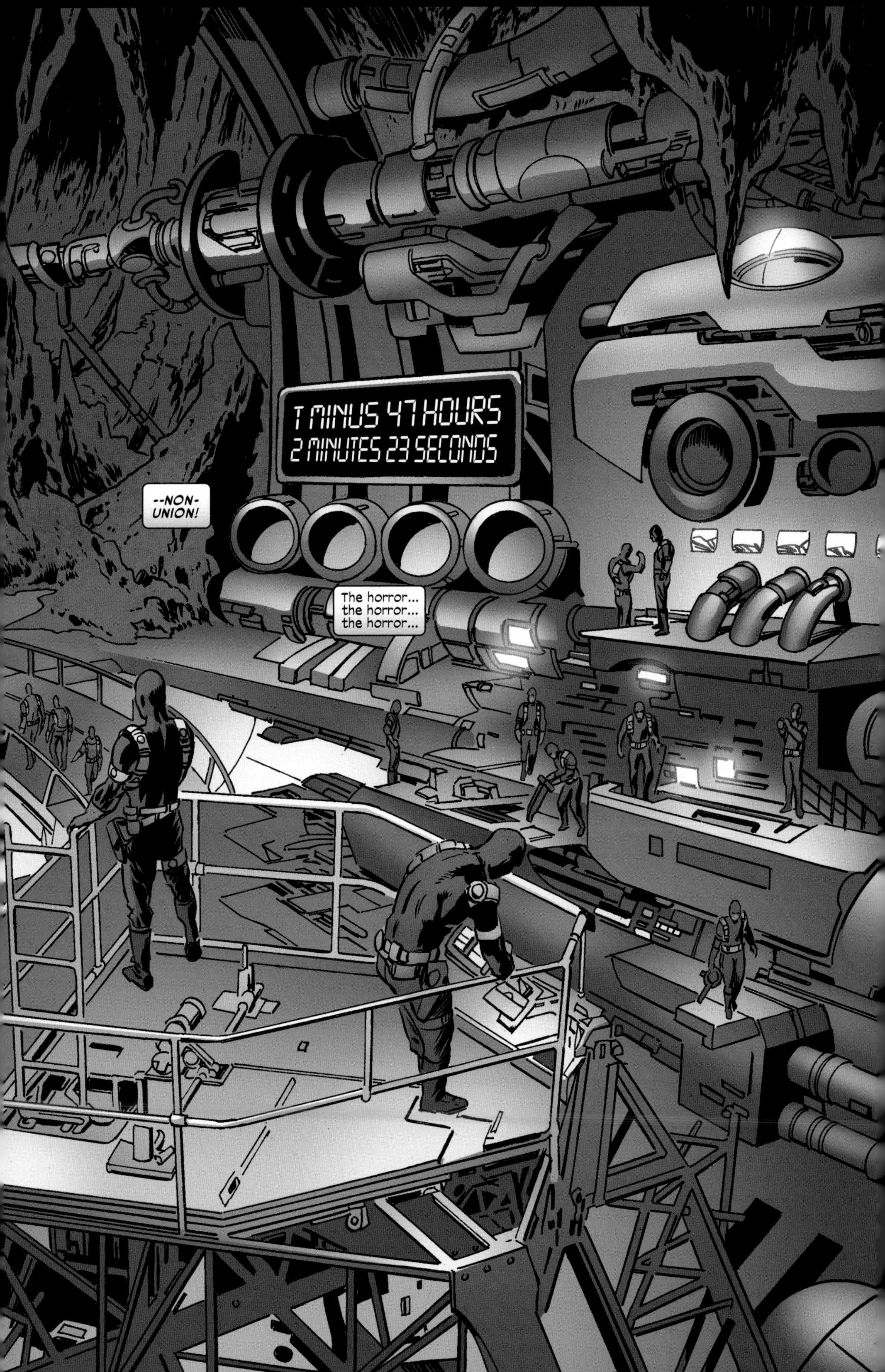
T MINUS 47 HOURS
2 MINUTES 23 SECONDS
--NON-UNION!
The horror... the horror... the horror...

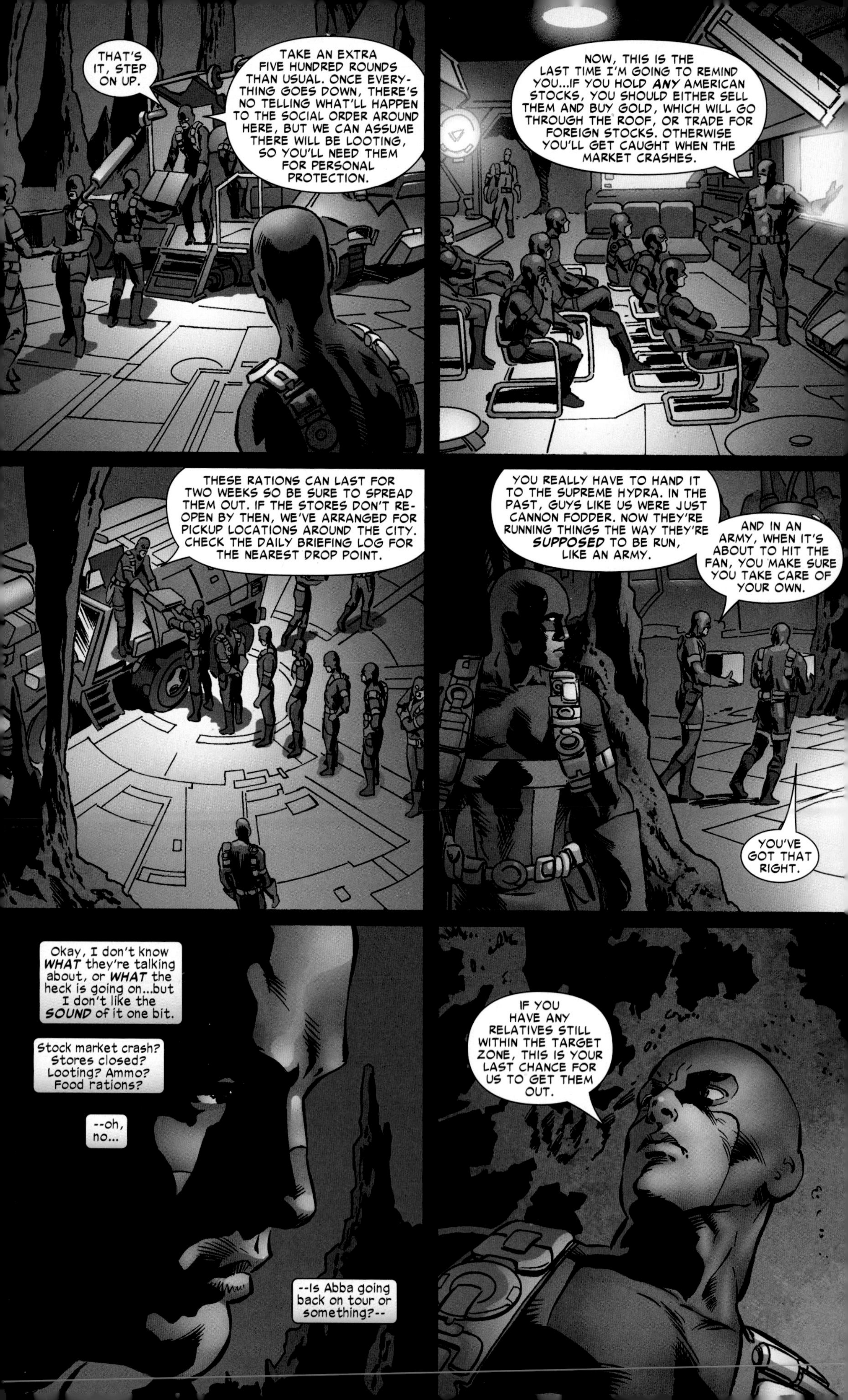
THAT'S IT, STEP ON UP.
TAKE AN EXTRA FIVE HUNDRED ROUNDS THAN USUAL. ONCE EVERYTHING GOES DOWN, THERE'S NO TELLING WHAT'LL HAPPEN TO THE SOCIAL ORDER AROUND HERE, BUT WE CAN ASSUME THERE WILL BE LOOTING, SO YOU'LL NEED THEM FOR PERSONAL PROTECTION.
NOW, THIS IS THE LAST TIME I'M GOING TO REMIND YOU...IF YOU HOLD ANY AMERICAN STOCKS, YOU SHOULD EITHER SELL THEM AND BUY GOLD, WHICH WILL GO THROUGH THE ROOF, OR TRADE FOR FOREIGN STOCKS. OTHERWISE YOU'LL GET CAUGHT WHEN THE MARKET CRASHES.
THESE RATIONS CAN LAST FOR TWO WEEKS SO BE SURE TO SPREAD THEM OUT. IF THE STORES DON'T RE-OPEN BY THEN, WE'VE ARRANGED FOR PICKUP LOCATIONS AROUND THE CITY. CHECK THE DAILY BRIEFING LOG FOR THE NEAREST DROP POINT.
YOU REALLY HAVE TO HAND IT TO THE SUPREME HYDRA. IN THE PAST, GUYS LIKE US WERE JUST CANNON FODDER. NOW THEY'RE RUNNING THINGS THE WAY THEY'RE SUPPOSED TO BE RUN, LIKE AN ARMY.
AND IN AN ARMY, WHEN IT'S ABOUT TO HIT THE FAN, YOU MAKE SURE YOU TAKE CARE OF YOUR OWN.
YOU'VE GOT THAT RIGHT.
Okay, I don't know WHAT they're talking about, or WHAT the heck is going on...but I don't like the SOUND of it one bit.
Stock market crash? Stores closed? Looting? Ammo? Food rations?
--oh, no...
--Is Abba going back on tour or something?--
IF YOU HAVE ANY RELATIVES STILL WITHIN THE TARGET ZONE, THIS IS YOUR LAST CHANCE FOR US TO GET THEM OUT.

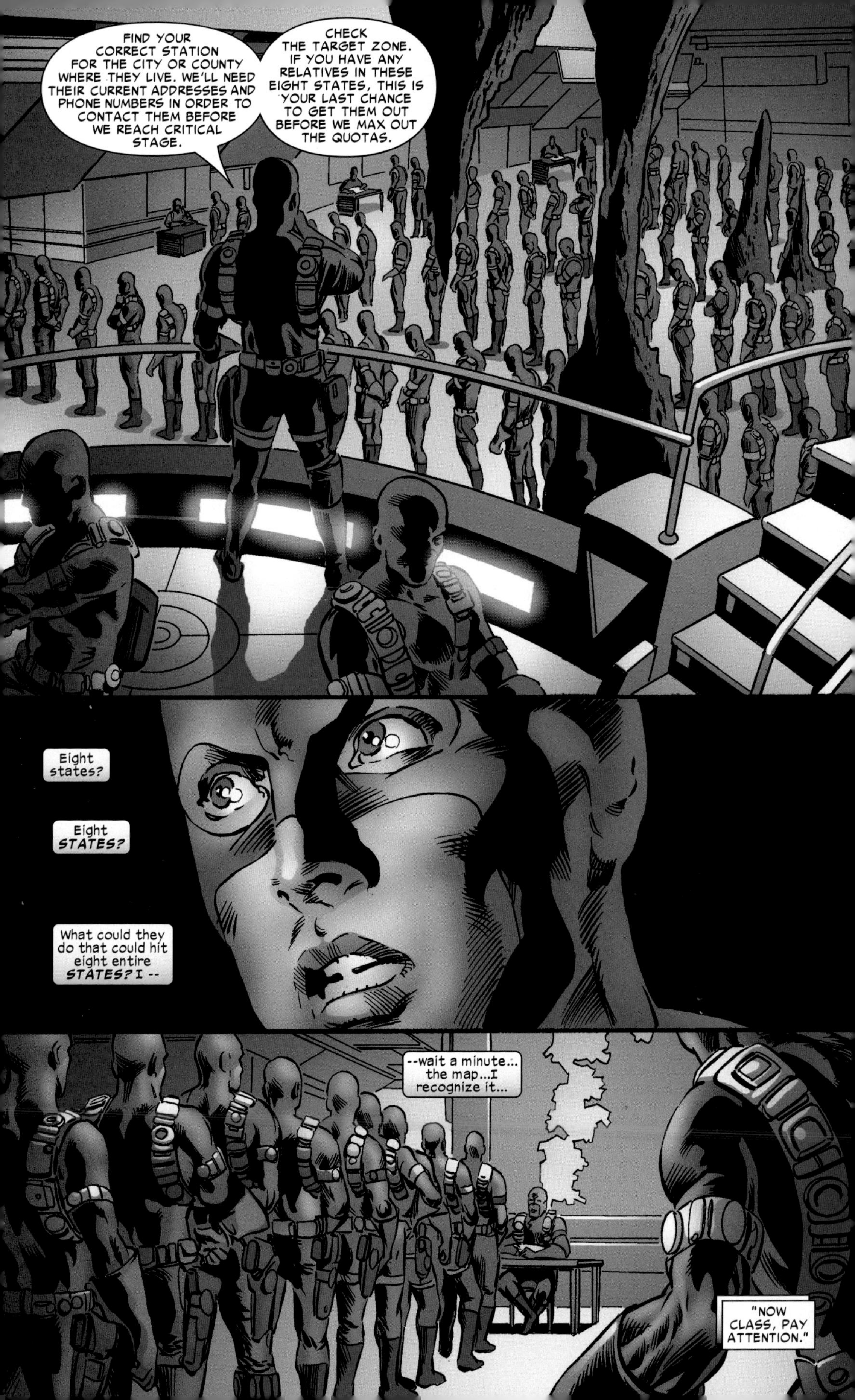
FIND YOUR CORRECT STATION FOR THE CITY OR COUNTY WHERE THEY LIVE. WE'LL NEED THEIR CURRENT ADDRESSES AND PHONE NUMBERS IN ORDER TO CONTACT THEM BEFORE WE REACH CRITICAL STAGE.
CHECK THE TARGET ZONE. IF YOU HAVE ANY RELATIVES IN THESE EIGHT STATES, THIS IS YOUR LAST CHANCE TO GET THEM OUT BEFORE WE MAX OUT THE QUOTAS.
Eight states?
Eight STATES?
What could they do that could hit eight entire STATES? I --
--wait a minute... the map...I recognize it...
"NOW CLASS, PAY ATTENTION."

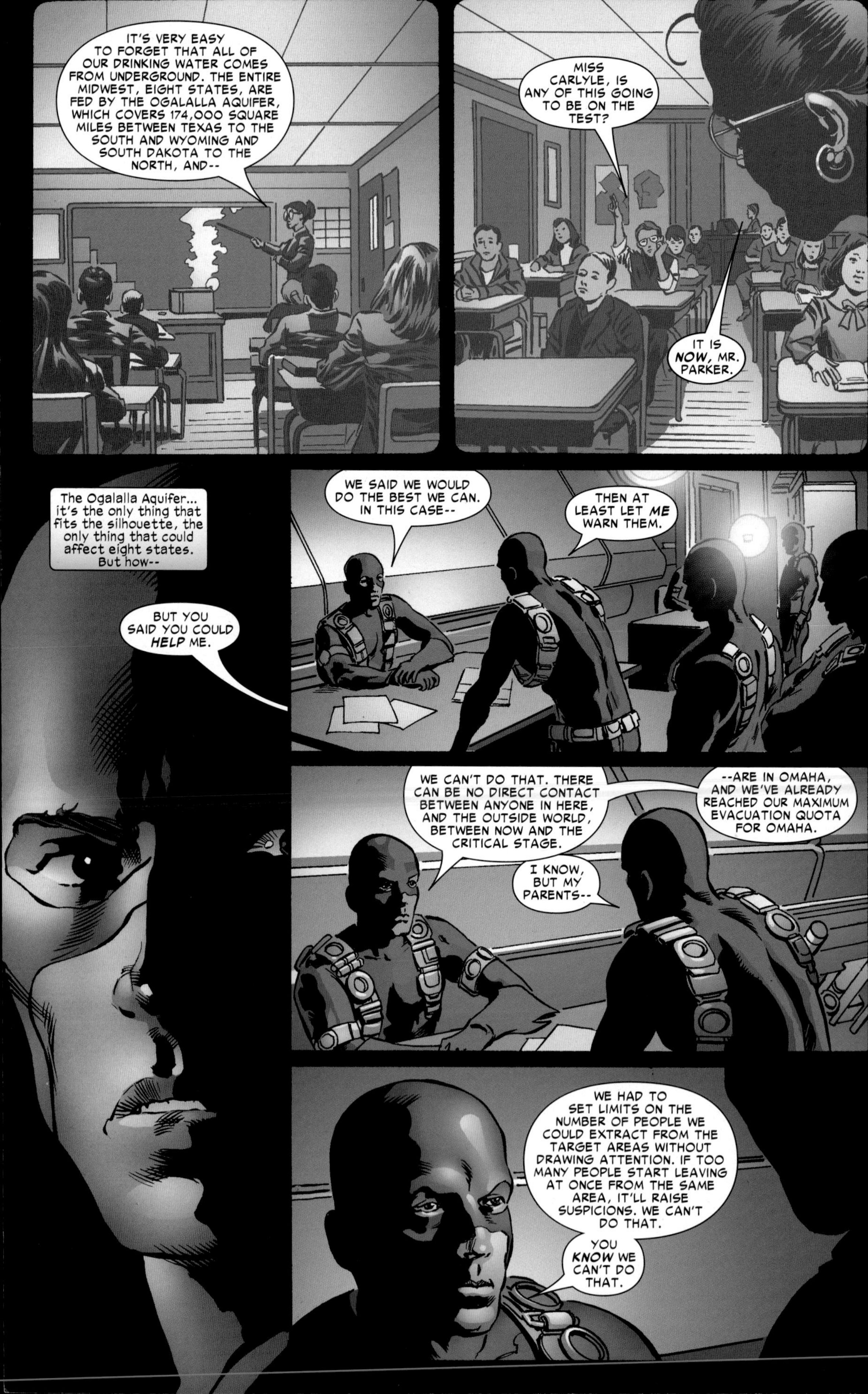
IT'S VERY EASY TO FORGET THAT ALL OF OUR DRINKING WATER COMES FROM UNDERGROUND. THE ENTIRE MIDWEST, EIGHT STATES, ARE FED BY THE OGALALLA AQUIFER, WHICH COVERS 174,000 SQUARE MILES BETWEEN TEXAS TO THE SOUTH AND WYOMING AND SOUTH DAKOTA TO THE NORTH, AND--
MISS CARLYLE, IS ANY OF THIS GOING TO BE ON THE TEST?
IT IS NOW, MR. PARKER.
The Ogalalla Aquifer... it's the only thing that fits the silhouette, the only thing that could affect eight states. But how--
WE SAID WE WOULD DO THE BEST WE CAN. IN THIS CASE--
THEN AT LEAST LET ME WARN THEM.
BUT YOU SAID YOU COULD HELP ME.
WE CAN'T DO THAT. THERE CAN BE NO DIRECT CONTACT BETWEEN ANYONE IN HERE, AND THE OUTSIDE WORLD, BETWEEN NOW AND THE CRITICAL STAGE.
I KNOW, BUT MY PARENTS--
--ARE IN OMAHA, AND WE'VE ALREADY REACHED OUR MAXIMUM EVACUATION QUOTA FOR OMAHA.
WE HAD TO SET LIMITS ON THE NUMBER OF PEOPLE WE COULD EXTRACT FROM THE TARGET AREAS WITHOUT DRAWING ATTENTION. IF TOO MANY PEOPLE START LEAVING AT ONCE FROM THE SAME AREA, IT'LL RAISE SUSPICIONS. WE CAN'T DO THAT.
YOU KNOW WE CAN'T DO THAT.

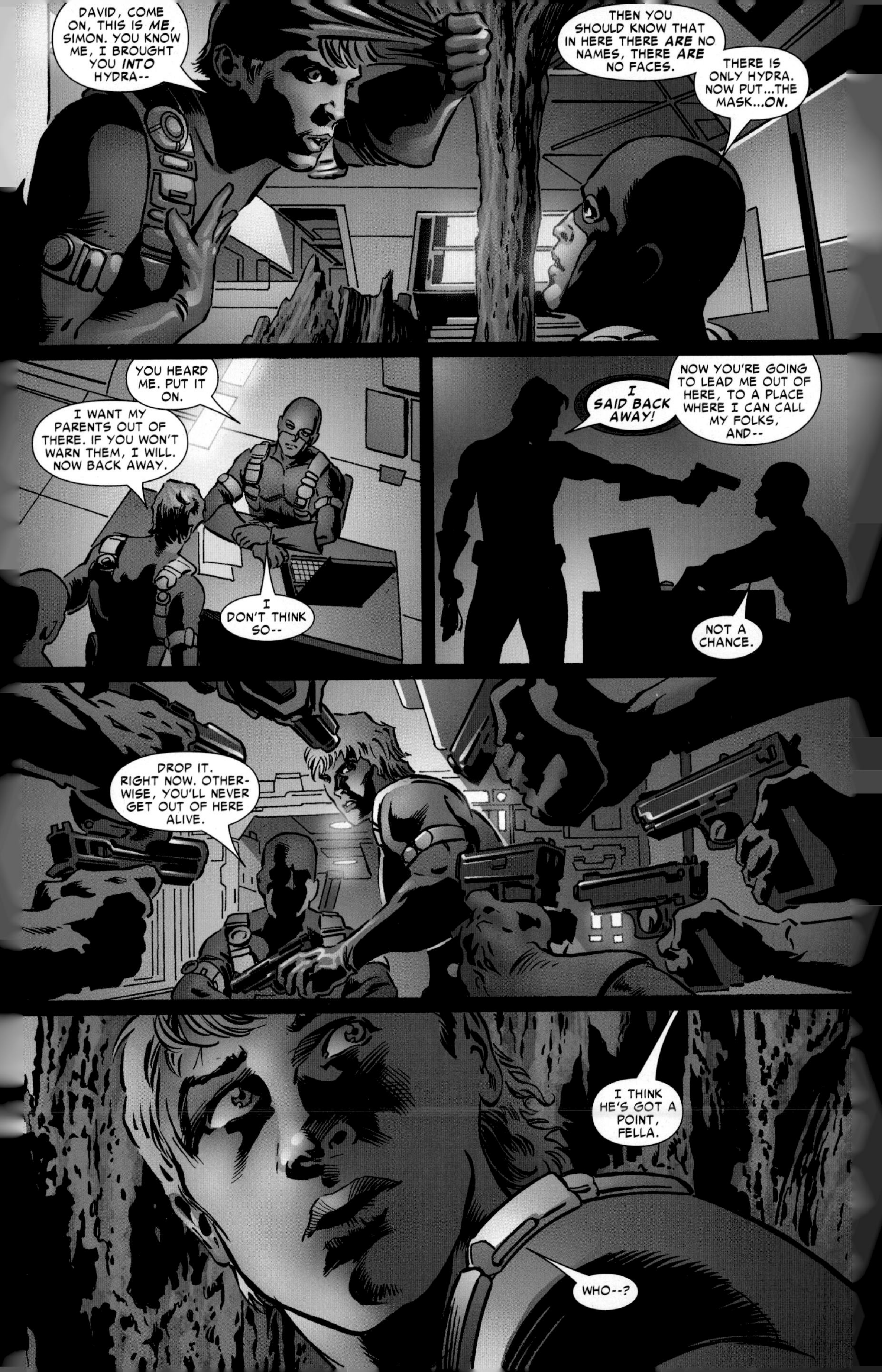
DAVID, COME ON, THIS IS ME, SIMON. YOU KNOW ME, I BROUGHT YOU INTO HYDRA--
THEN YOU SHOULD KNOW THAT IN HERE THERE ARE NO NAMES, THERE ARE NO FACES.
THERE IS ONLY HYDRA. NOW PUT...THE MASK...ON.
YOU HEARD ME. PUT IT ON.
I WANT MY PARENTS OUT OF THERE. IF YOU WON'T WARN THEM, I WILL. NOW BACK AWAY.
I DON'T THINK SO--
I SAID BACK AWAY!
NOW YOU'RE GOING TO LEAD ME OUT OF HERE, TO A PLACE WHERE I CAN CALL MY FOLKS, AND--
NOT A CHANCE.
DROP IT. RIGHT NOW. OTHERWISE, YOU'LL NEVER GET OUT OF HERE ALIVE.
I THINK HE'S GOT A POINT, FELLA.
WHO--?

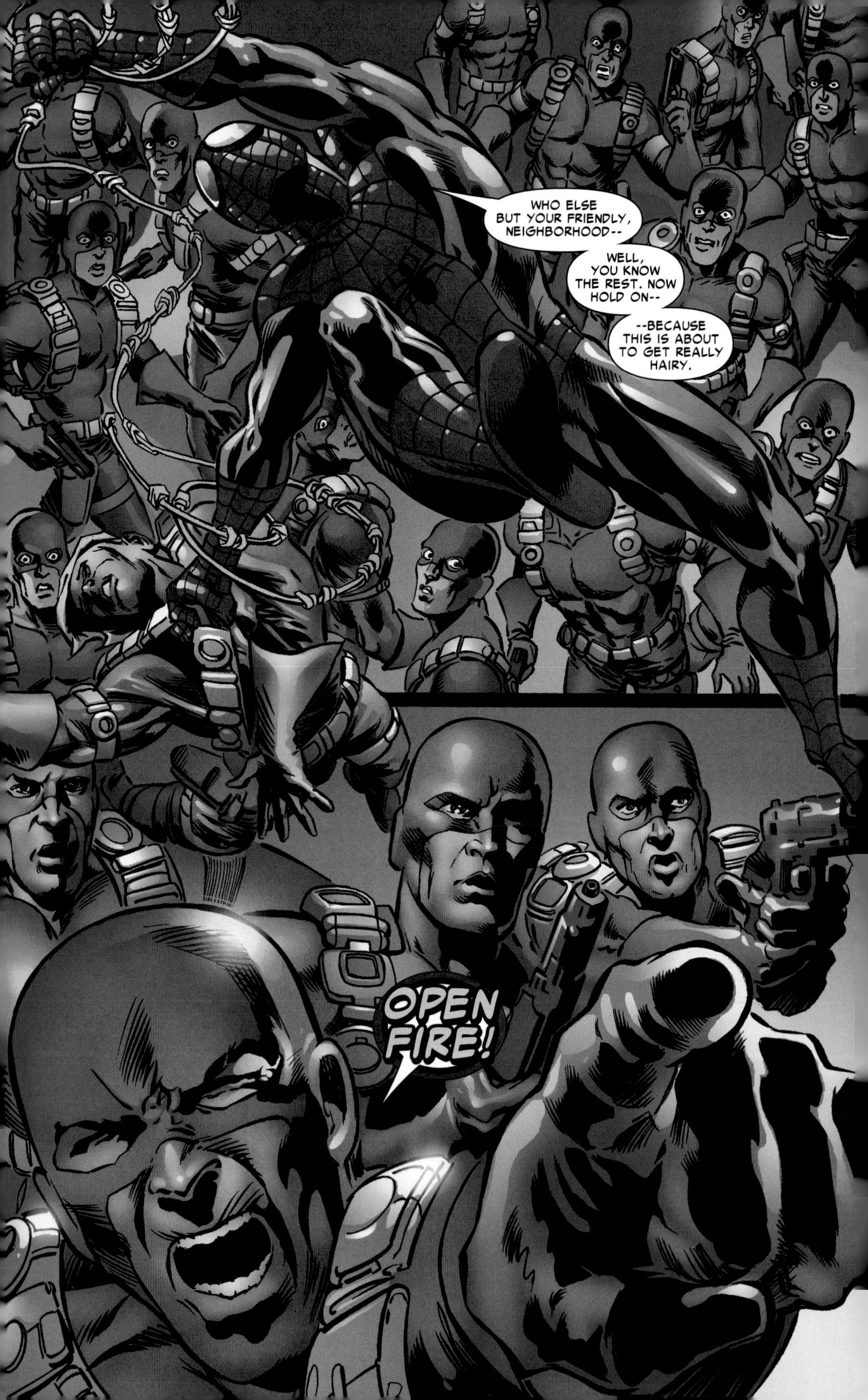
WHO ELSE BUT YOUR FRIENDLY, NEIGHBORHOOD--
WELL, YOU KNOW THE REST. NOW HOLD ON--
--BECAUSE THIS IS ABOUT TO GET REALLY HAIRY.
OPEN FIRE!

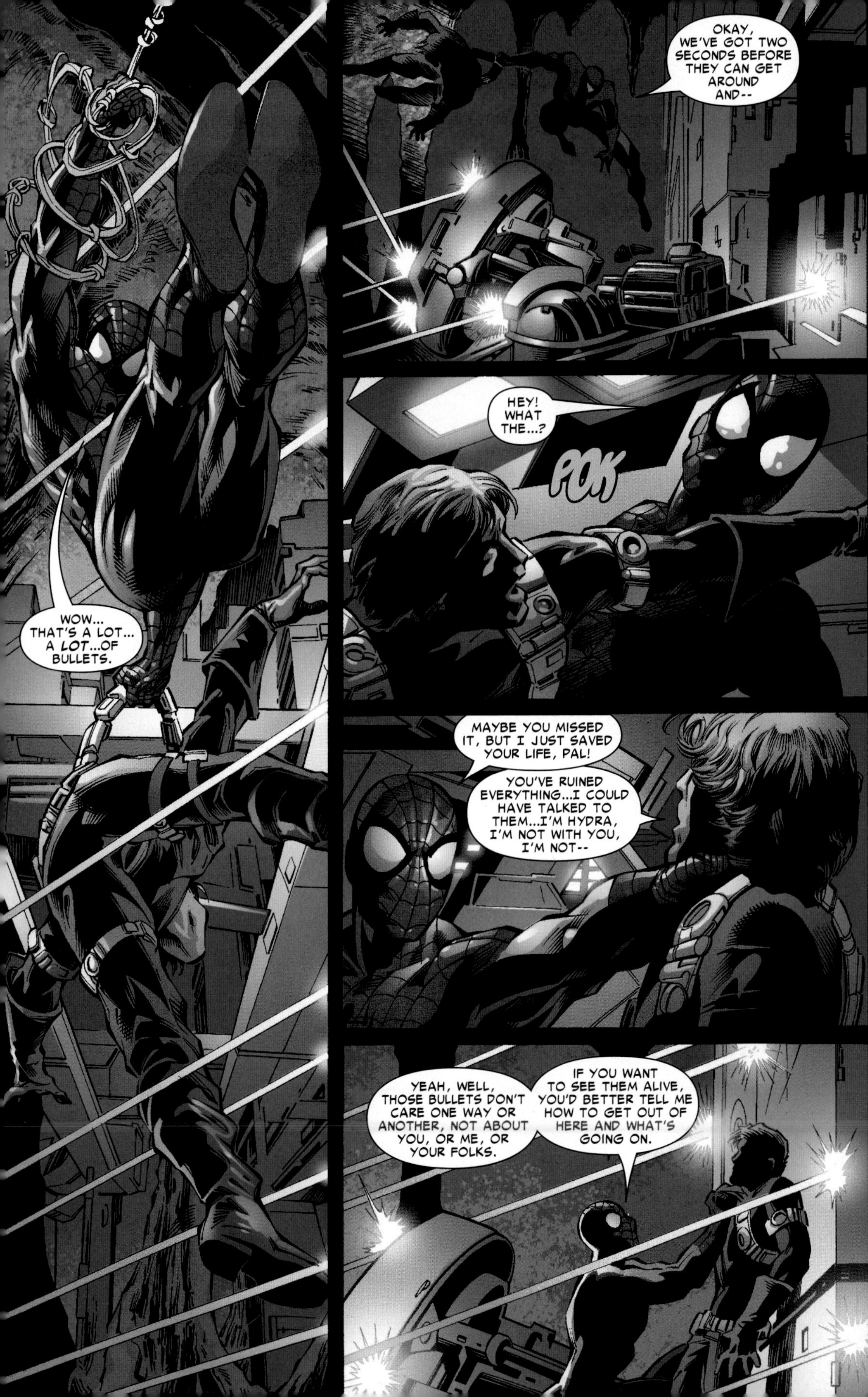
WOW... THAT'S A LOT... A *LOT*...OF BULLETS.
OKAY, WE'VE GOT TWO SECONDS BEFORE THEY CAN GET AROUND AND--
HEY! WHAT THE...?
POK
MAYBE YOU MISSED IT, BUT I JUST SAVED YOUR LIFE, PAL!
YOU'VE RUINED EVERYTHING...I COULD HAVE TALKED TO THEM...I'M HYDRA, I'M NOT WITH YOU, I'M NOT--
YEAH, WELL, THOSE BULLETS DON'T CARE ONE WAY OR ANOTHER, NOT ABOUT YOU, OR ME, OR YOUR FOLKS.
IF YOU WANT TO SEE THEM ALIVE, YOU'D BETTER TELL ME HOW TO GET OUT OF HERE AND WHAT'S GOING ON.

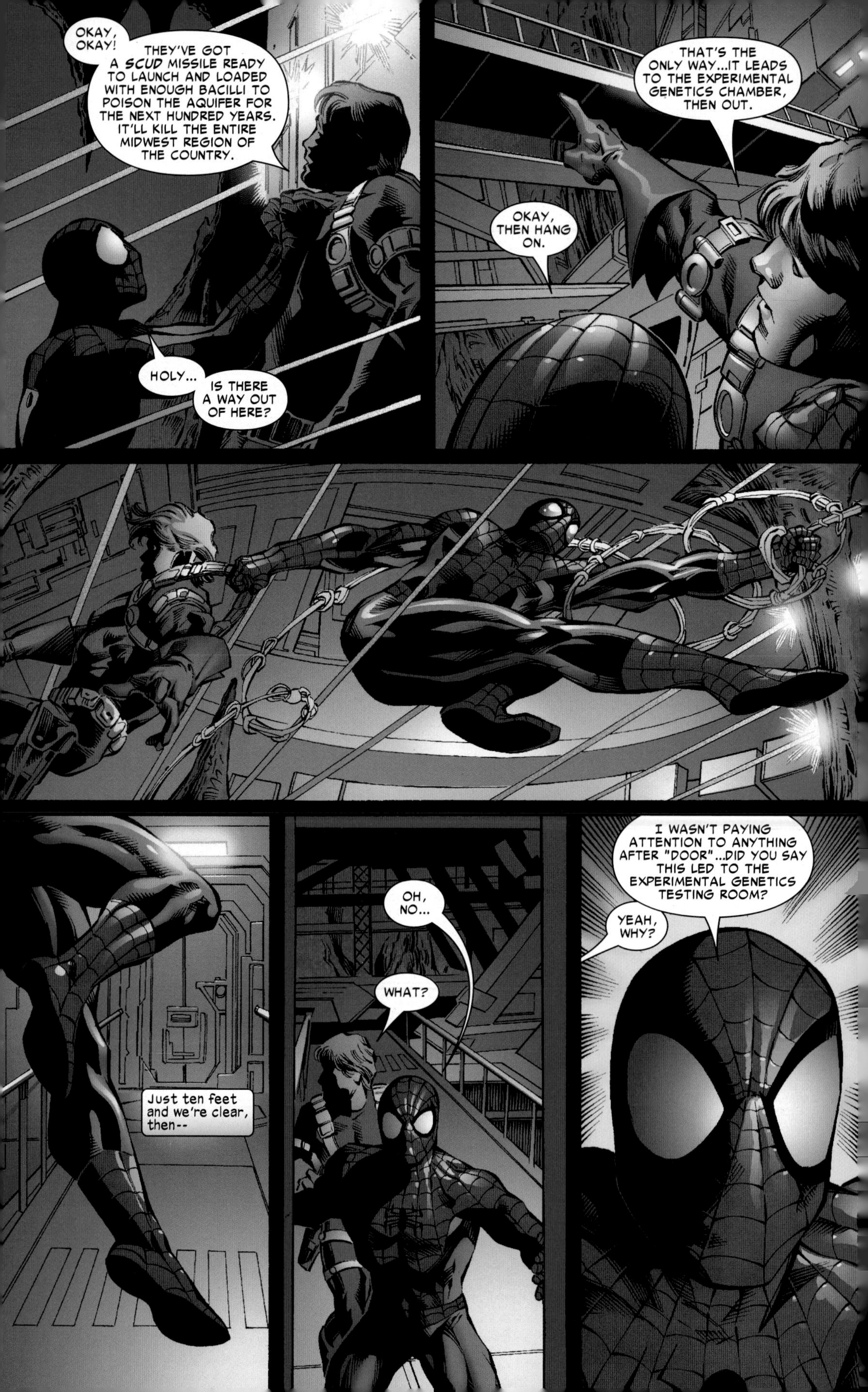
OKAY, OKAY!
THEY'VE GOT A SCUD MISSILE READY TO LAUNCH AND LOADED WITH ENOUGH BACILLI TO POISON THE AQUIFER FOR THE NEXT HUNDRED YEARS. IT'LL KILL THE ENTIRE MIDWEST REGION OF THE COUNTRY.
HOLY...
IS THERE A WAY OUT OF HERE?
THAT'S THE ONLY WAY...IT LEADS TO THE EXPERIMENTAL GENETICS CHAMBER, THEN OUT.
OKAY, THEN HANG ON.
Just ten feet and we're clear, then--
OH, NO...
WHAT?
I WASN'T PAYING ATTENTION TO ANYTHING AFTER "DOOR"...DID YOU SAY THIS LED TO THE EXPERIMENTAL GENETICS TESTING ROOM?
YEAH, WHY?

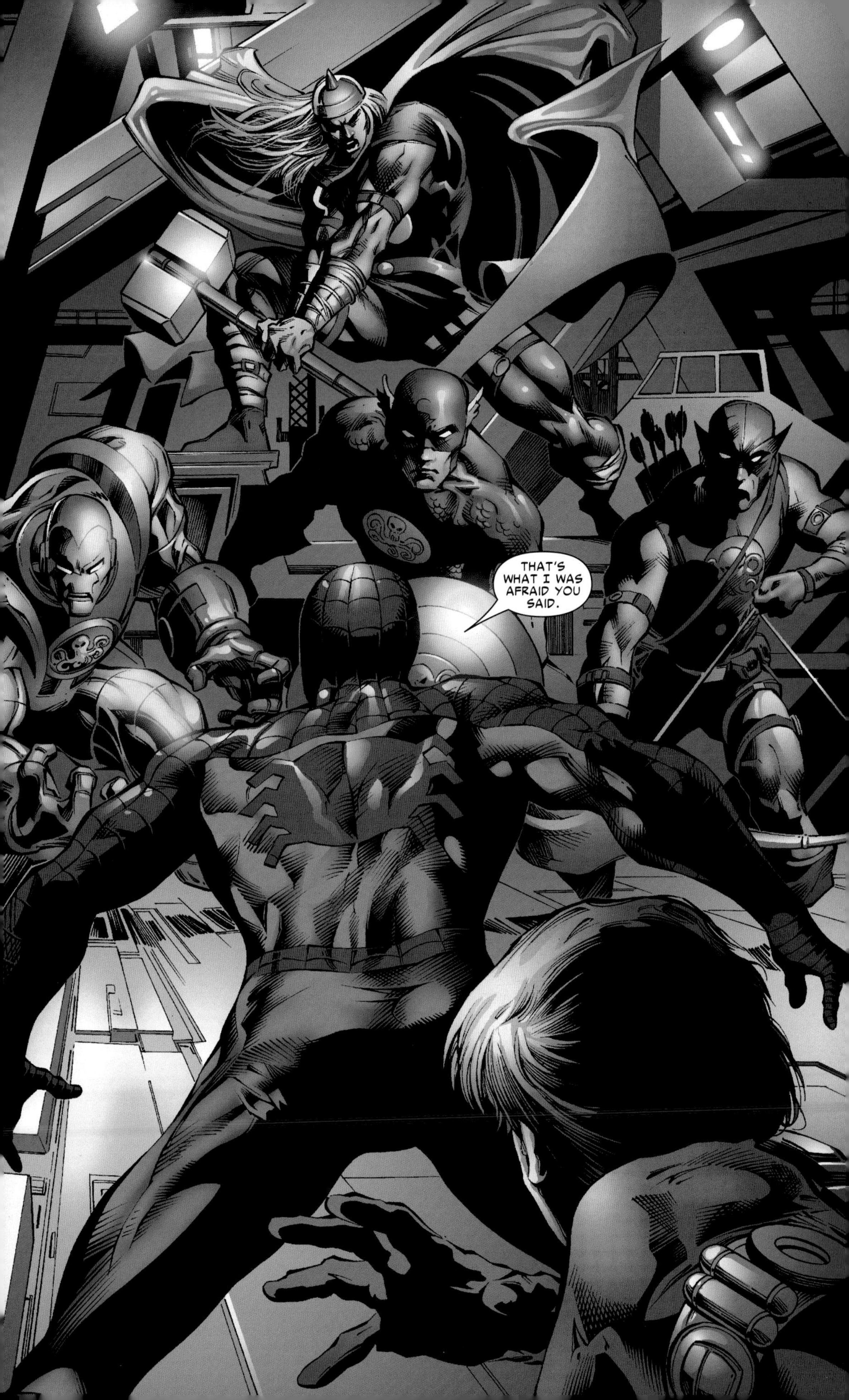
THAT'S WHAT I WAS AFRAID YOU SAID.

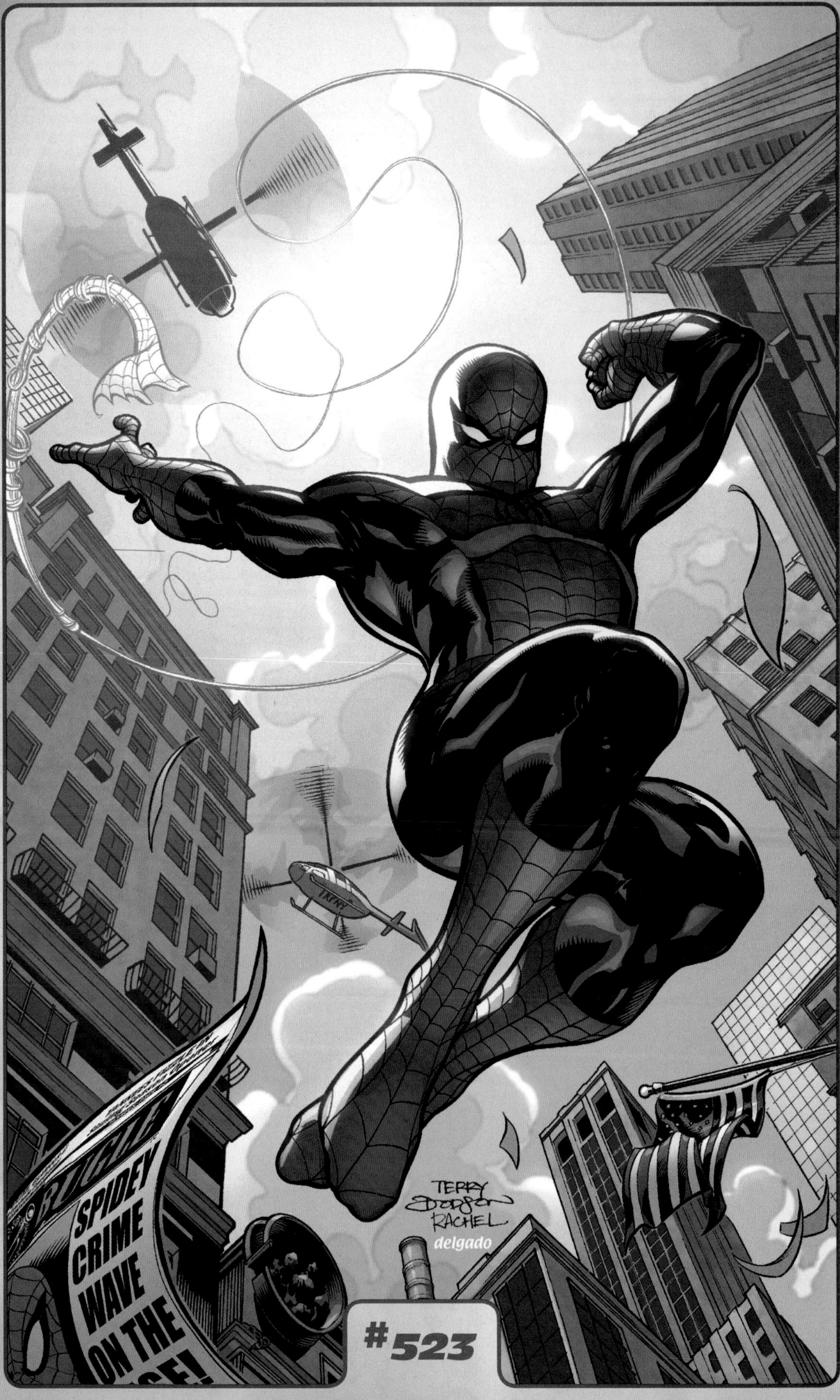

SPIDEY
CRIME
WAVE
ON THE
TERRY
RACHEL
delgado
#523

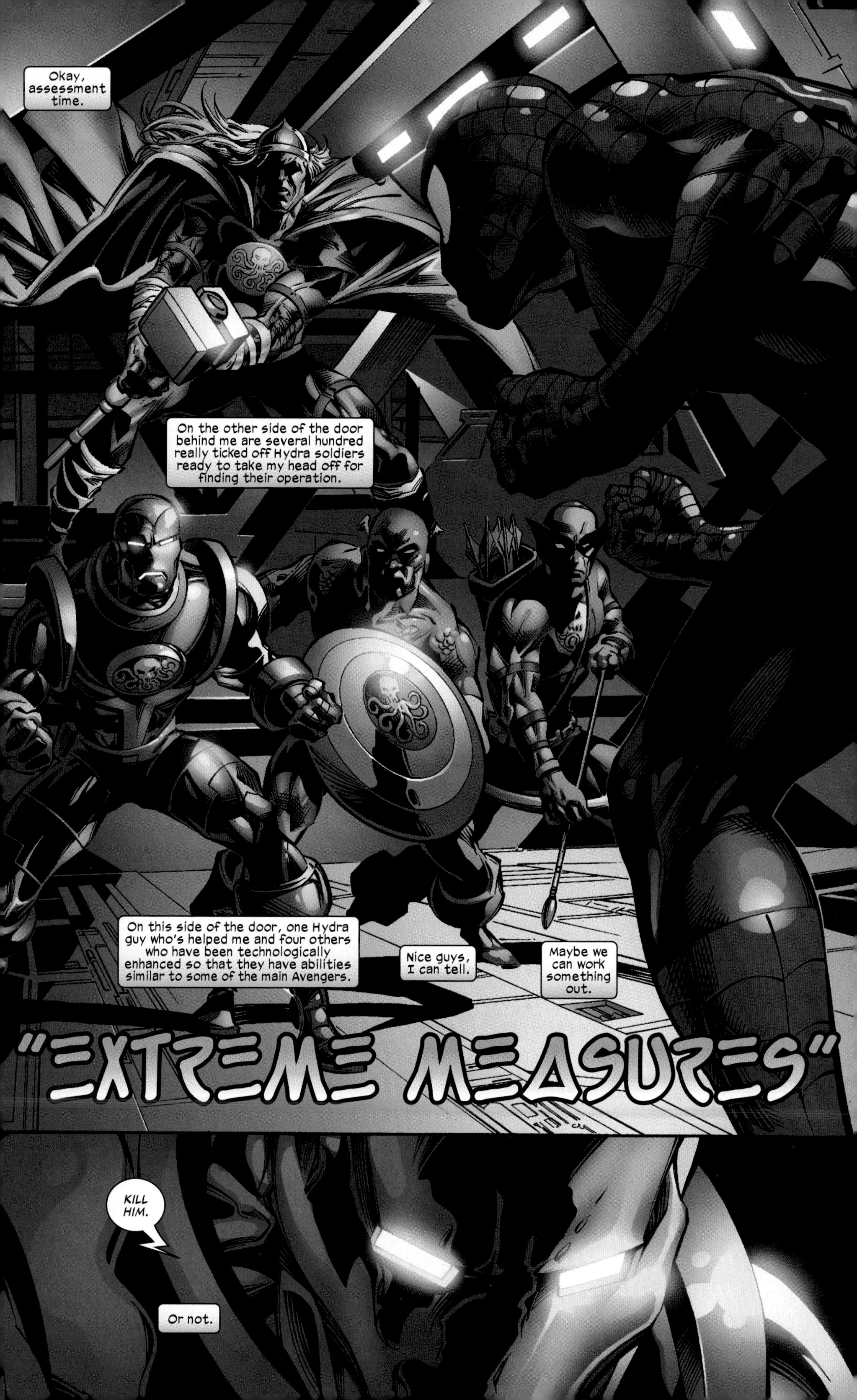
Okay, assessment time.
On the other side of the door behind me are several hundred really ticked off Hydra soldiers ready to take my head off for finding their operation.
On this side of the door, one Hydra guy who's helped me and four others who have been technologically enhanced so that they have abilities similar to some of the main Avengers.
Nice guys, I can tell.
Maybe we can work something out.
"EXTREME MEASURES"
KILL HIM.
Or not.

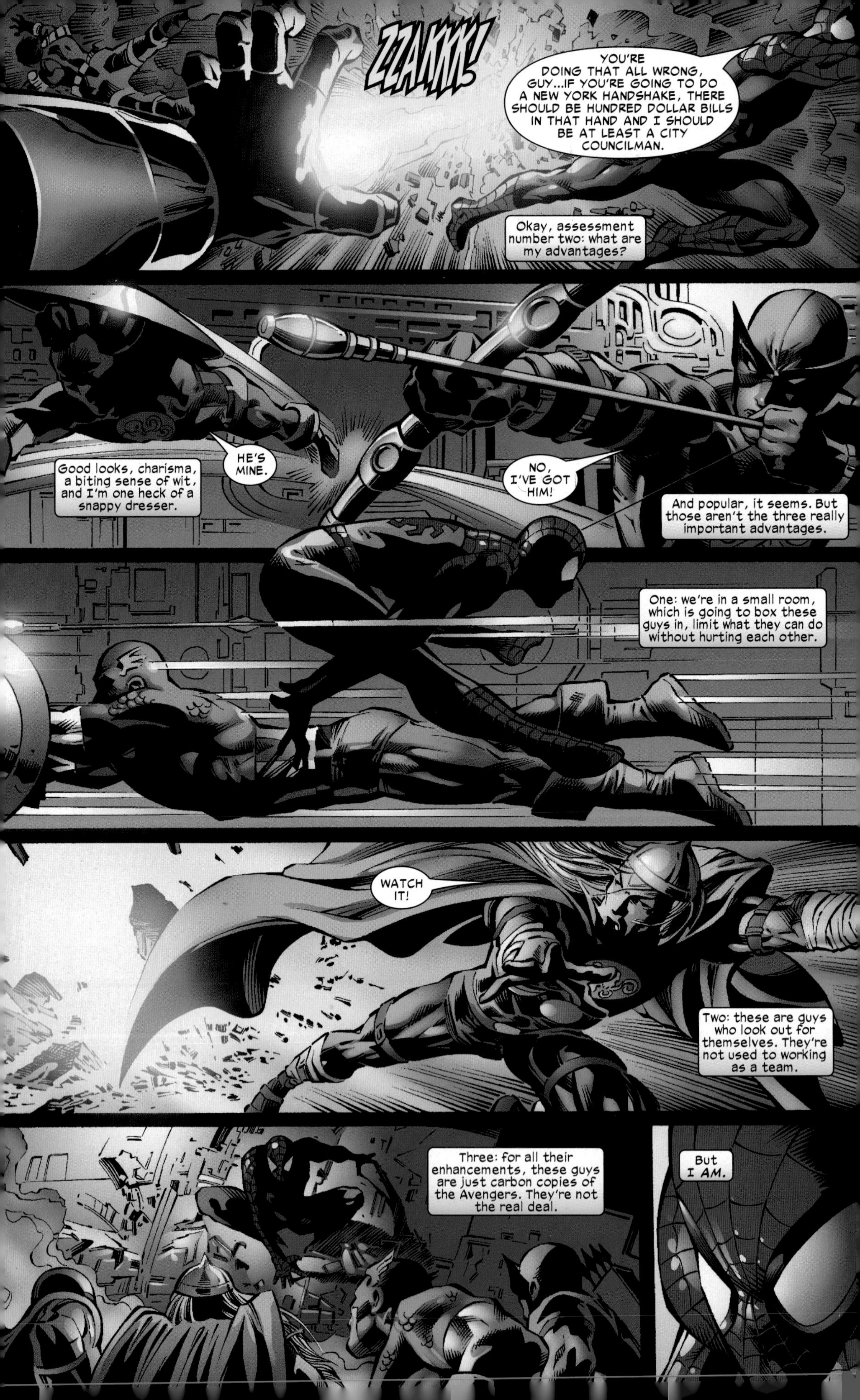
ZZAKKK!
YOU'RE DOING THAT ALL WRONG, GUY...IF YOU'RE GOING TO DO A NEW YORK HANDSHAKE, THERE SHOULD BE HUNDRED DOLLAR BILLS IN THAT HAND AND I SHOULD BE AT LEAST A CITY COUNCILMAN.
Okay, assessment number two: what are my advantages?
Good looks, charisma, a biting sense of wit, and I'm one heck of a snappy dresser.
HE'S MINE.
NO, I'VE GOT HIM!
And popular, it seems. But those aren't the three really important advantages.
One: we're in a small room, which is going to box these guys in, limit what they can do without hurting each other.
WATCH IT!
Two: these are guys who look out for themselves. They're not used to working as a team.
Three: for all their enhancements, these guys are just carbon copies of the Avengers. They're not the real deal.
But I AM.

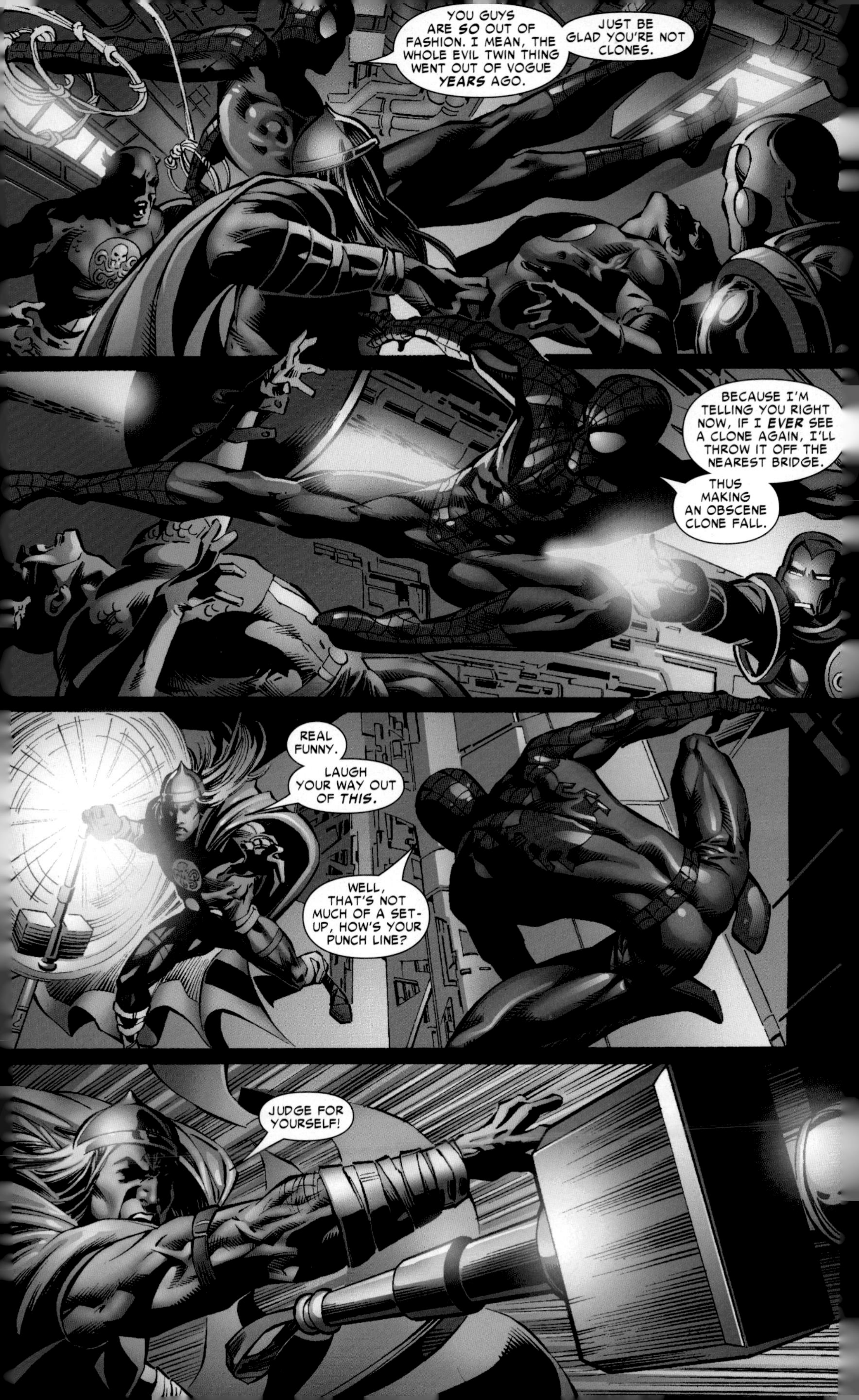
YOU GUYS ARE SO OUT OF FASHION. I MEAN, THE WHOLE EVIL TWIN THING WENT OUT OF VOGUE YEARS AGO.
JUST BE GLAD YOU'RE NOT CLONES.
BECAUSE I'M TELLING YOU RIGHT NOW, IF I EVER SEE A CLONE AGAIN, I'LL THROW IT OFF THE NEAREST BRIDGE.
THUS MAKING AN OBSCENE CLONE FALL.
REAL FUNNY.
LAUGH YOUR WAY OUT OF THIS.
WELL, THAT'S NOT MUCH OF A SET-UP, HOW'S YOUR PUNCH LINE?
JUDGE FOR YOURSELF!

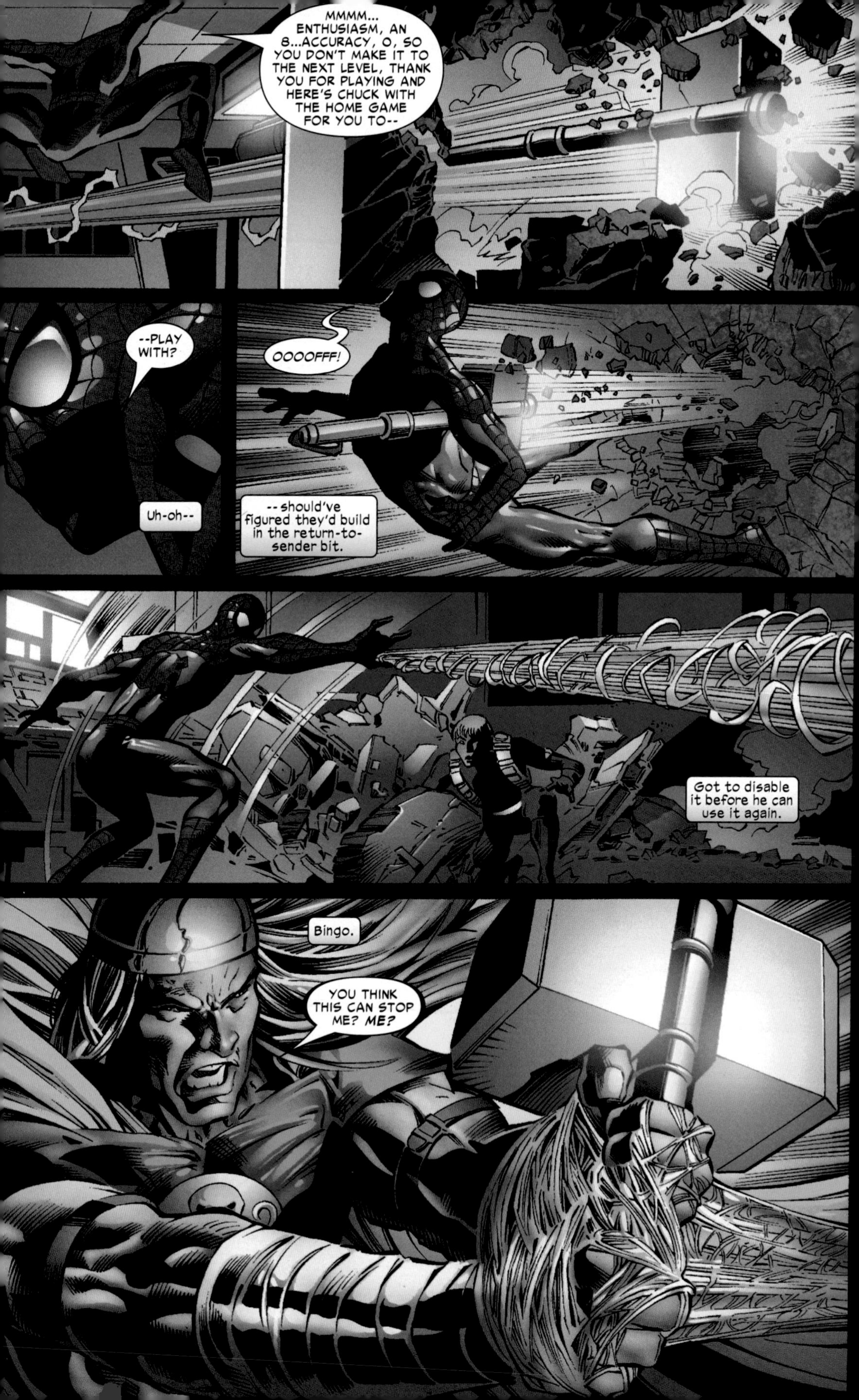
MMMM... ENTHUSIASM, AN 8...ACCURACY, 0, SO YOU DON'T MAKE IT TO THE NEXT LEVEL, THANK YOU FOR PLAYING AND HERE'S CHUCK WITH THE HOME GAME FOR YOU TO--
--PLAY WITH?
Uh-oh--
OOOOFFF!
--should've figured they'd build in the return-to-sender bit.
Got to disable it before he can use it again.
Bingo.
YOU THINK THIS CAN STOP ME? *ME?*

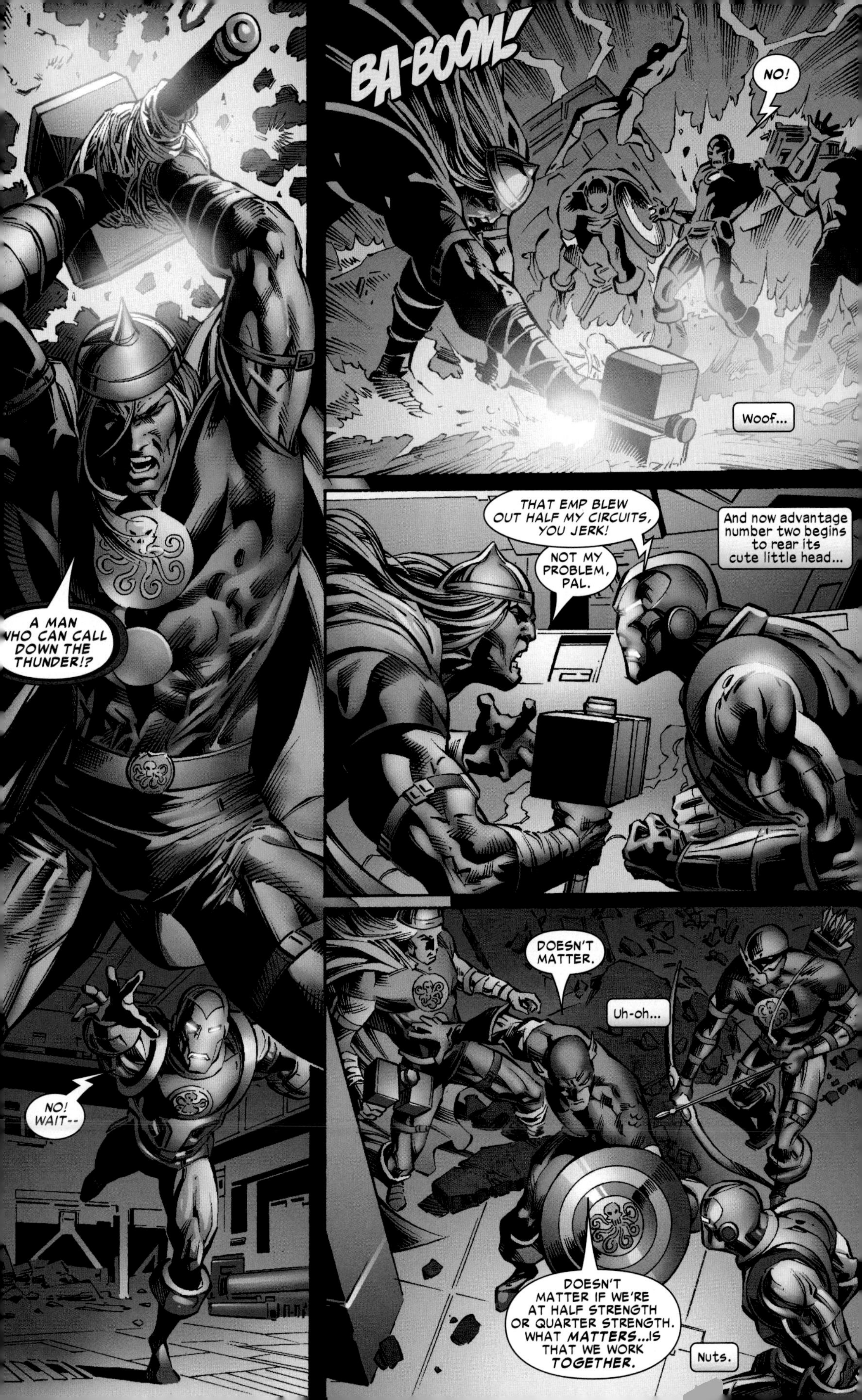
A MAN WHO CAN CALL DOWN THE THUNDER!?
NO! WAIT--
BA-BOOM!
NO!
Woof...
THAT EMP BLEW OUT HALF MY CIRCUITS, YOU JERK!
NOT MY PROBLEM, PAL.
And now advantage number two begins to rear its cute little head...
DOESN'T MATTER.
Uh-oh...
DOESN'T MATTER IF WE'RE AT HALF STRENGTH OR QUARTER STRENGTH. WHAT MATTERS...IS THAT WE WORK TOGETHER.
Nuts.

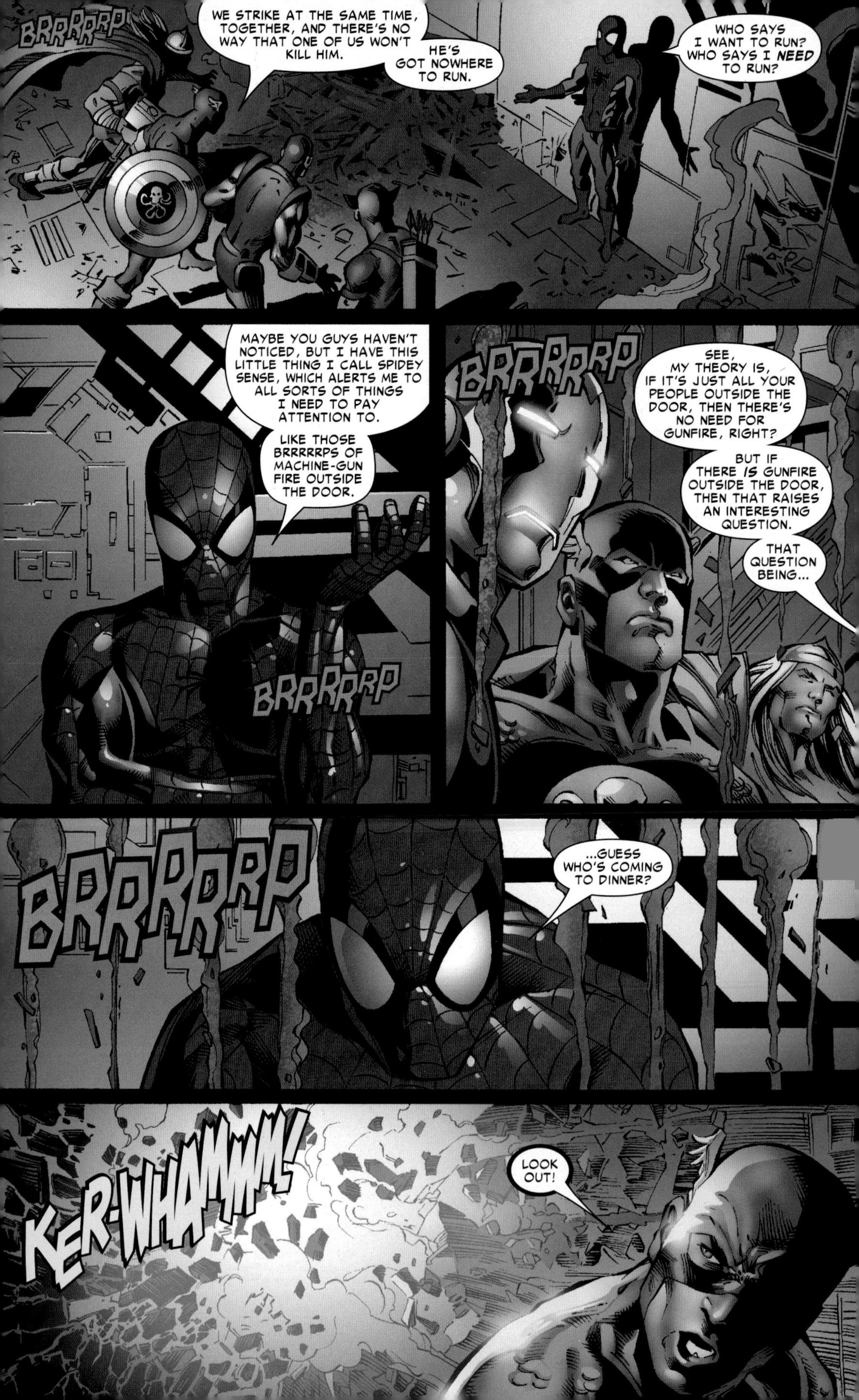
BRRRRRP
WE STRIKE AT THE SAME TIME, TOGETHER, AND THERE'S NO WAY THAT ONE OF US WON'T KILL HIM.
HE'S GOT NOWHERE TO RUN.
WHO SAYS I WANT TO RUN? WHO SAYS I NEED TO RUN?
MAYBE YOU GUYS HAVEN'T NOTICED, BUT I HAVE THIS LITTLE THING I CALL SPIDEY SENSE, WHICH ALERTS ME TO ALL SORTS OF THINGS I NEED TO PAY ATTENTION TO.
LIKE THOSE BRRRRRPS OF MACHINE-GUN FIRE OUTSIDE THE DOOR.
BRRRRRP
BRRRRRP
SEE, MY THEORY IS, IF IT'S JUST ALL YOUR PEOPLE OUTSIDE THE DOOR, THEN THERE'S NO NEED FOR GUNFIRE, RIGHT?
BUT IF THERE IS GUNFIRE OUTSIDE THE DOOR, THEN THAT RAISES AN INTERESTING QUESTION.
THAT QUESTION BEING...
BRRRRRP
...GUESS WHO'S COMING TO DINNER?
KER-WHAMMM!
LOOK OUT!

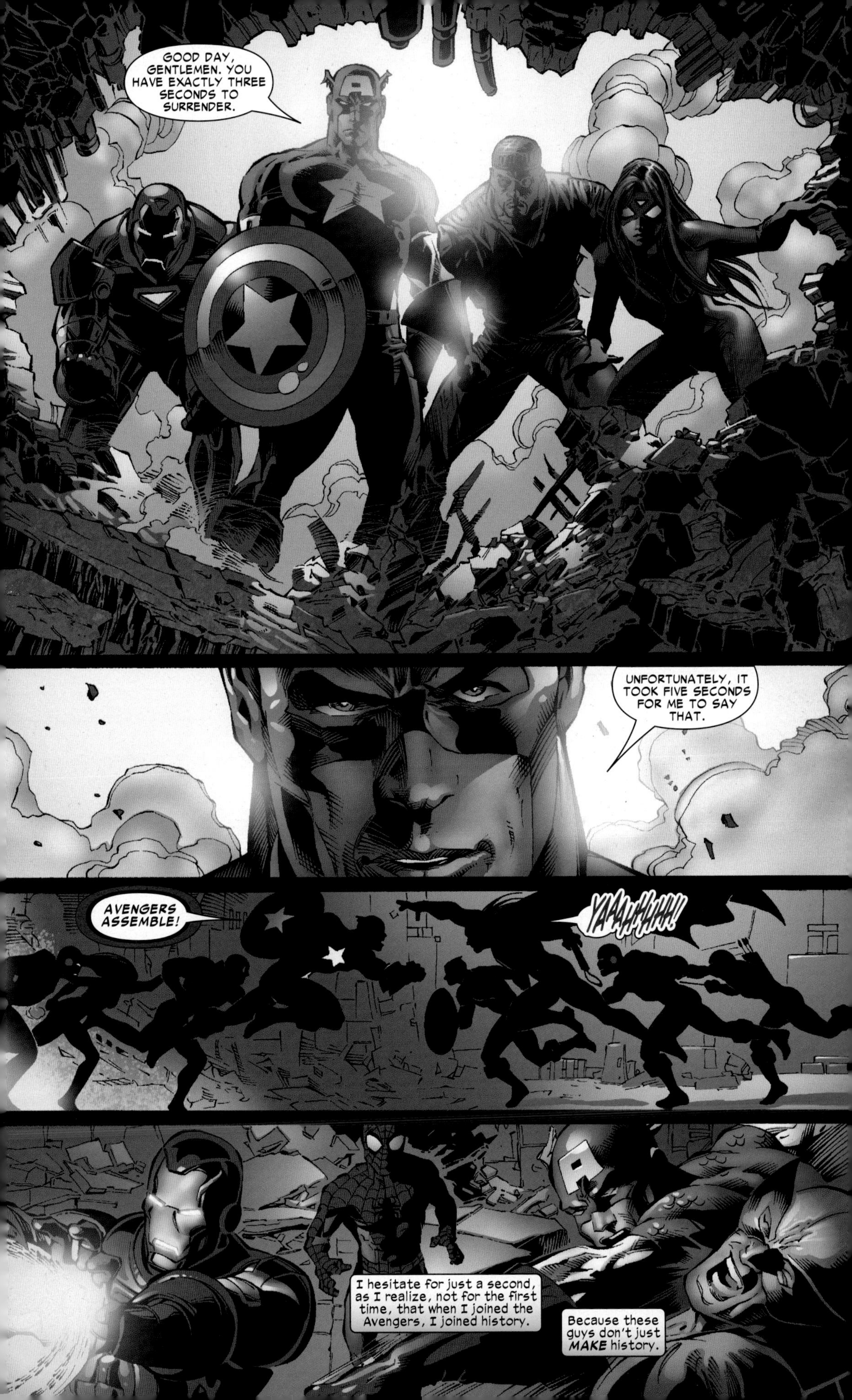

GOOD DAY, GENTLEMEN. YOU HAVE EXACTLY THREE SECONDS TO SURRENDER.
UNFORTUNATELY, IT TOOK FIVE SECONDS FOR ME TO SAY THAT.
AVENGERS ASSEMBLE!
YAAAHHHH!
I hesitate for just a second, as I realize, not for the first time, that when I joined the Avengers, I joined history.
Because these guys don't just MAKE history.

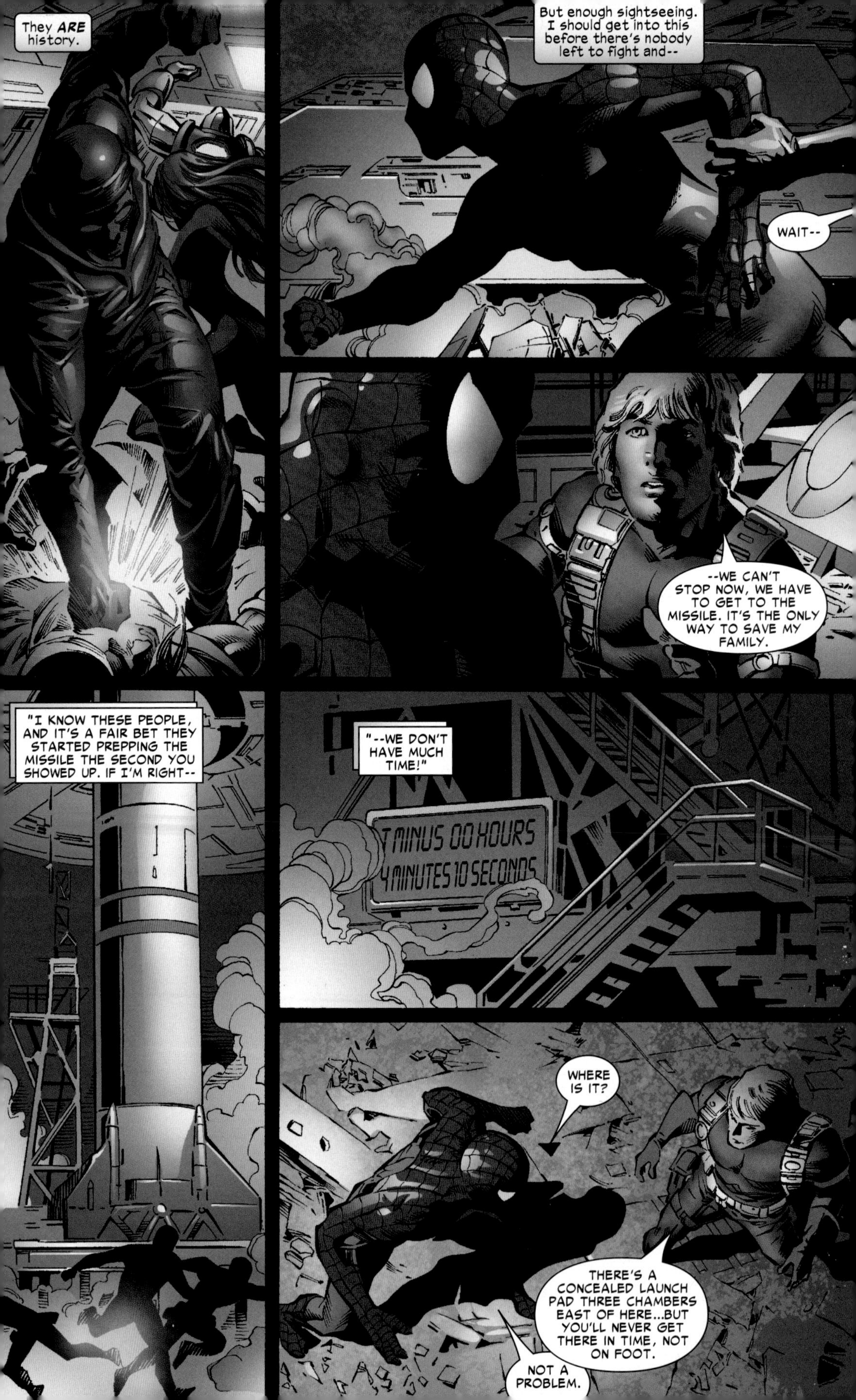
They ARE history.
But enough sightseeing. I should get into this before there's nobody left to fight and--
WAIT--
--WE CAN'T STOP NOW, WE HAVE TO GET TO THE MISSILE. IT'S THE ONLY WAY TO SAVE MY FAMILY.
"I KNOW THESE PEOPLE, AND IT'S A FAIR BET THEY STARTED PREPPING THE MISSILE THE SECOND YOU SHOWED UP. IF I'M RIGHT--
"--WE DON'T HAVE MUCH TIME!"
T MINUS 00 HOURS
4 MINUTES 10 SECONDS
WHERE IS IT?
THERE'S A CONCEALED LAUNCH PAD THREE CHAMBERS EAST OF HERE...BUT YOU'LL NEVER GET THERE IN TIME, NOT ON FOOT.
NOT A PROBLEM.

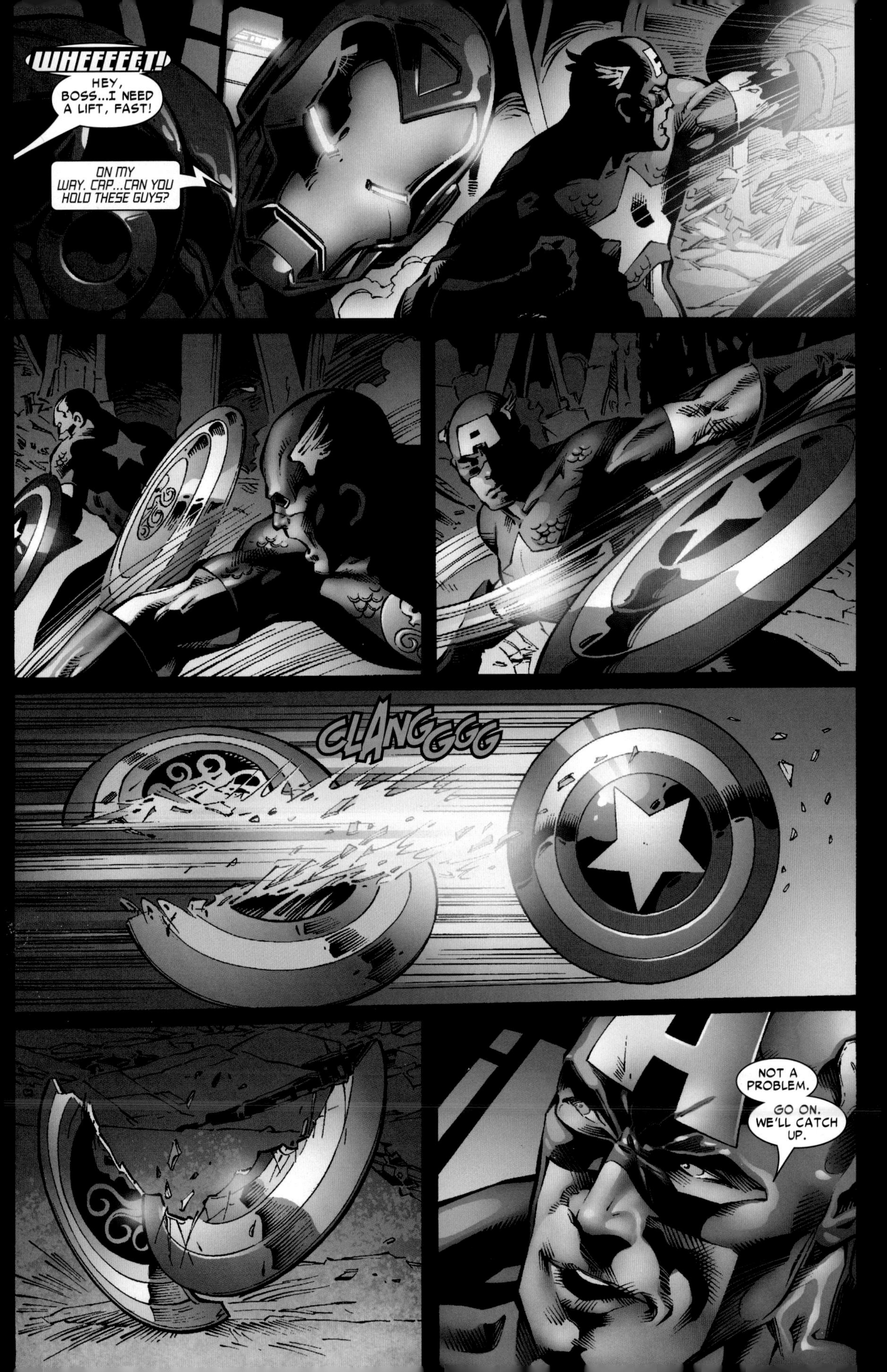
WHEEEEET!
HEY, BOSS...I NEED A LIFT, FAST!
ON MY WAY. CAP...CAN YOU HOLD THESE GUYS?
CLANGGGG
NOT A PROBLEM.
GO ON. WE'LL CATCH UP.

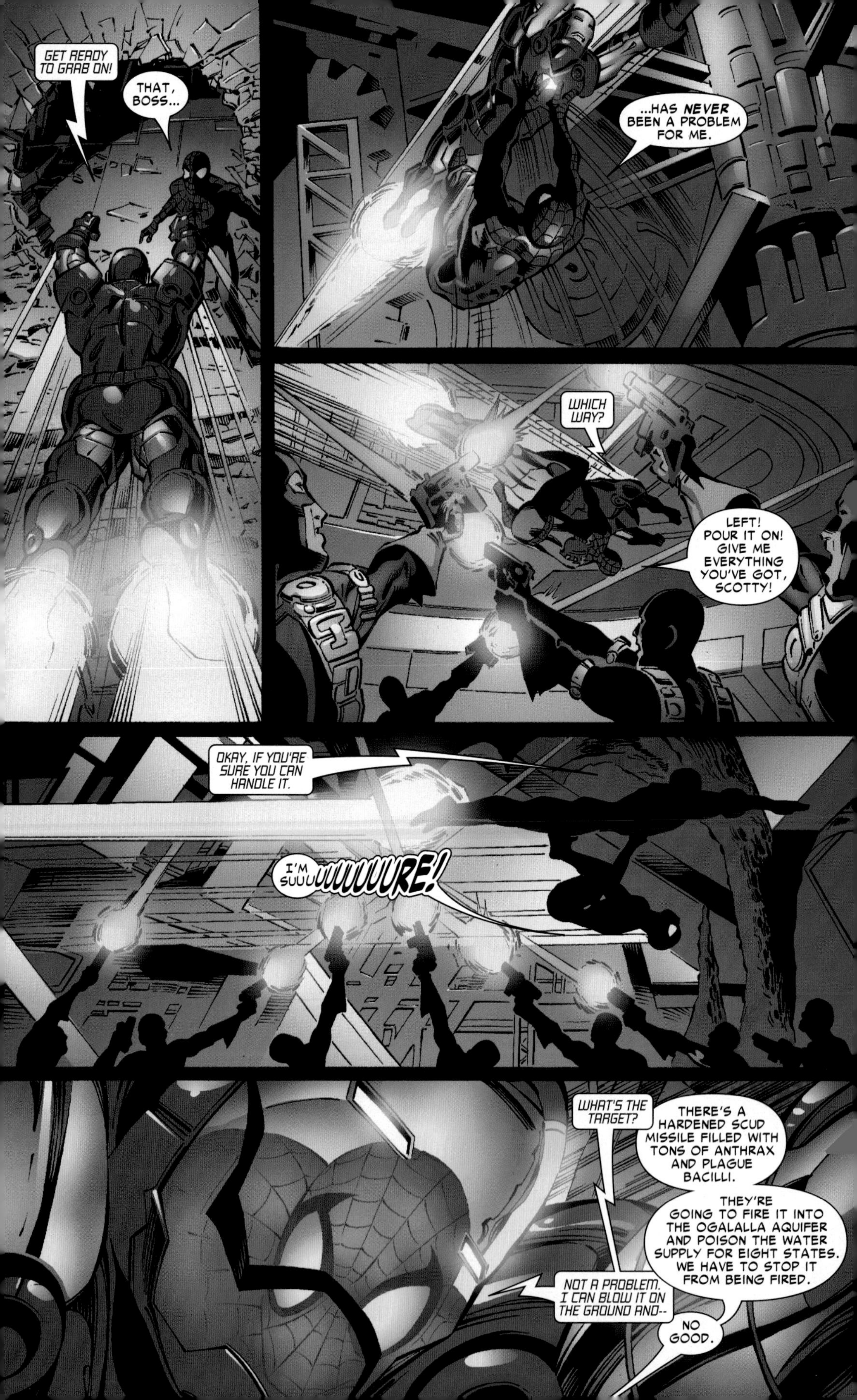
GET READY TO GRAB ON!
THAT, BOSS...
...HAS NEVER BEEN A PROBLEM FOR ME.
WHICH WAY?
LEFT! POUR IT ON! GIVE ME EVERYTHING YOU'VE GOT, SCOTTY!
OKAY, IF YOU'RE SURE YOU CAN HANDLE IT.
I'M SUUUUUUUUUURE!
WHAT'S THE TARGET?
THERE'S A HARDENED SCUD MISSILE FILLED WITH TONS OF ANTHRAX AND PLAGUE BACILLI.
THEY'RE GOING TO FIRE IT INTO THE OGALALLA AQUIFER AND POISON THE WATER SUPPLY FOR EIGHT STATES. WE HAVE TO STOP IT FROM BEING FIRED.
NOT A PROBLEM. I CAN BLOW IT ON THE GROUND AND--
NO GOOD.

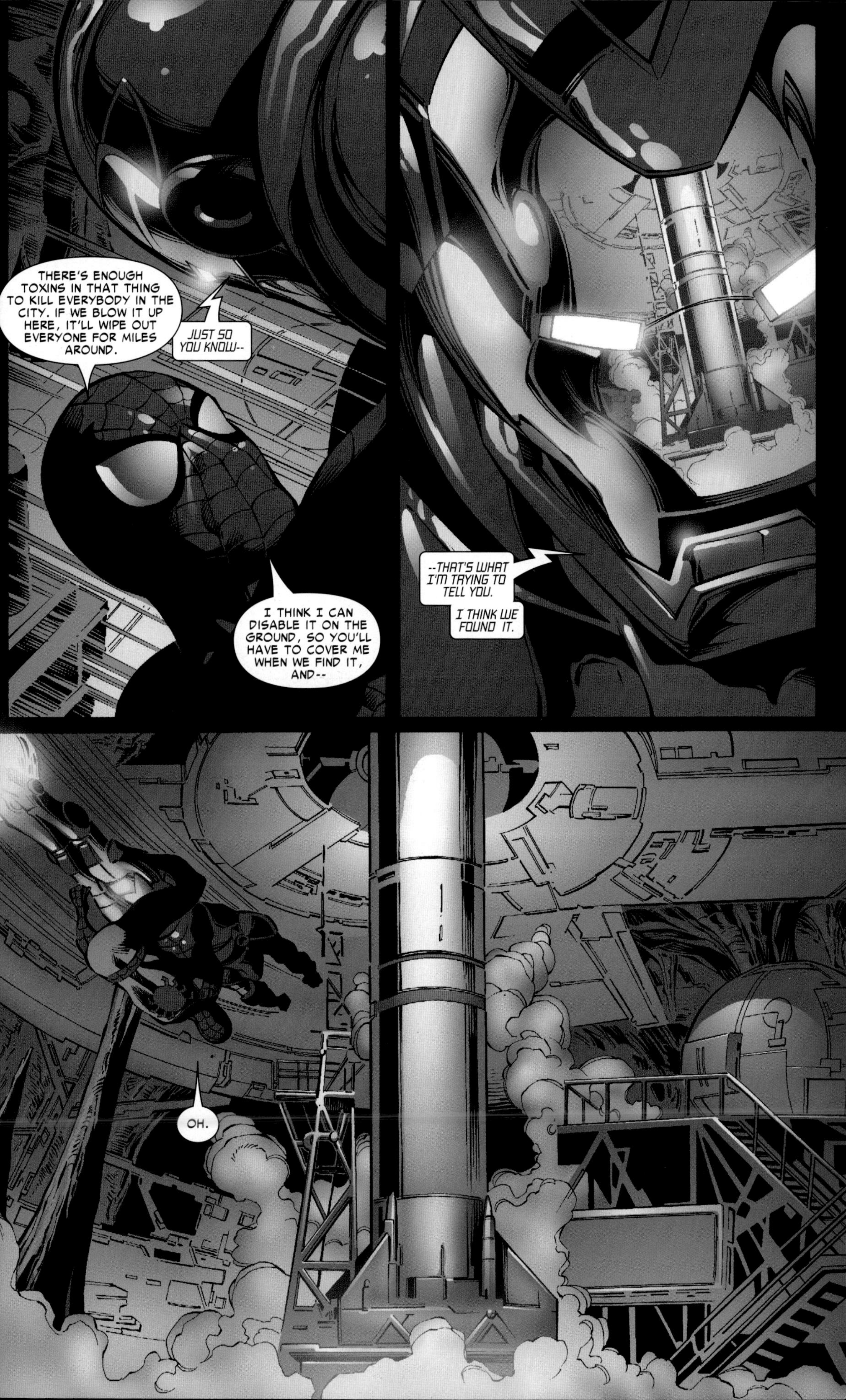
THERE'S ENOUGH TOXINS IN THAT THING TO KILL EVERYBODY IN THE CITY. IF WE BLOW IT UP HERE, IT'LL WIPE OUT EVERYONE FOR MILES AROUND.
JUST SO YOU KNOW--
I THINK I CAN DISABLE IT ON THE GROUND, SO YOU'LL HAVE TO COVER ME WHEN WE FIND IT, AND--
--THAT'S WHAT I'M TRYING TO TELL YOU.
I THINK WE FOUND IT.
OH.

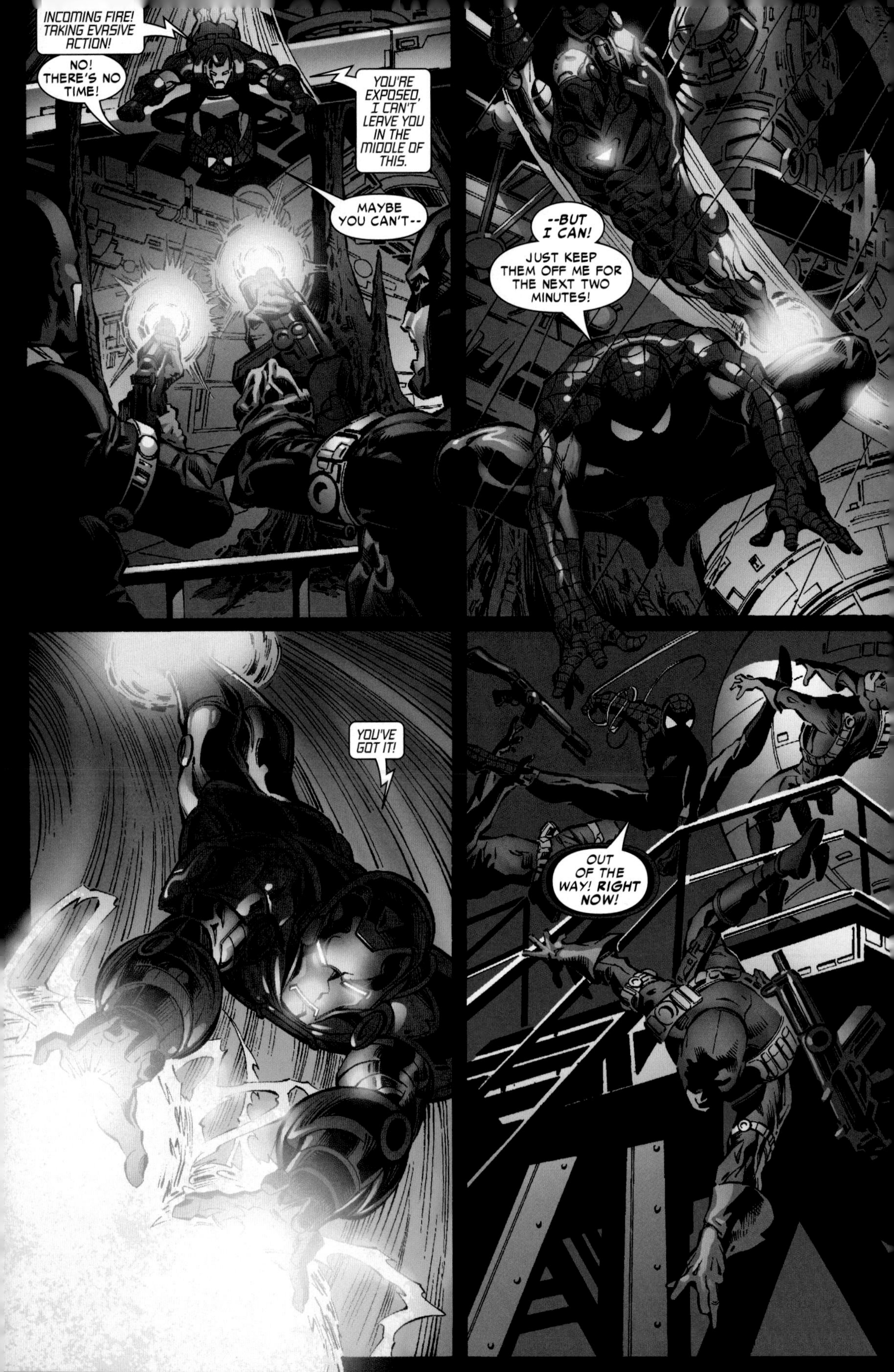
INCOMING FIRE! TAKING EVASIVE ACTION!
NO! THERE'S NO TIME!
YOU'RE EXPOSED, I CAN'T LEAVE YOU IN THE MIDDLE OF THIS.
MAYBE YOU CAN'T--
--BUT I CAN!
JUST KEEP THEM OFF ME FOR THE NEXT TWO MINUTES!
YOU'VE GOT IT!
OUT OF THE WAY! **RIGHT NOW!**

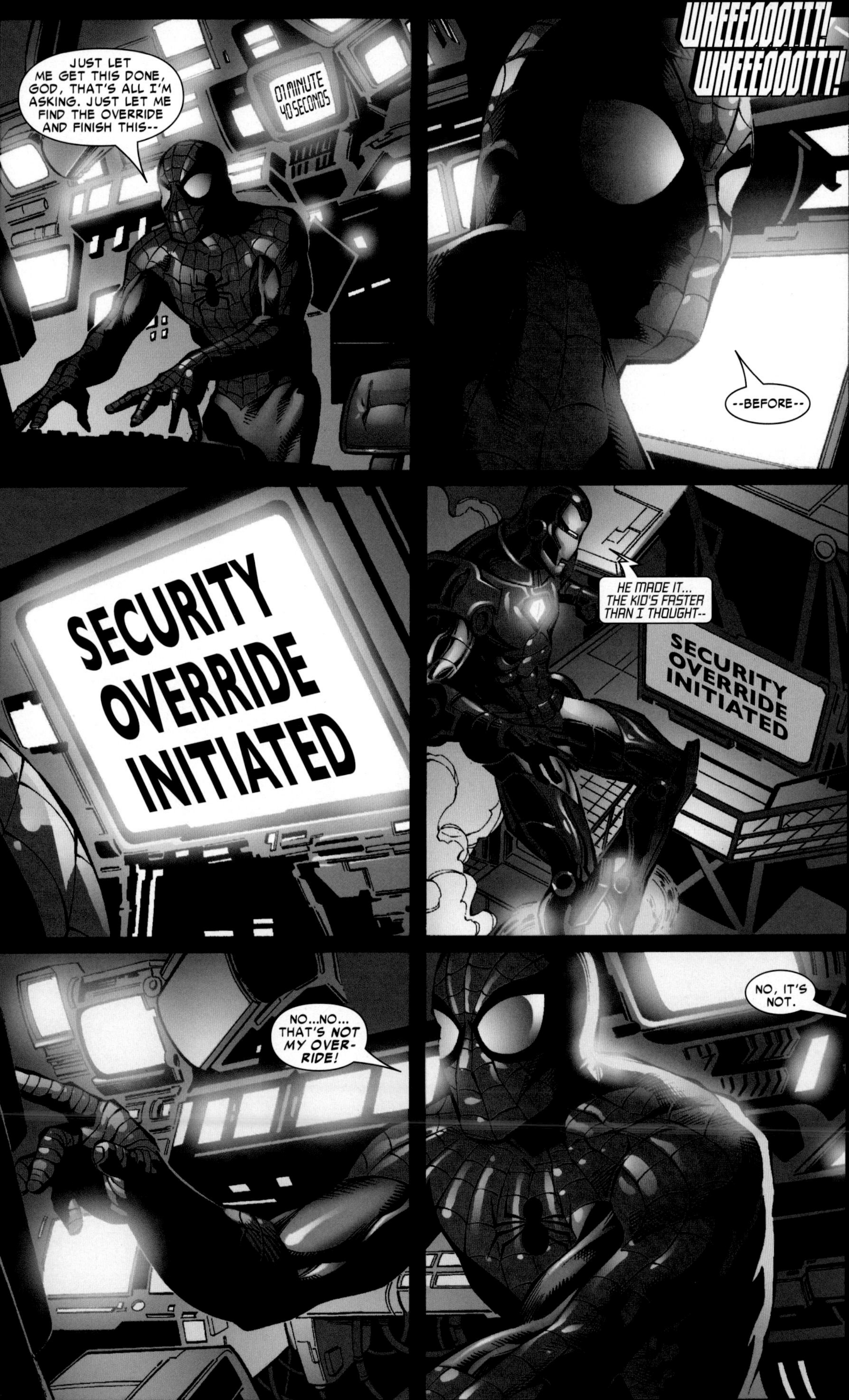
JUST LET ME GET THIS DONE, GOD, THAT'S ALL I'M ASKING. JUST LET ME FIND THE OVERRIDE AND FINISH THIS--
01 MINUTE 40 SECONDS
WHEEEOOOTTT! WHEEEOOOTTT!
--BEFORE--
SECURITY OVERRIDE INITIATED
HE MADE IT... THE KID'S FASTER THAN I THOUGHT--
SECURITY OVERRIDE INITIATED
NO...NO... THAT'S NOT MY OVER-RIDE!
NO, IT'S NOT.

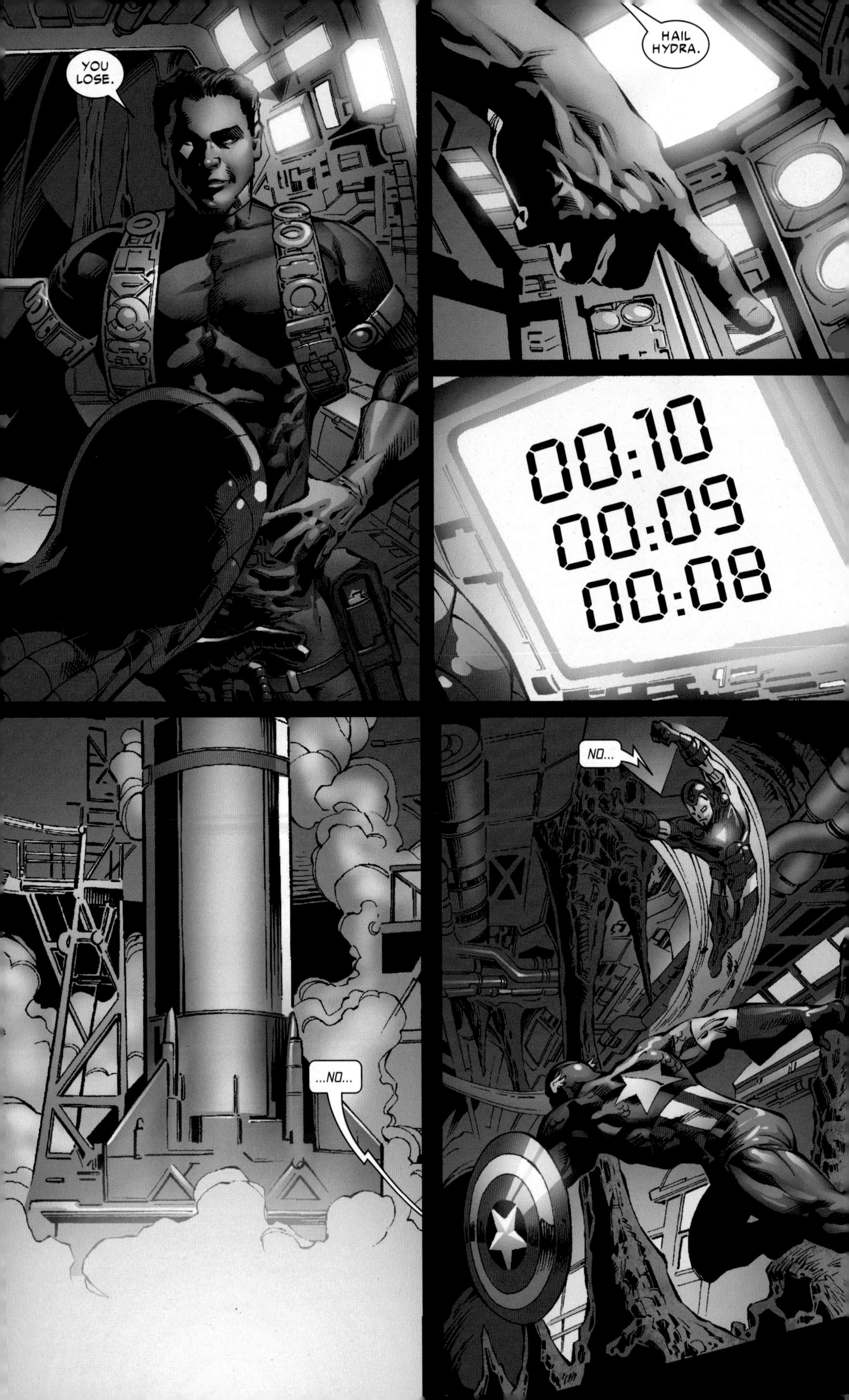
YOU LOSE.
HAIL HYDRA.
00:10
00:09
00:08
...NO...
NO...

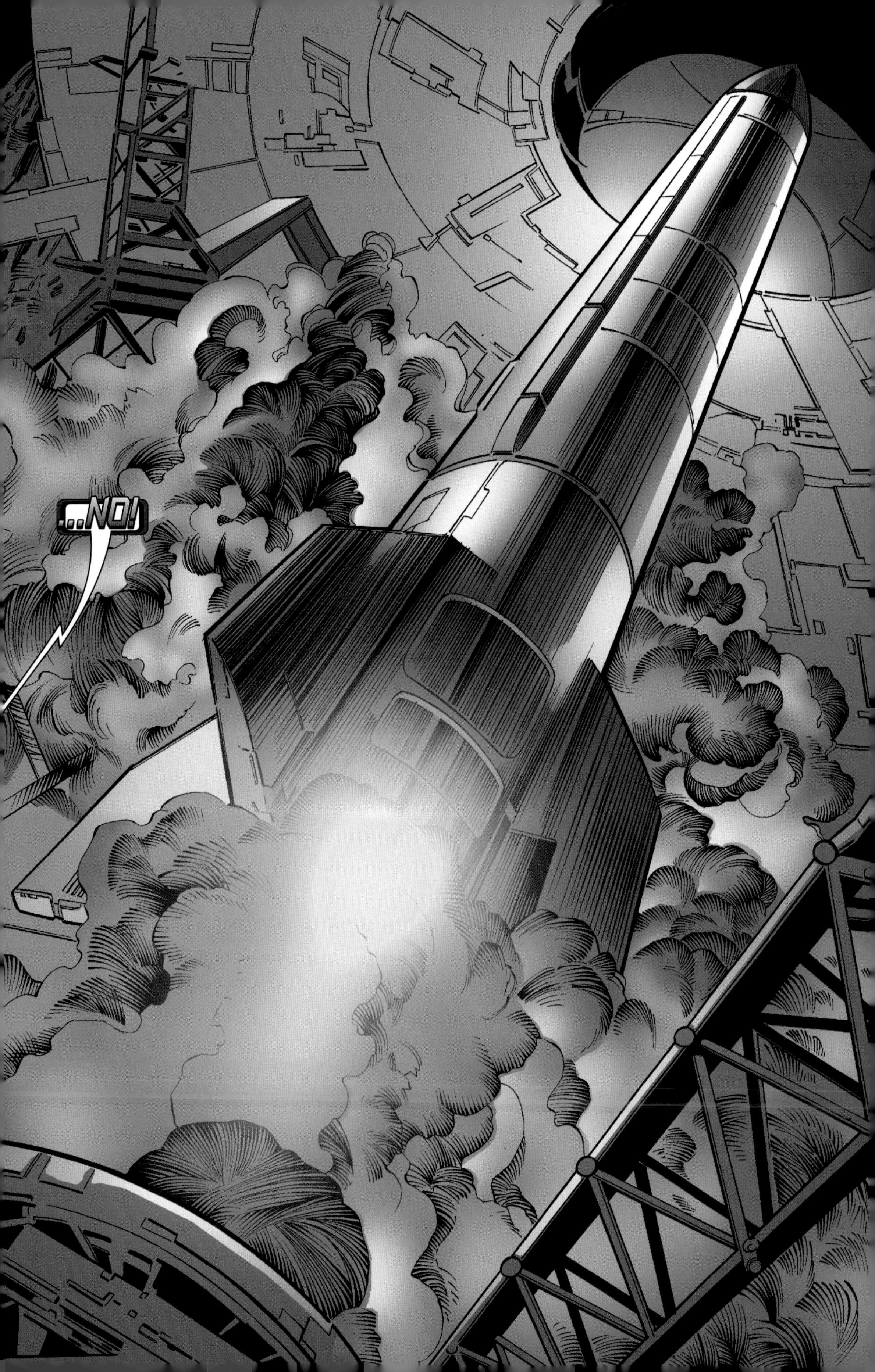
...NO!

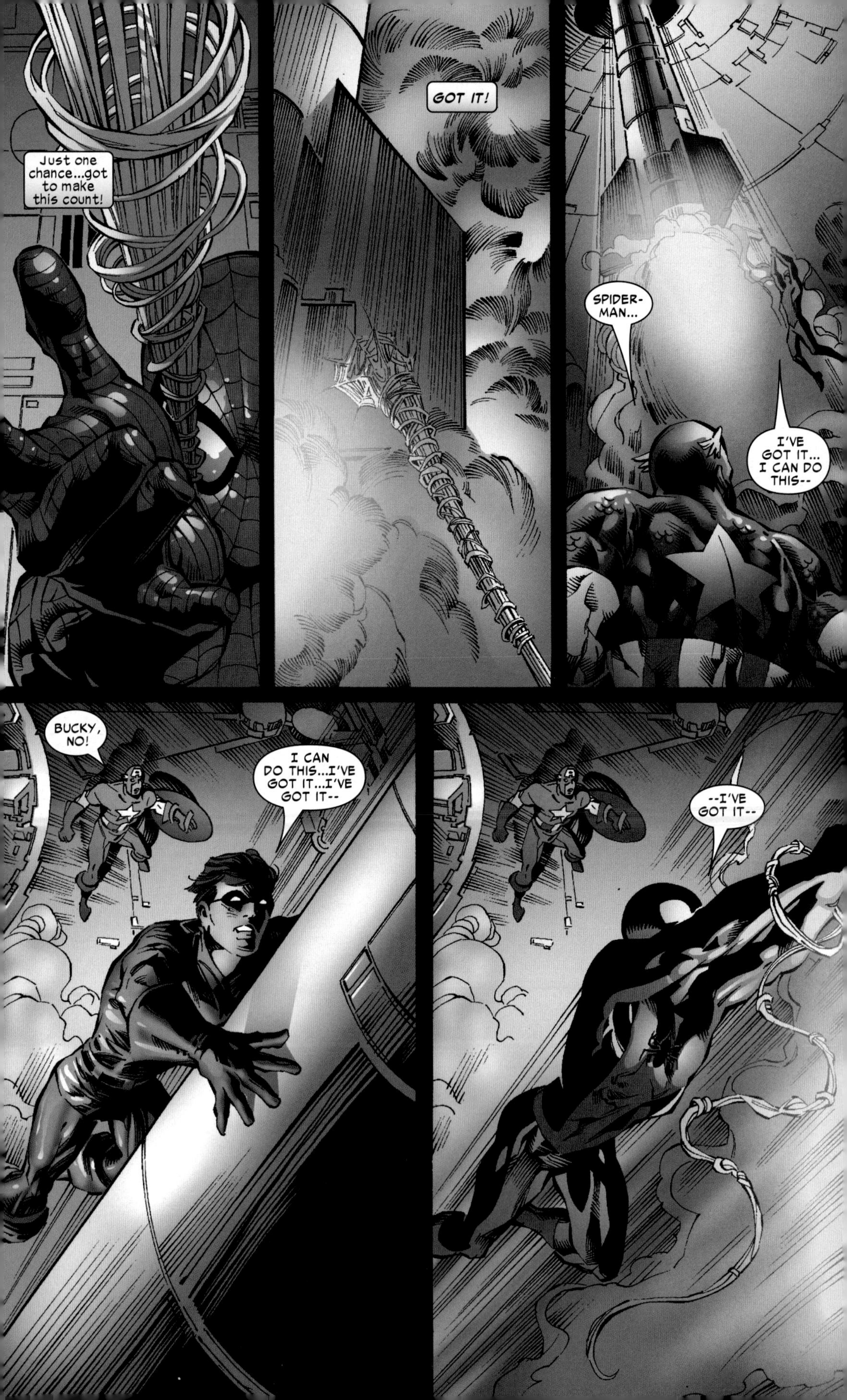
Just one chance...got to make this count!
GOT IT!
SPIDER-MAN...
I'VE GOT IT... I CAN DO THIS--
BUCKY, NO!
I CAN DO THIS...I'VE GOT IT...I'VE GOT IT--
--I'VE GOT IT--

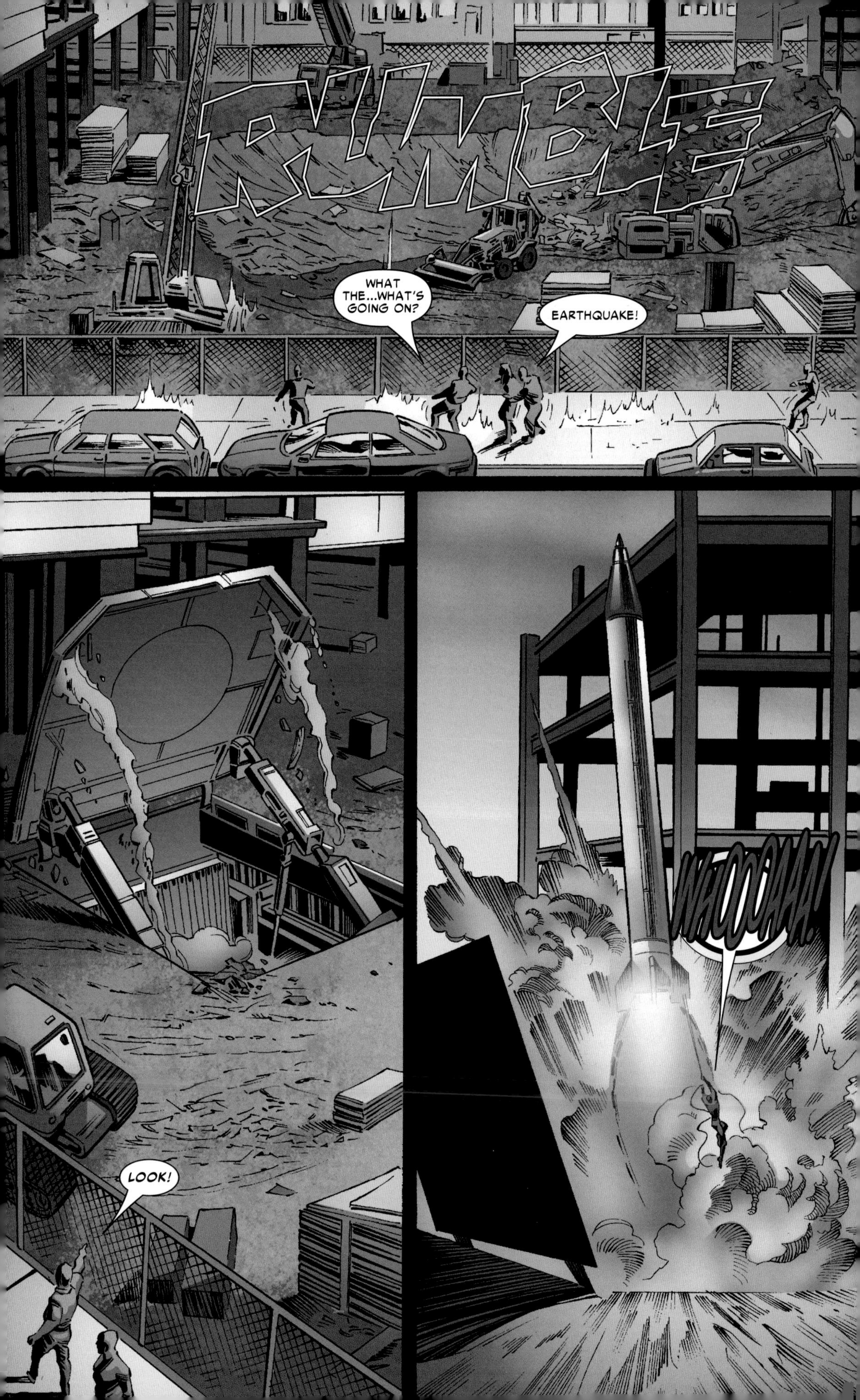
RUMBLE
WHAT THE...WHAT'S GOING ON?
EARTHQUAKE!
LOOK!
WHOOOAAA!

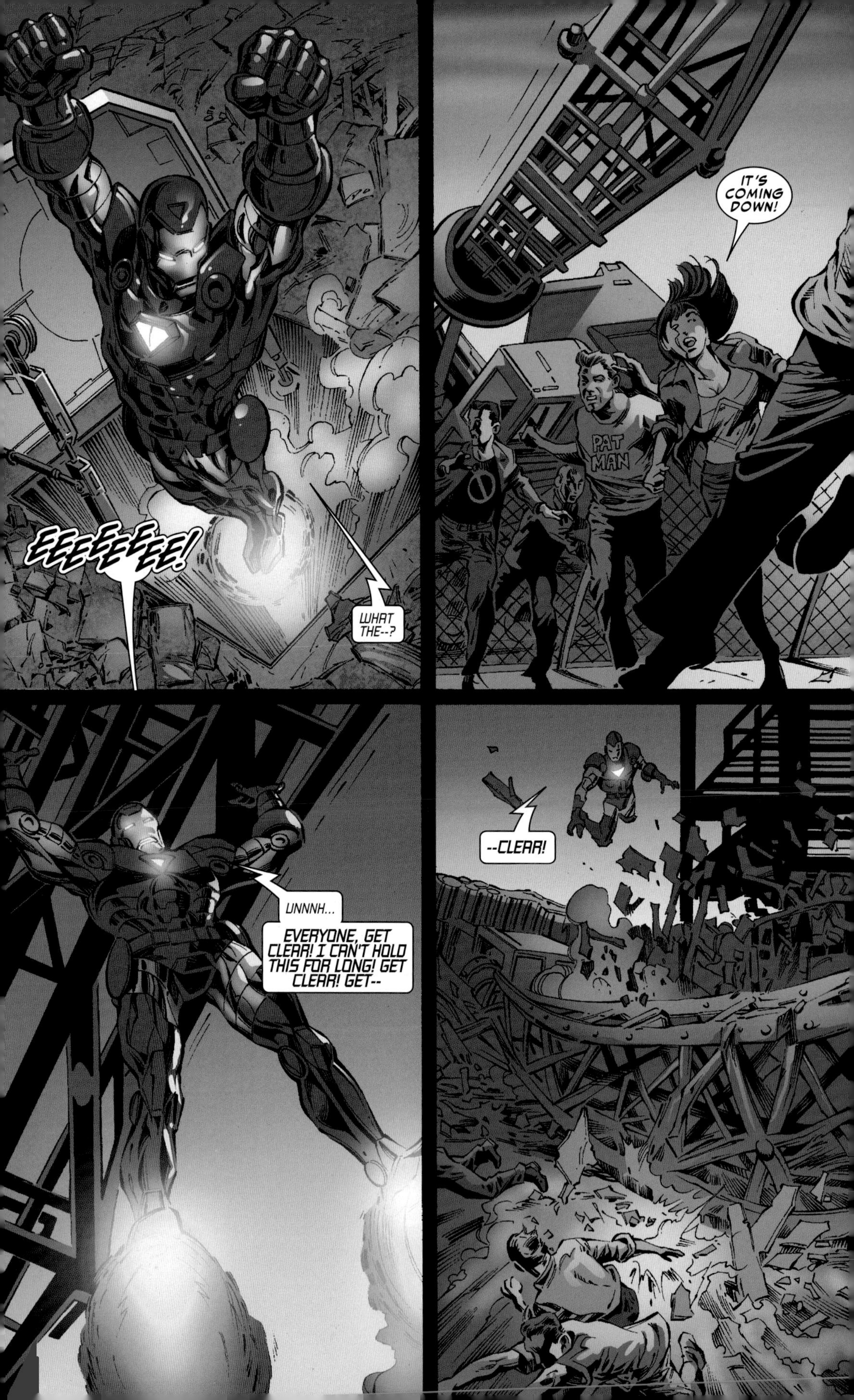
EEEEEEEEE!
WHAT THE--?
IT'S COMING DOWN!
PAT MAN
UNNNH...
EVERYONE, GET CLEAR! I CAN'T HOLD THIS FOR LONG! GET CLEAR! GET--
--CLEAR!

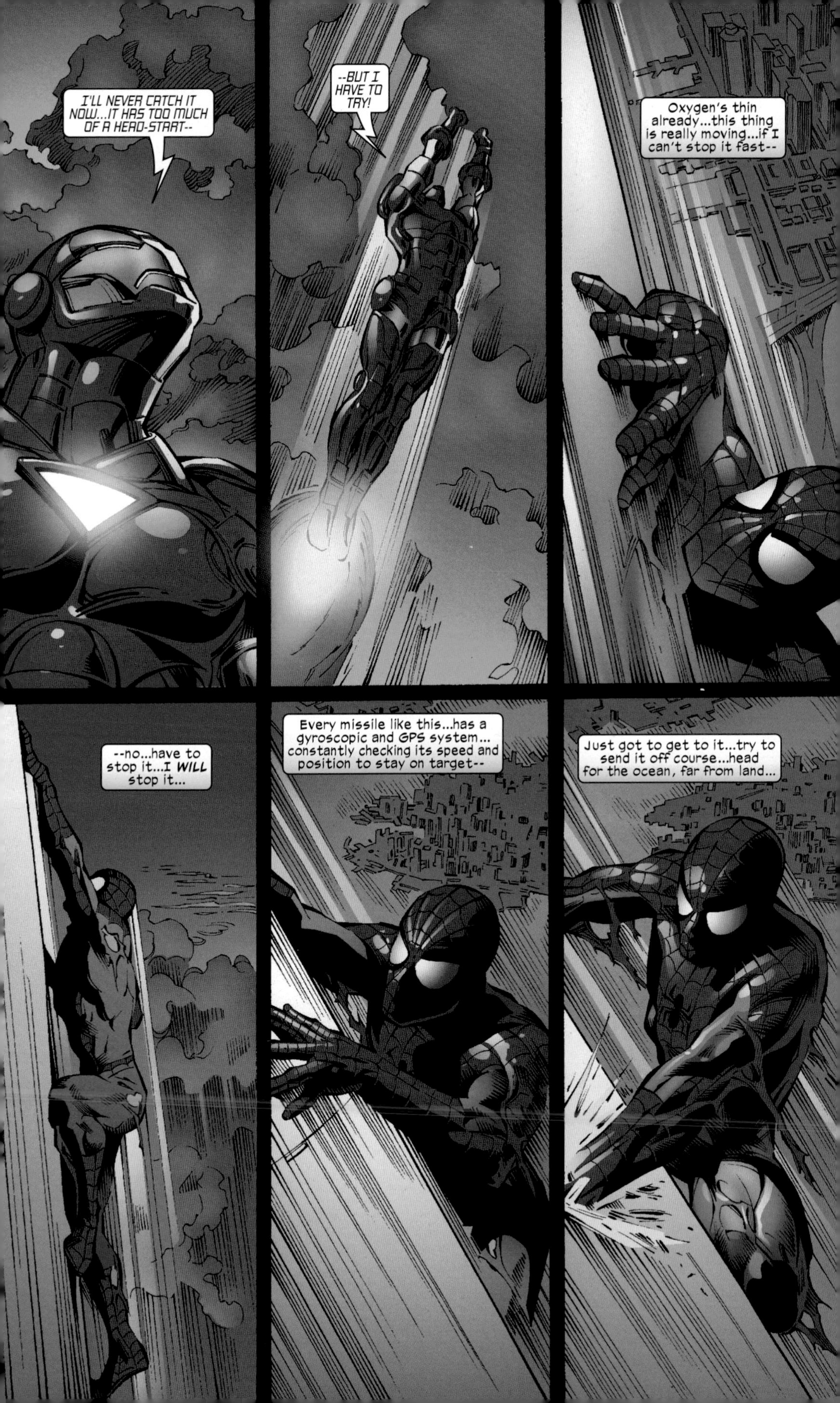

I'LL NEVER CATCH IT NOW...IT HAS TOO MUCH OF A HEAD-START--
--BUT I HAVE TO TRY!
Oxygen's thin already...this thing is really moving...if I can't stop it fast--
--no...have to stop it...I **WILL** stop it...
Every missile like this...has a gyroscopic and GPS system... constantly checking its speed and position to stay on target--
Just got to get to it...try to send it off course...head for the ocean, far from land...

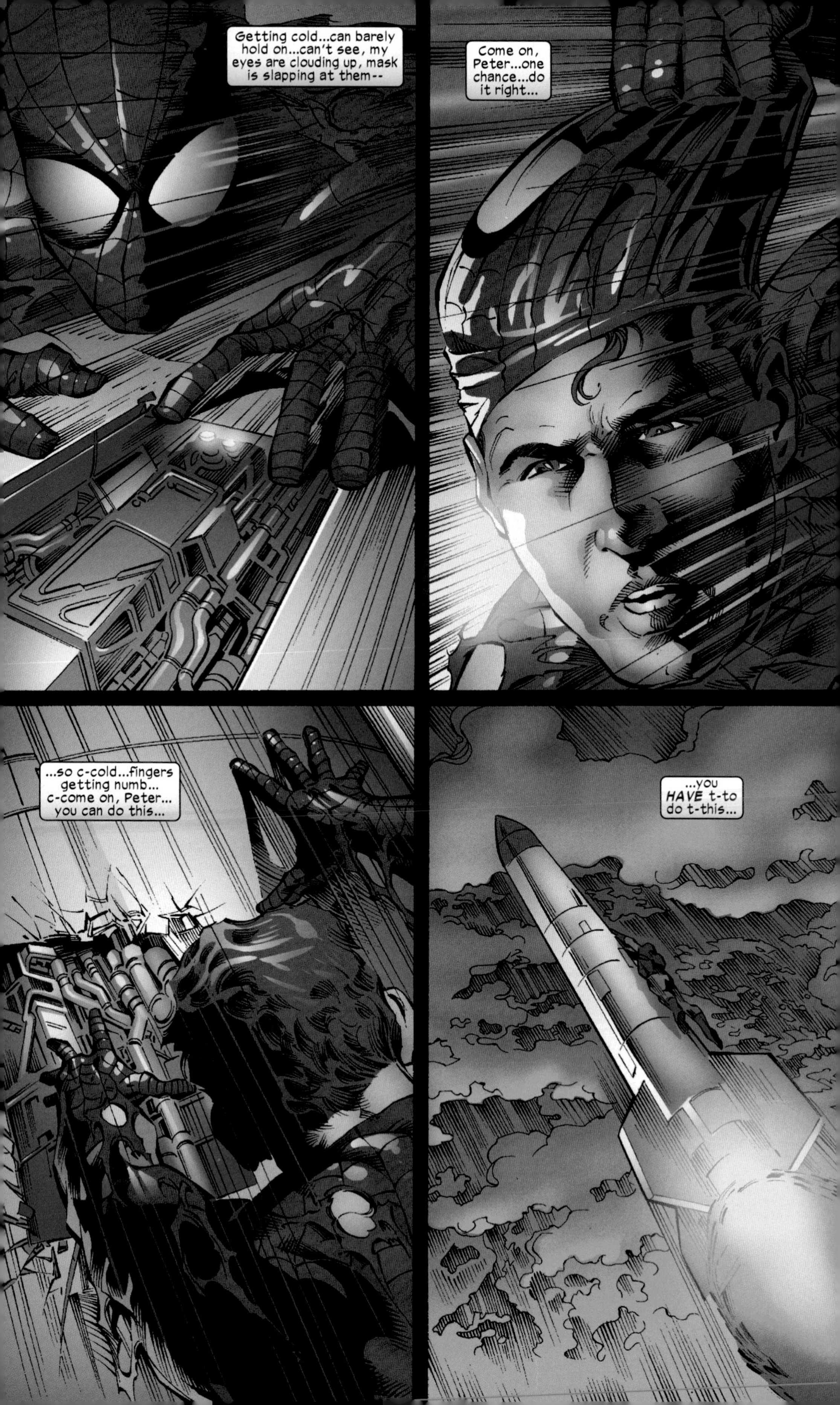
Getting cold...can barely hold on...can't see, my eyes are clouding up, mask is slapping at them--
Come on, Peter...one chance...do it right...
...so c-cold...fingers getting numb... c-come on, Peter... you can do this...
...you *HAVE* t-to do t-this...

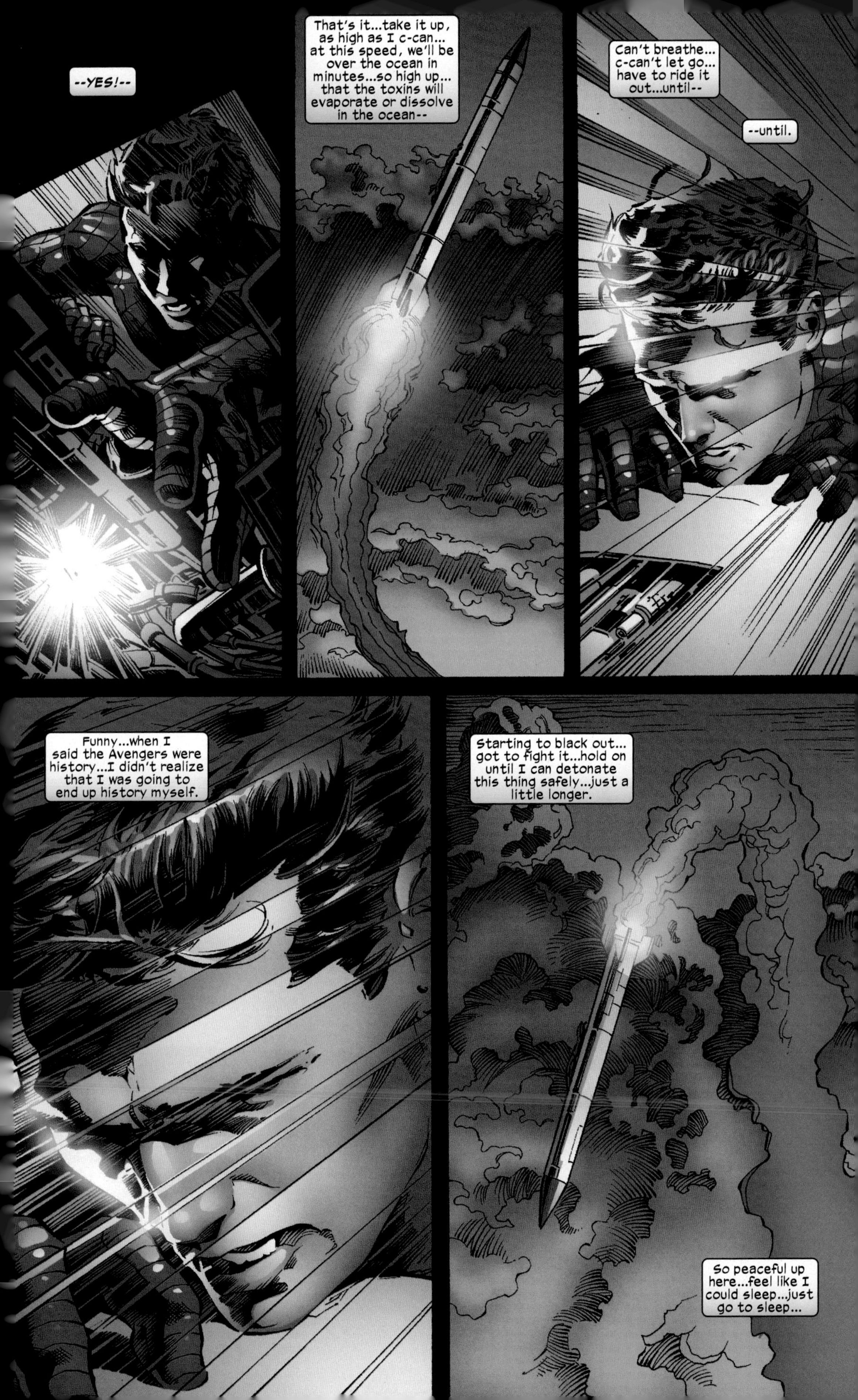
--YES!--
That's it...take it up, as high as I c-can... at this speed, we'll be over the ocean in minutes...so high up... that the toxins will evaporate or dissolve in the ocean--
Can't breathe... c-can't let go... have to ride it out...until--
--until.
Funny...when I said the Avengers were history...I didn't realize that I was going to end up history myself.
Starting to black out... got to fight it...hold on until I can detonate this thing safely...just a little longer.
So peaceful up here...feel like I could sleep...just go to sleep...

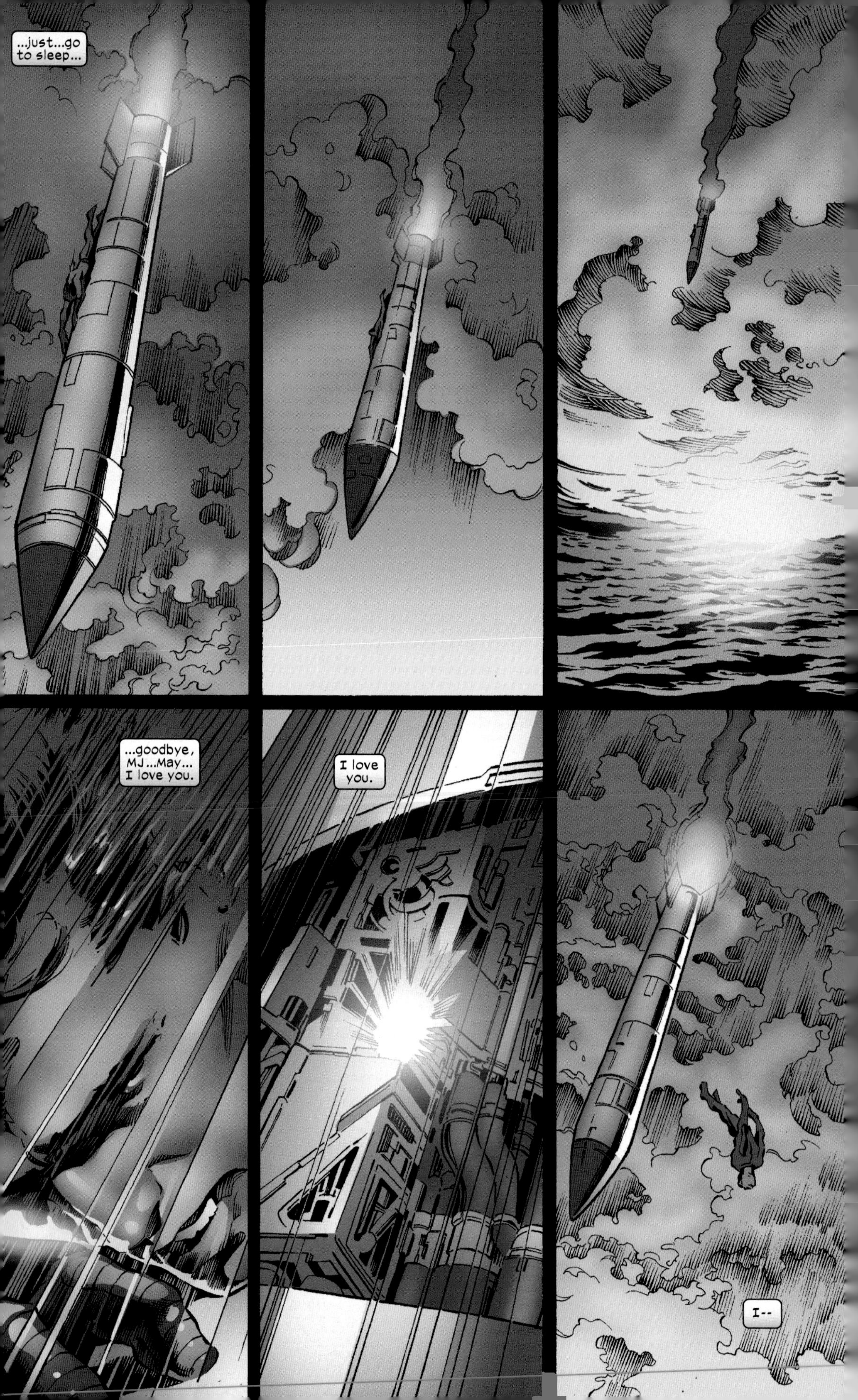
...just...go to sleep...
...goodbye, MJ...May... I love you.
I love you.
I--

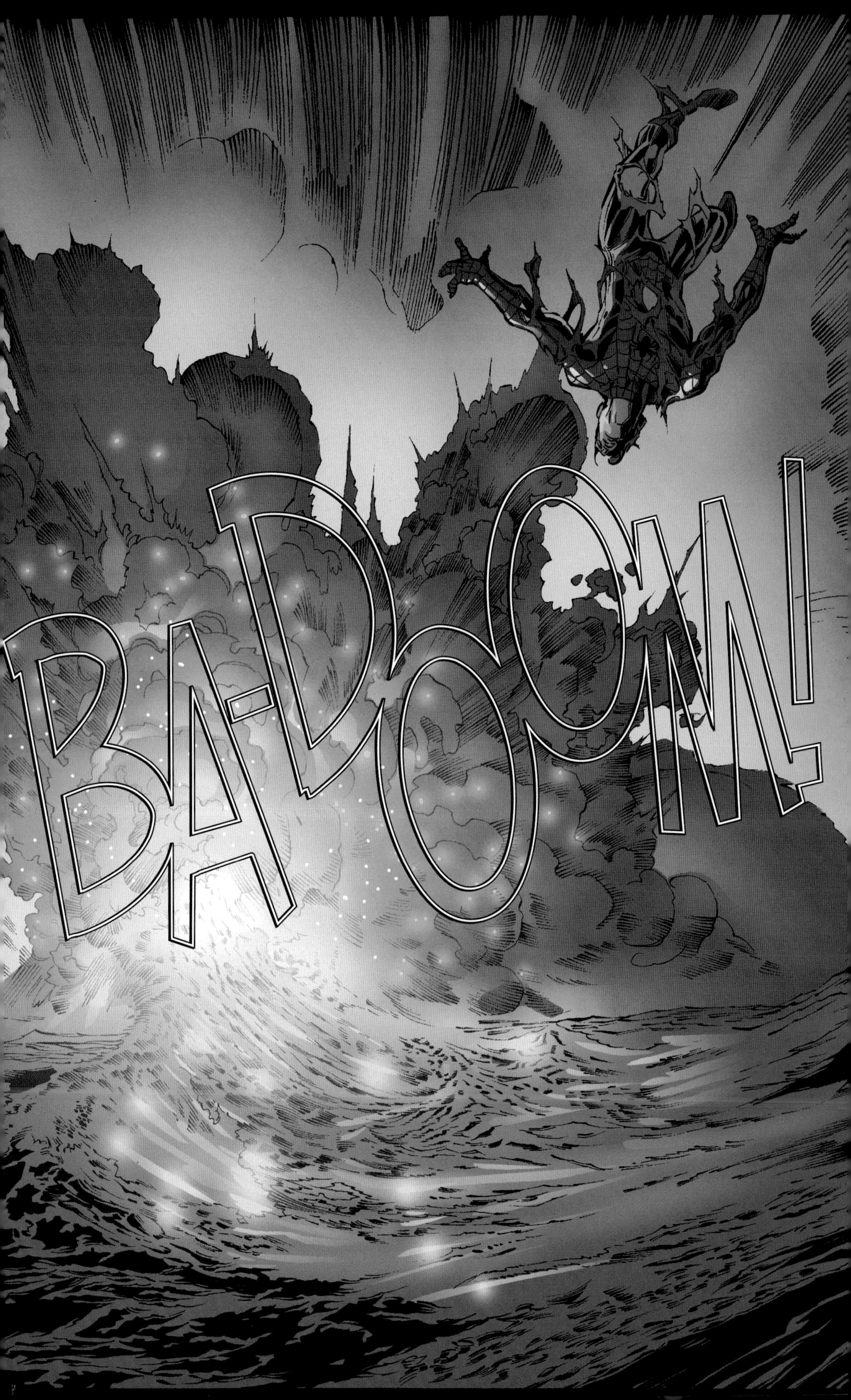
BA-DOOM!

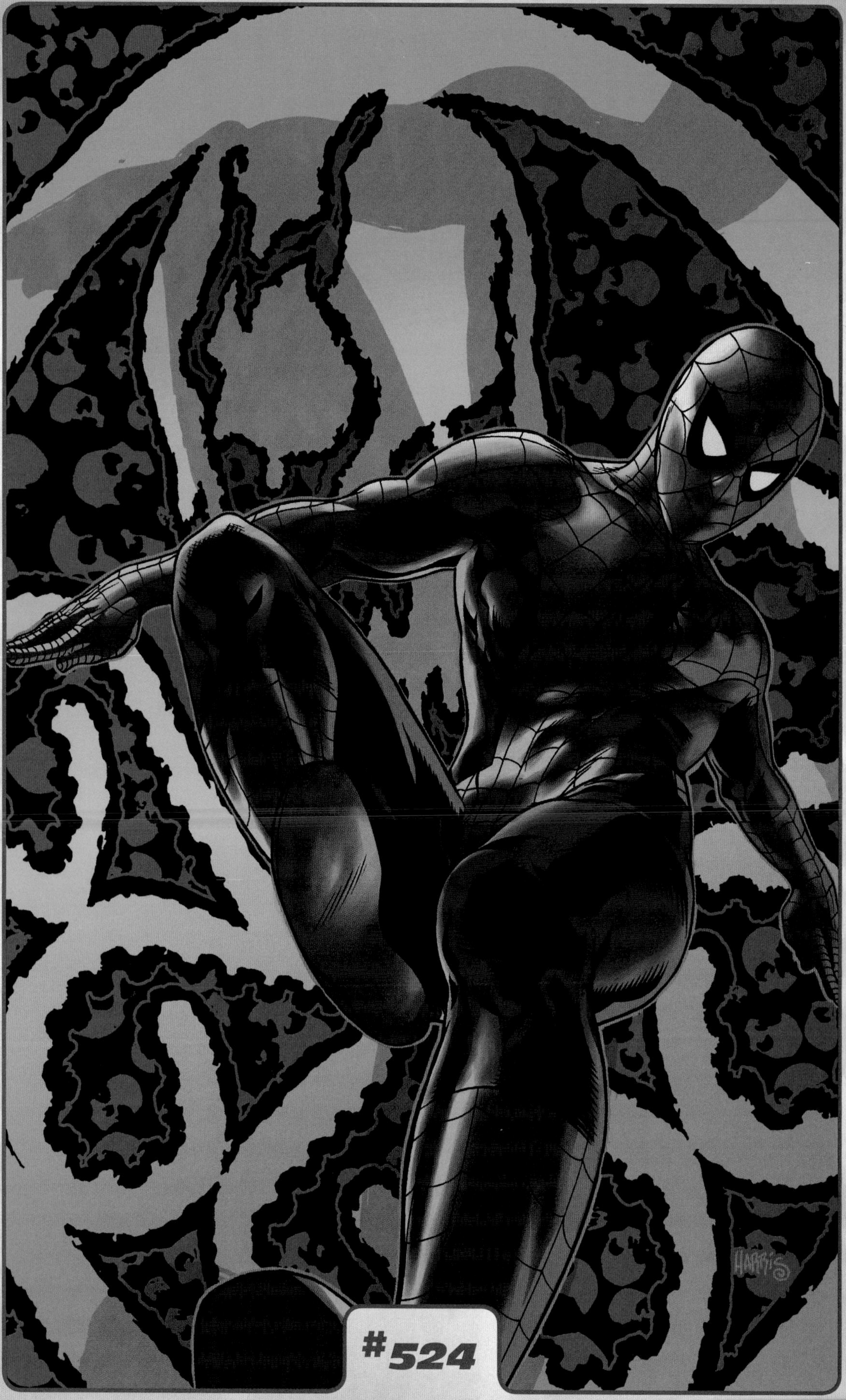

HARRIS
#524

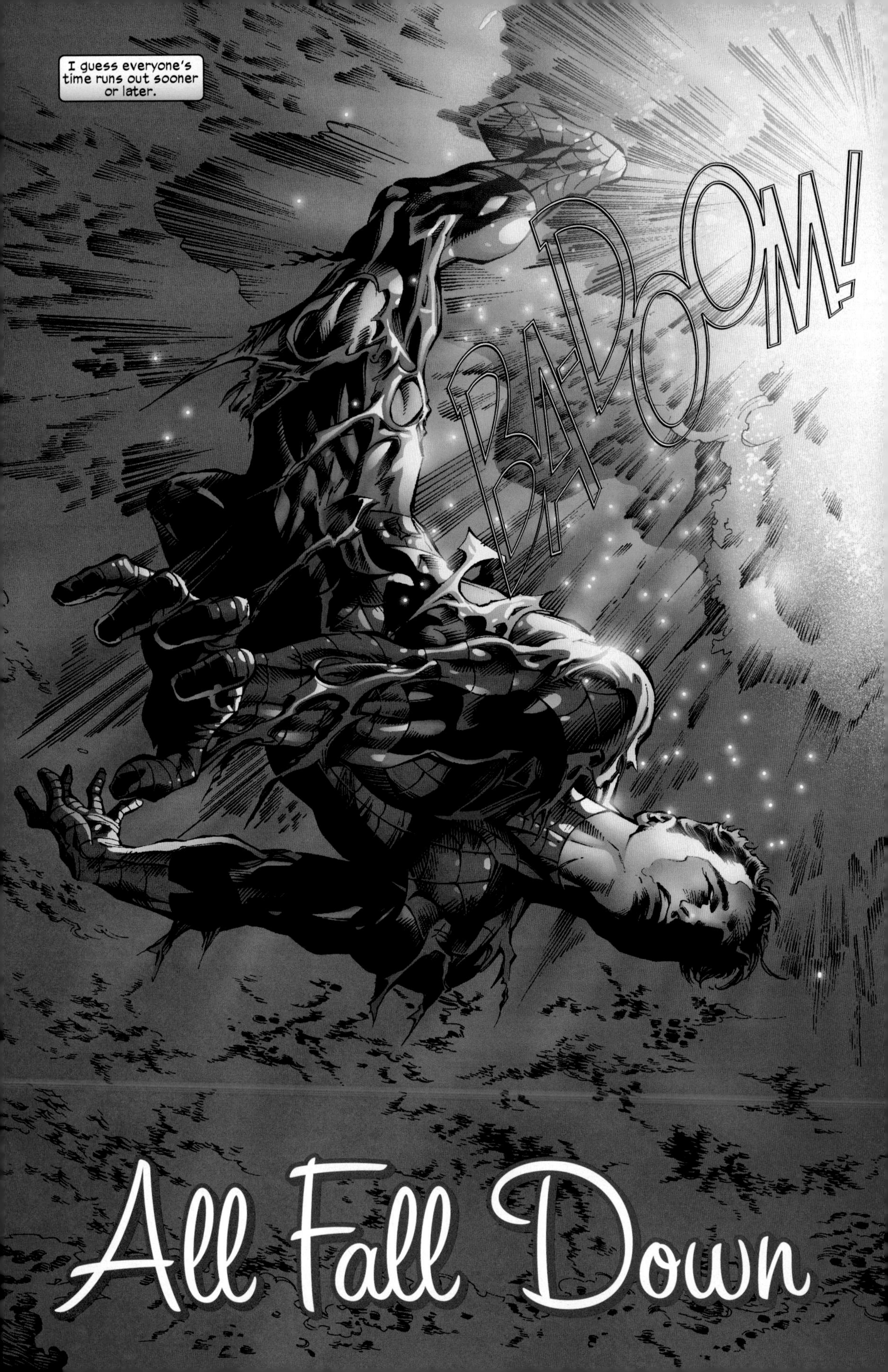
I guess everyone's time runs out sooner or later.
BA-DOOM!
All Fall Down

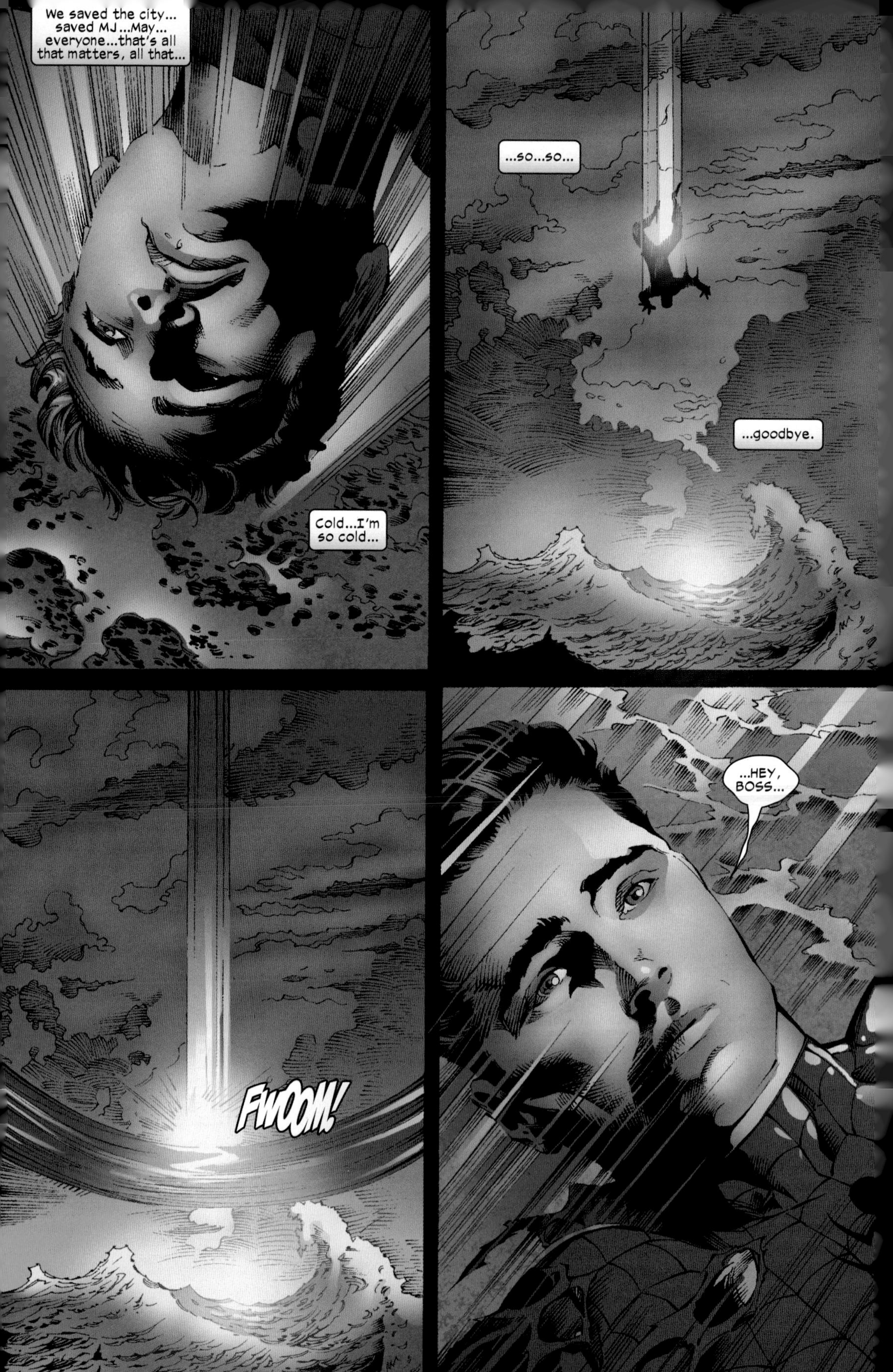
We saved the city... saved MJ...May... everyone...that's all that matters, all that...
Cold...I'm so cold...
...so...so...
...goodbye.
FWOOM!
...HEY, BOSS...

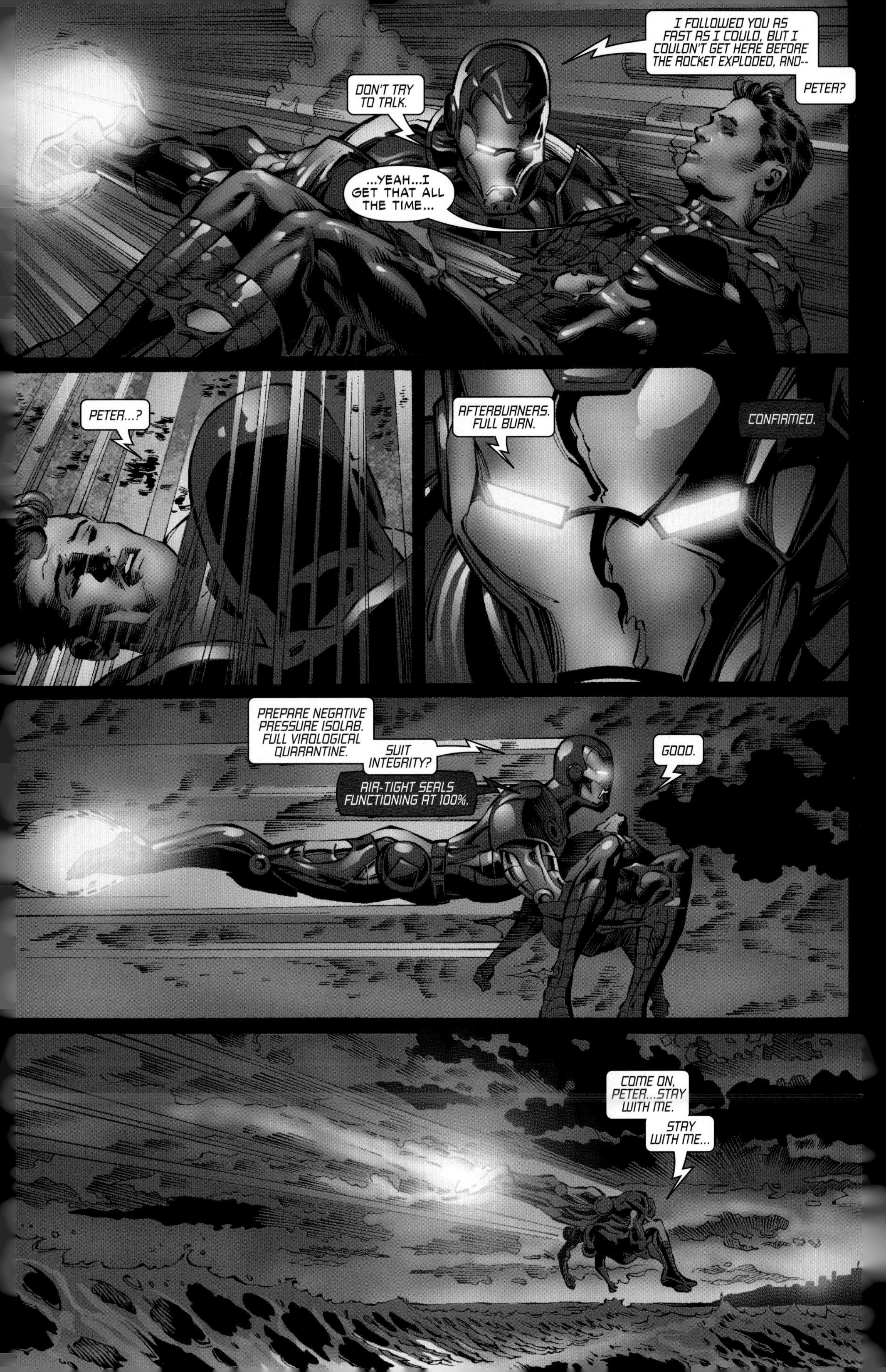
I FOLLOWED YOU AS FAST AS I COULD, BUT I COULDN'T GET HERE BEFORE THE ROCKET EXPLODED, AND--
PETER?
DON'T TRY TO TALK.
...YEAH...I GET THAT ALL THE TIME...
PETER...?
AFTERBURNERS. FULL BURN.
CONFIRMED.
PREPARE NEGATIVE PRESSURE ISOLAB. FULL VIROLOGICAL QUARANTINE.
SUIT INTEGRITY?
AIR-TIGHT SEALS FUNCTIONING AT 100%.
GOOD.
COME ON, PETER...STAY WITH ME.
STAY WITH ME...

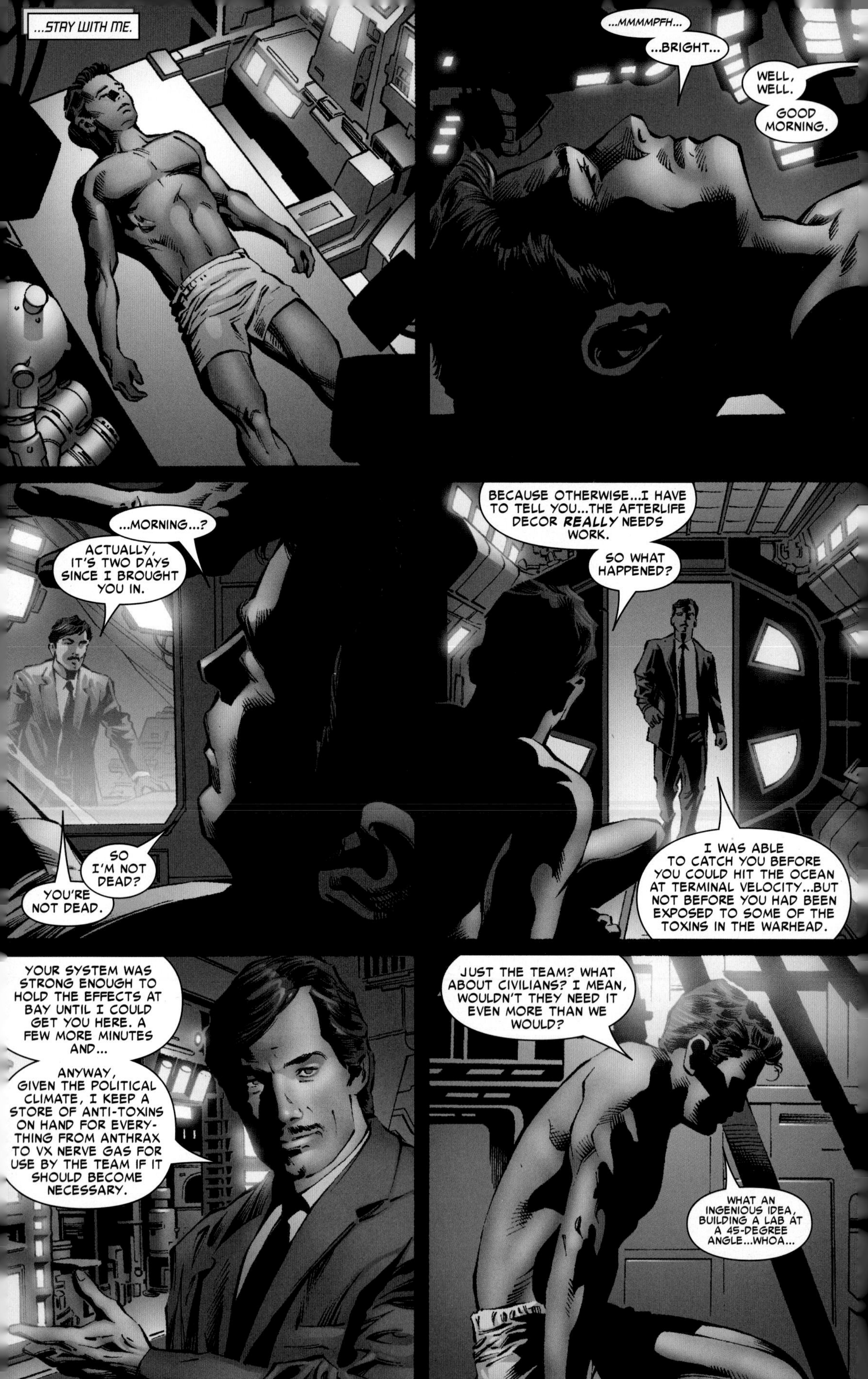
...STAY WITH ME.
...MMMMPFH...
...BRIGHT...
WELL, WELL.
GOOD MORNING.
...MORNING...?
ACTUALLY, IT'S TWO DAYS SINCE I BROUGHT YOU IN.
SO I'M NOT DEAD?
YOU'RE NOT DEAD.
BECAUSE OTHERWISE...I HAVE TO TELL YOU...THE AFTERLIFE DECOR REALLY NEEDS WORK.
SO WHAT HAPPENED?
I WAS ABLE TO CATCH YOU BEFORE YOU COULD HIT THE OCEAN AT TERMINAL VELOCITY...BUT NOT BEFORE YOU HAD BEEN EXPOSED TO SOME OF THE TOXINS IN THE WARHEAD.
YOUR SYSTEM WAS STRONG ENOUGH TO HOLD THE EFFECTS AT BAY UNTIL I COULD GET YOU HERE. A FEW MORE MINUTES AND...
ANYWAY, GIVEN THE POLITICAL CLIMATE, I KEEP A STORE OF ANTI-TOXINS ON HAND FOR EVERYTHING FROM ANTHRAX TO VX NERVE GAS FOR USE BY THE TEAM IF IT SHOULD BECOME NECESSARY.
JUST THE TEAM? WHAT ABOUT CIVILIANS? I MEAN, WOULDN'T THEY NEED IT EVEN MORE THAN WE WOULD?
WHAT AN INGENIOUS IDEA, BUILDING A LAB AT A 45-DEGREE ANGLE...WHOA...

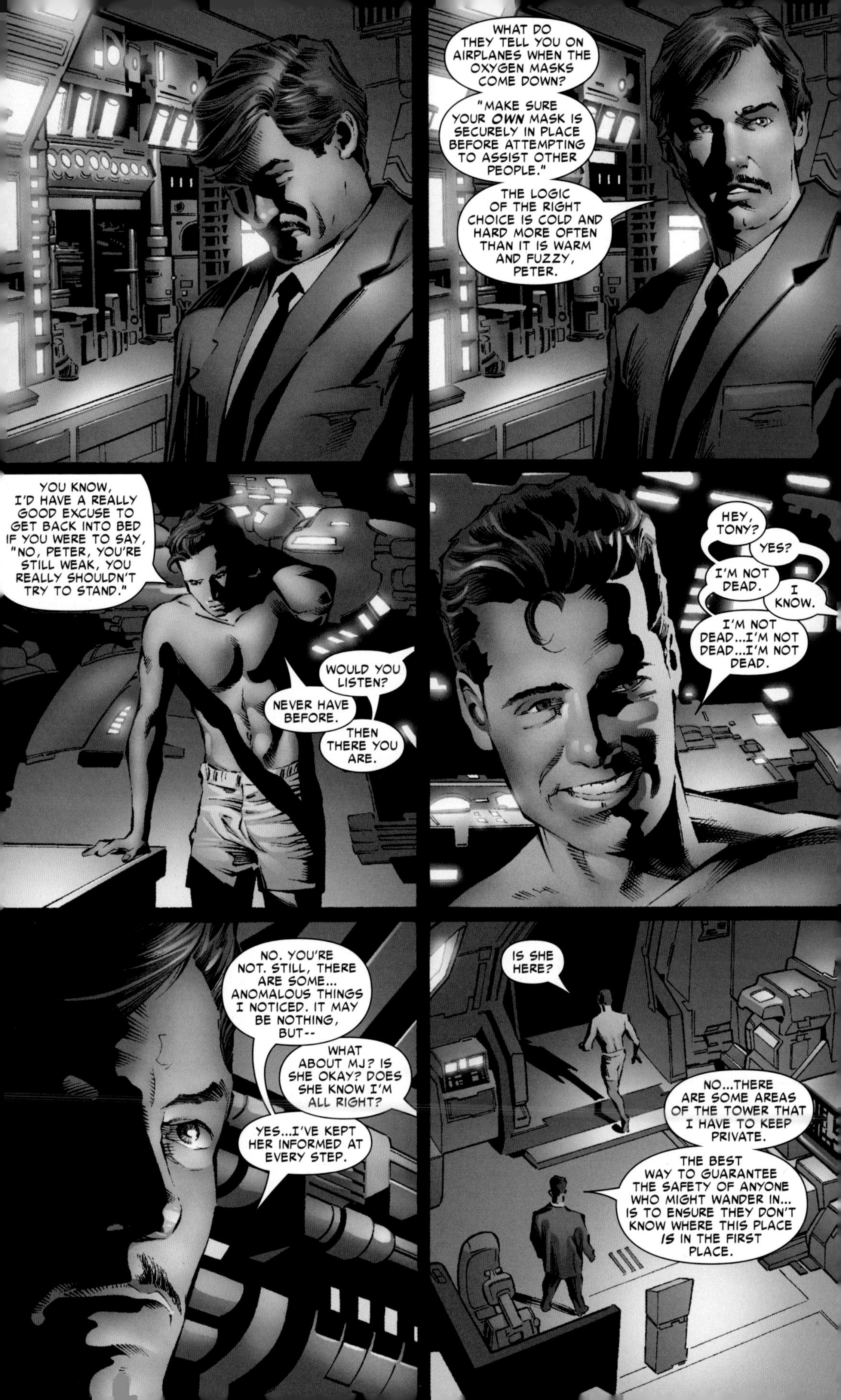

WHAT DO THEY TELL YOU ON AIRPLANES WHEN THE OXYGEN MASKS COME DOWN?
"MAKE SURE YOUR *OWN* MASK IS SECURELY IN PLACE BEFORE ATTEMPTING TO ASSIST OTHER PEOPLE."
THE LOGIC OF THE RIGHT CHOICE IS COLD AND HARD MORE OFTEN THAN IT IS WARM AND FUZZY, PETER.
YOU KNOW, I'D HAVE A REALLY GOOD EXCUSE TO GET BACK INTO BED IF YOU WERE TO SAY, "NO, PETER, YOU'RE STILL WEAK, YOU REALLY SHOULDN'T TRY TO STAND."
WOULD YOU LISTEN?
NEVER HAVE BEFORE.
THEN THERE YOU ARE.
HEY, TONY?
YES?
I'M NOT DEAD.
I KNOW.
I'M NOT DEAD...I'M NOT DEAD...I'M NOT DEAD.
NO. YOU'RE NOT. STILL, THERE ARE SOME... ANOMALOUS THINGS I NOTICED. IT MAY BE NOTHING, BUT--
WHAT ABOUT MJ? IS SHE OKAY? DOES SHE KNOW I'M ALL RIGHT?
YES...I'VE KEPT HER INFORMED AT EVERY STEP.
IS SHE HERE?
NO...THERE ARE SOME AREAS OF THE TOWER THAT I HAVE TO KEEP PRIVATE.
THE BEST WAY TO GUARANTEE THE SAFETY OF ANYONE WHO MIGHT WANDER IN... IS TO ENSURE THEY DON'T KNOW WHERE THIS PLACE *IS* IN THE FIRST PLACE.

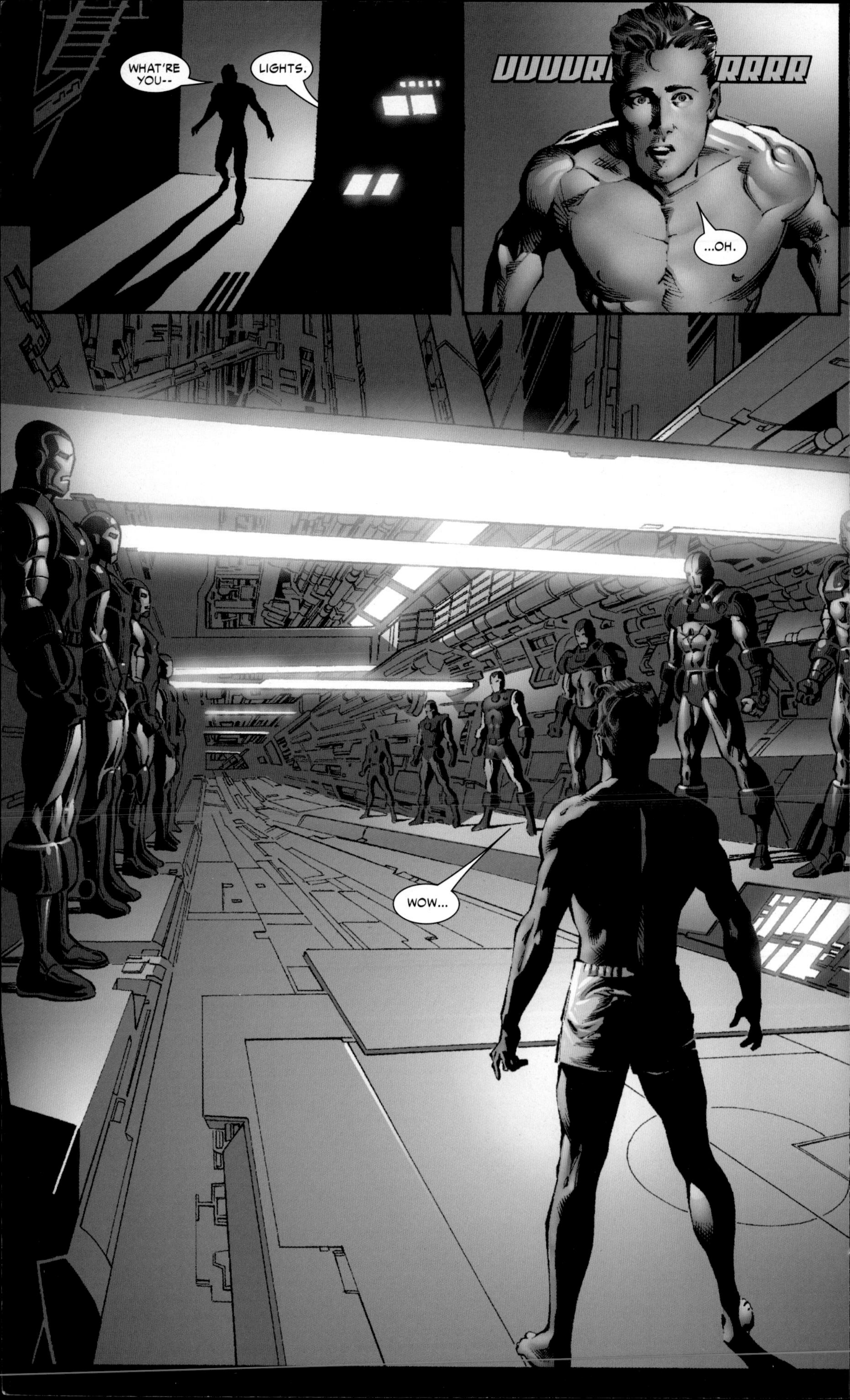
WHAT'RE YOU--
LIGHTS.
VVVVR
RRRRR
...OH.
WOW...

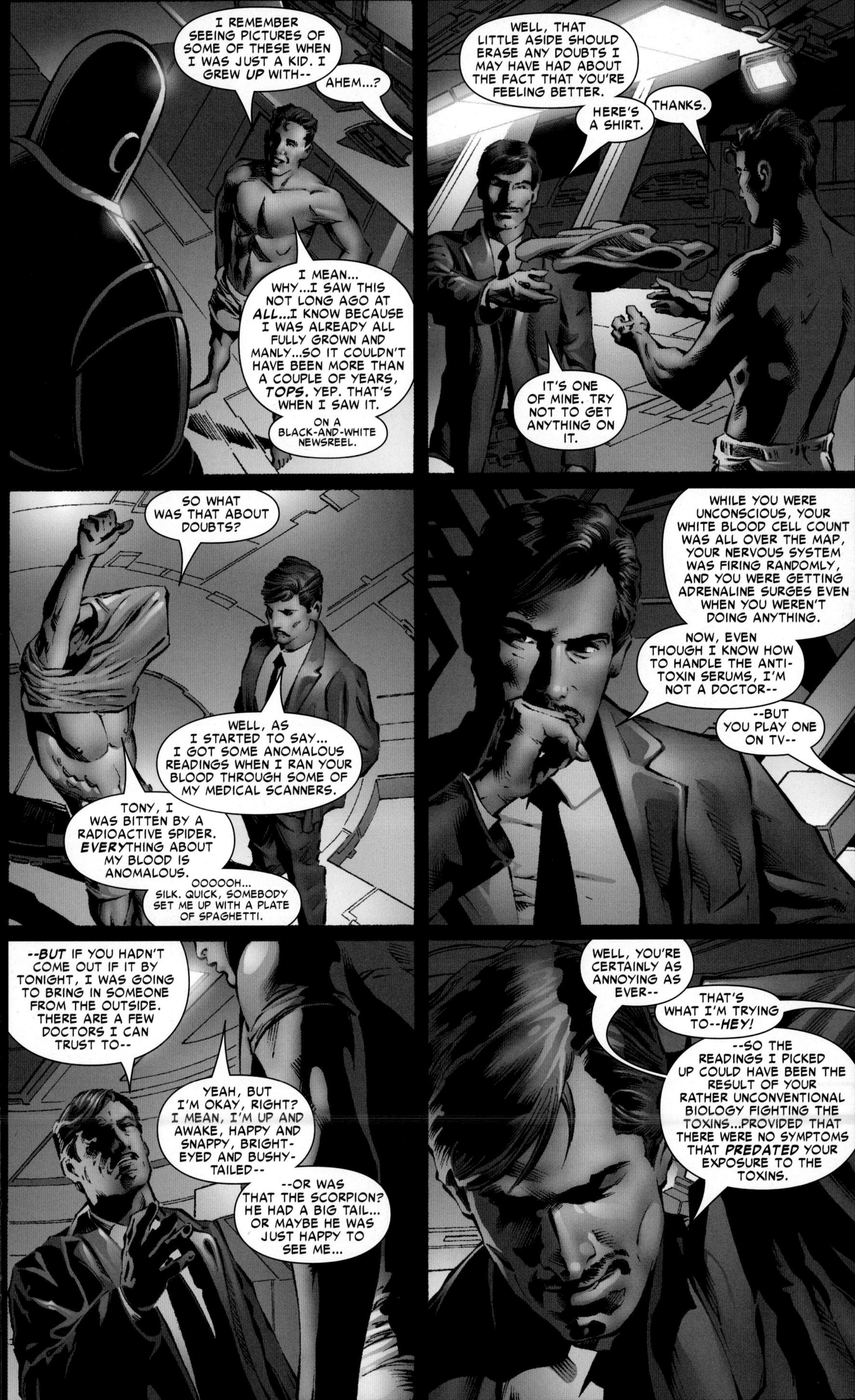

I REMEMBER SEEING PICTURES OF SOME OF THESE WHEN I WAS JUST A KID. I GREW UP WITH--
AHEM...?
I MEAN... WHY...I SAW THIS NOT LONG AGO AT ALL...I KNOW BECAUSE I WAS ALREADY ALL FULLY GROWN AND MANLY...SO IT COULDN'T HAVE BEEN MORE THAN A COUPLE OF YEARS, TOPS. YEP. THAT'S WHEN I SAW IT.
ON A BLACK-AND-WHITE NEWSREEL.
WELL, THAT LITTLE ASIDE SHOULD ERASE ANY DOUBTS I MAY HAVE HAD ABOUT THE FACT THAT YOU'RE FEELING BETTER.
HERE'S A SHIRT.
THANKS.
IT'S ONE OF MINE. TRY NOT TO GET ANYTHING ON IT.
SO WHAT WAS THAT ABOUT DOUBTS?
WELL, AS I STARTED TO SAY... I GOT SOME ANOMALOUS READINGS WHEN I RAN YOUR BLOOD THROUGH SOME OF MY MEDICAL SCANNERS.
TONY, I WAS BITTEN BY A RADIOACTIVE SPIDER. EVERYTHING ABOUT MY BLOOD IS ANOMALOUS.
OOOOOH... SILK. QUICK, SOMEBODY SET ME UP WITH A PLATE OF SPAGHETTI.
WHILE YOU WERE UNCONSCIOUS, YOUR WHITE BLOOD CELL COUNT WAS ALL OVER THE MAP, YOUR NERVOUS SYSTEM WAS FIRING RANDOMLY, AND YOU WERE GETTING ADRENALINE SURGES EVEN WHEN YOU WEREN'T DOING ANYTHING.
NOW, EVEN THOUGH I KNOW HOW TO HANDLE THE ANTI-TOXIN SERUMS, I'M NOT A DOCTOR--
--BUT YOU PLAY ONE ON TV--
--BUT IF YOU HADN'T COME OUT IF IT BY TONIGHT, I WAS GOING TO BRING IN SOMEONE FROM THE OUTSIDE. THERE ARE A FEW DOCTORS I CAN TRUST TO--
YEAH, BUT I'M OKAY, RIGHT? I MEAN, I'M UP AND AWAKE, HAPPY AND SNAPPY, BRIGHT-EYED AND BUSHY-TAILED--
--OR WAS THAT THE SCORPION? HE HAD A BIG TAIL... OR MAYBE HE WAS JUST HAPPY TO SEE ME...
WELL, YOU'RE CERTAINLY AS ANNOYING AS EVER--
THAT'S WHAT I'M TRYING TO--HEY!
--SO THE READINGS I PICKED UP COULD HAVE BEEN THE RESULT OF YOUR RATHER UNCONVENTIONAL BIOLOGY FIGHTING THE TOXINS...PROVIDED THAT THERE WERE NO SYMPTOMS THAT PREDATED YOUR EXPOSURE TO THE TOXINS.

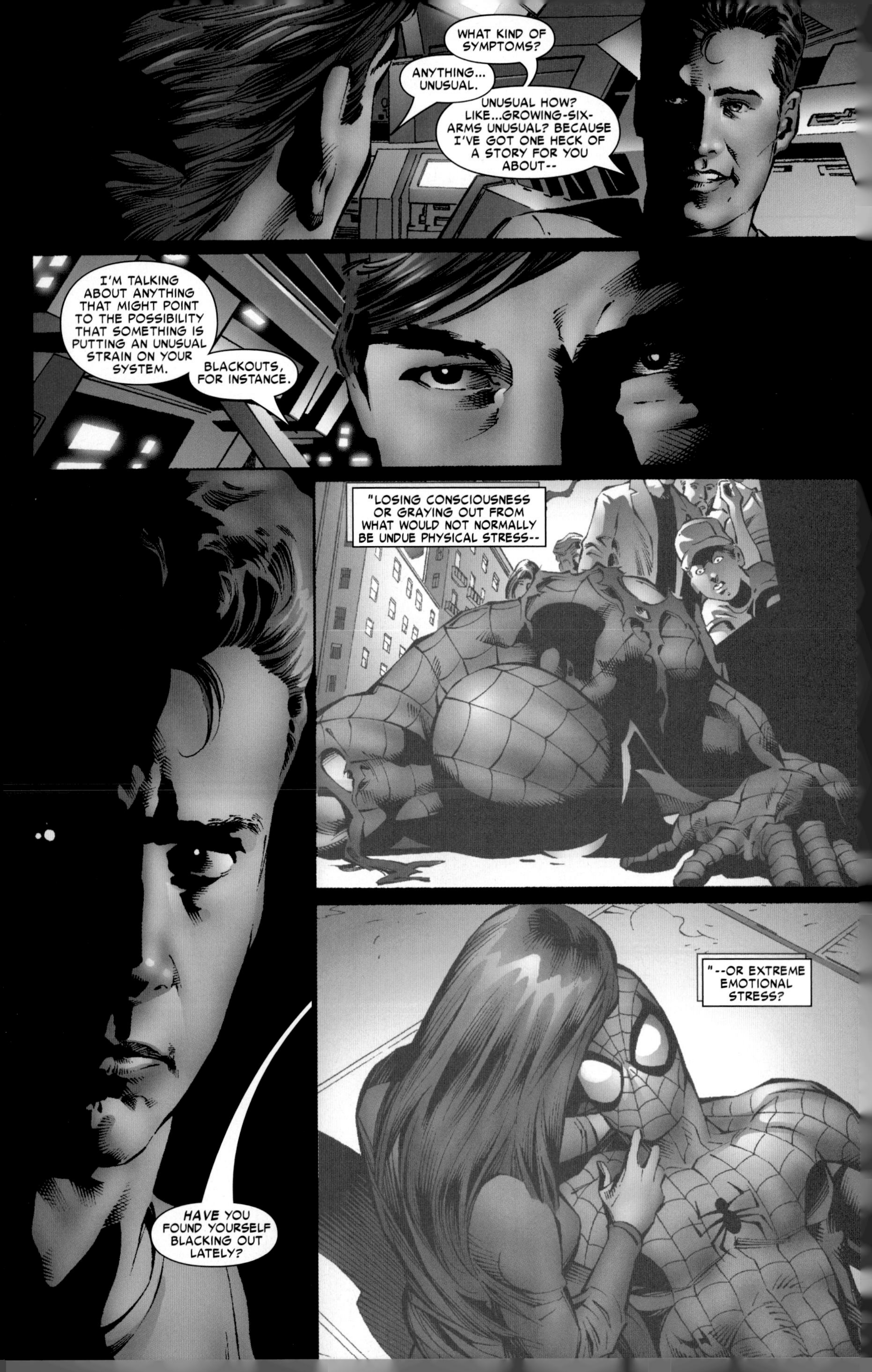
WHAT KIND OF SYMPTOMS?
ANYTHING... UNUSUAL.
UNUSUAL HOW? LIKE...GROWING-SIX-ARMS UNUSUAL? BECAUSE I'VE GOT ONE HECK OF A STORY FOR YOU ABOUT--
I'M TALKING ABOUT ANYTHING THAT MIGHT POINT TO THE POSSIBILITY THAT SOMETHING IS PUTTING AN UNUSUAL STRAIN ON YOUR SYSTEM.
BLACKOUTS, FOR INSTANCE.
"LOSING CONSCIOUSNESS OR GRAYING OUT FROM WHAT WOULD NOT NORMALLY BE UNDUE PHYSICAL STRESS--
"--OR EXTREME EMOTIONAL STRESS?
HAVE YOU FOUND YOURSELF BLACKING OUT LATELY?

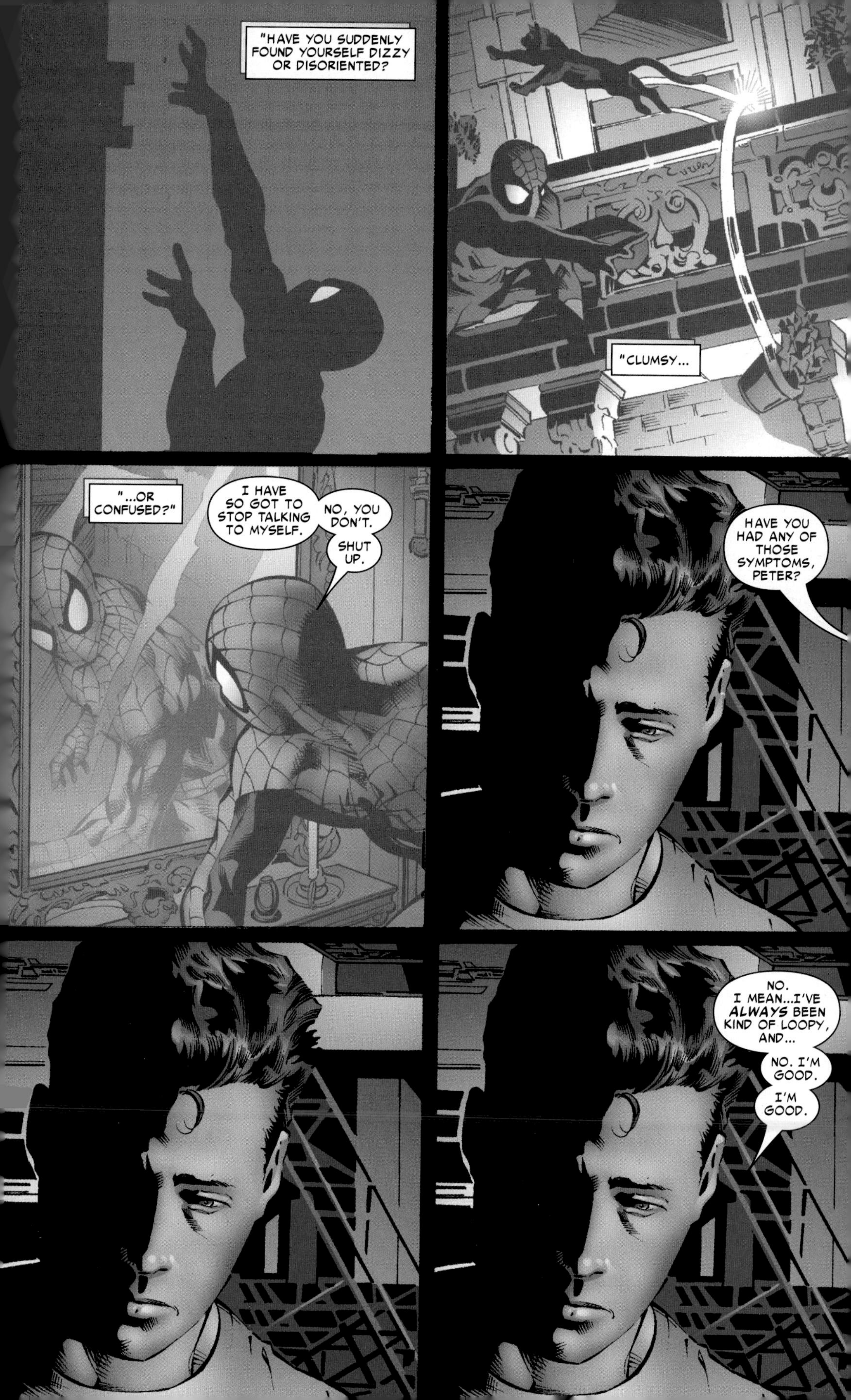
"HAVE YOU SUDDENLY FOUND YOURSELF DIZZY OR DISORIENTED?
"CLUMSY...
"...OR CONFUSED?"
I HAVE SO GOT TO STOP TALKING TO MYSELF.
NO, YOU DON'T.
SHUT UP.
HAVE YOU HAD ANY OF THOSE SYMPTOMS, PETER?
NO. I MEAN...I'VE ALWAYS BEEN KIND OF LOOPY, AND...
NO. I'M GOOD.
I'M GOOD.

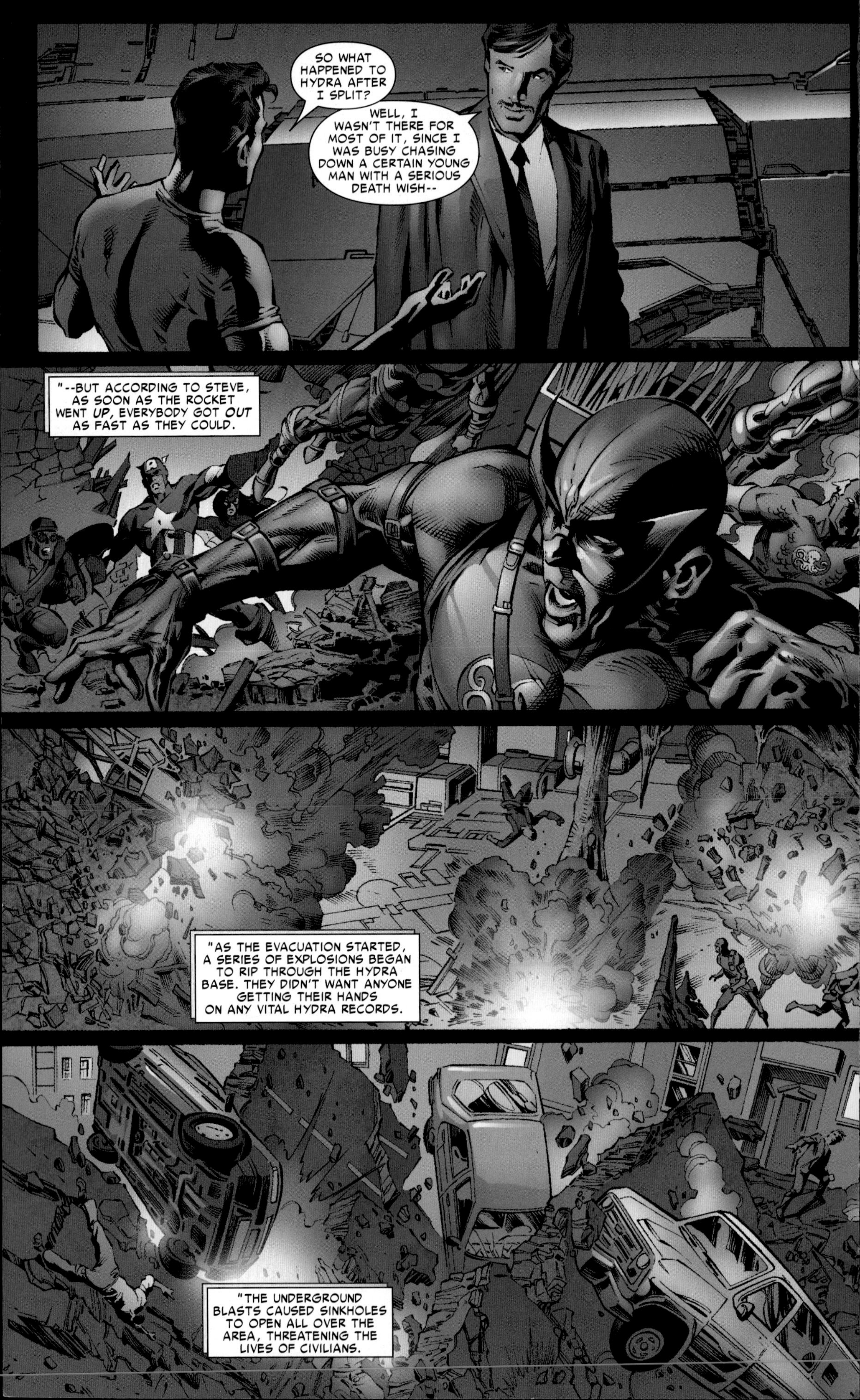
SO WHAT HAPPENED TO HYDRA AFTER I SPLIT?
WELL, I WASN'T THERE FOR MOST OF IT, SINCE I WAS BUSY CHASING DOWN A CERTAIN YOUNG MAN WITH A SERIOUS DEATH WISH--
"--BUT ACCORDING TO STEVE, AS SOON AS THE ROCKET WENT *UP*, EVERYBODY GOT *OUT* AS FAST AS THEY COULD.
"AS THE EVACUATION STARTED, A SERIES OF EXPLOSIONS BEGAN TO RIP THROUGH THE HYDRA BASE. THEY DIDN'T WANT ANYONE GETTING THEIR HANDS ON ANY VITAL HYDRA RECORDS.
"THE UNDERGROUND BLASTS CAUSED SINKHOLES TO OPEN ALL OVER THE AREA, THREATENING THE LIVES OF CIVILIANS.

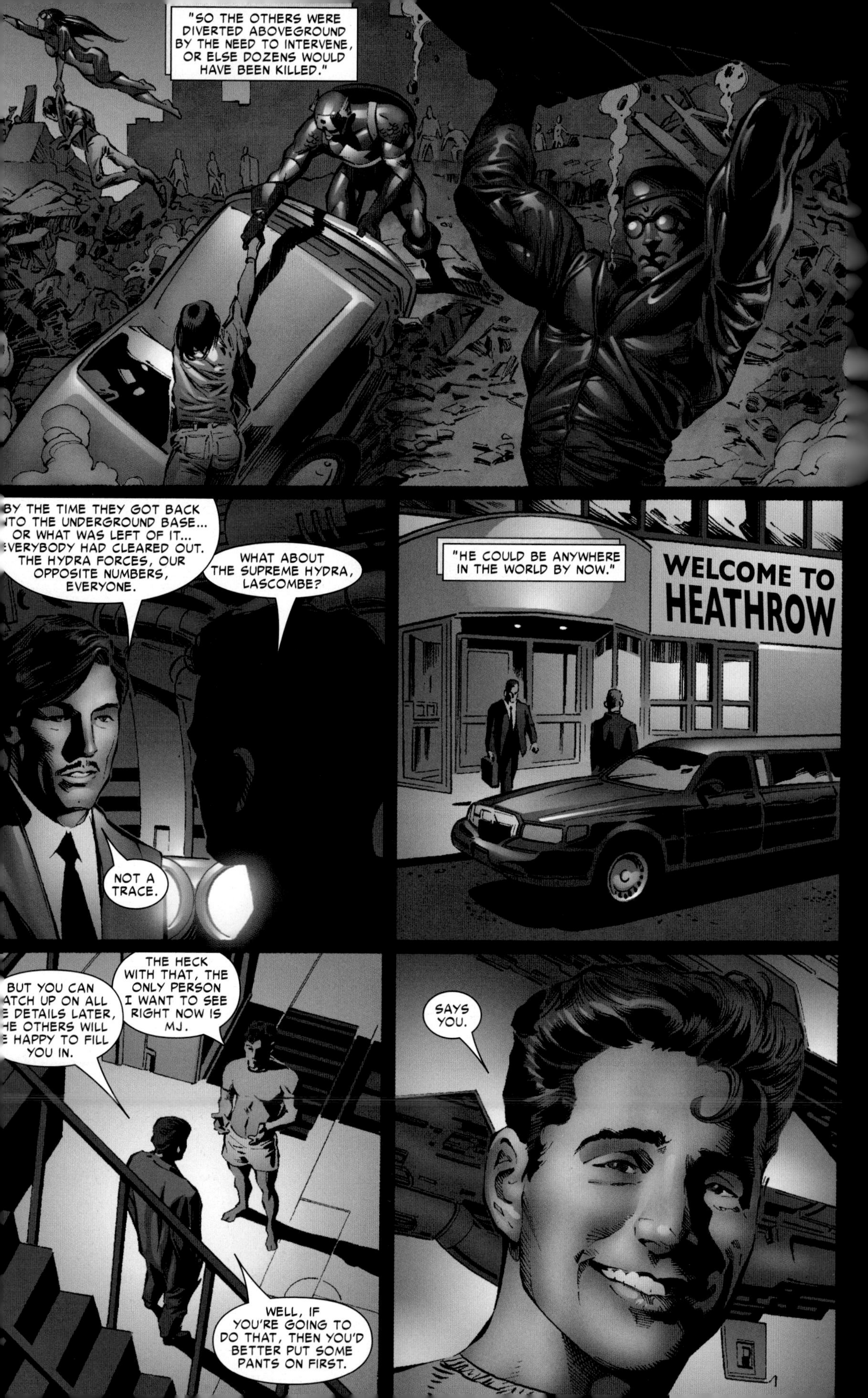
"SO THE OTHERS WERE DIVERTED ABOVEGROUND BY THE NEED TO INTERVENE, OR ELSE DOZENS WOULD HAVE BEEN KILLED."
BY THE TIME THEY GOT BACK TO THE UNDERGROUND BASE... OR WHAT WAS LEFT OF IT... EVERYBODY HAD CLEARED OUT. THE HYDRA FORCES, OUR OPPOSITE NUMBERS, EVERYONE.
WHAT ABOUT THE SUPREME HYDRA, LASCOMBE?
NOT A TRACE.
"HE COULD BE ANYWHERE IN THE WORLD BY NOW."
WELCOME TO HEATHROW
BUT YOU CAN ATCH UP ON ALL E DETAILS LATER, HE OTHERS WILL E HAPPY TO FILL YOU IN.
THE HECK WITH THAT, THE ONLY PERSON I WANT TO SEE RIGHT NOW IS MJ.
WELL, IF YOU'RE GOING TO DO THAT, THEN YOU'D BETTER PUT SOME PANTS ON FIRST.
SAYS YOU.

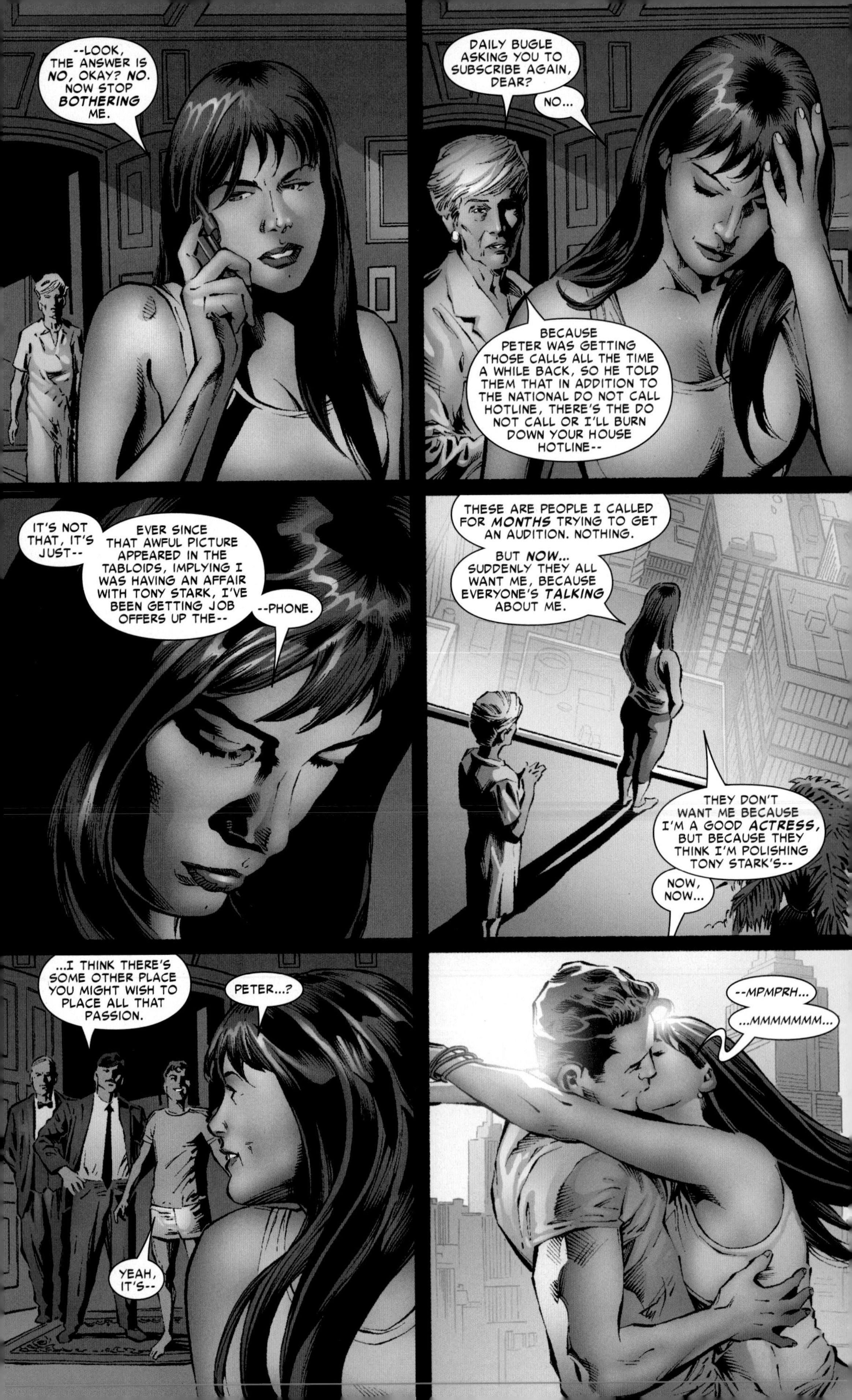
--LOOK, THE ANSWER IS NO, OKAY? NO. NOW STOP BOTHERING ME.
DAILY BUGLE ASKING YOU TO SUBSCRIBE AGAIN, DEAR?
NO...
BECAUSE PETER WAS GETTING THOSE CALLS ALL THE TIME A WHILE BACK, SO HE TOLD THEM THAT IN ADDITION TO THE NATIONAL DO NOT CALL HOTLINE, THERE'S THE DO NOT CALL OR I'LL BURN DOWN YOUR HOUSE HOTLINE--
IT'S NOT THAT, IT'S JUST--
EVER SINCE THAT AWFUL PICTURE APPEARED IN THE TABLOIDS, IMPLYING I WAS HAVING AN AFFAIR WITH TONY STARK, I'VE BEEN GETTING JOB OFFERS UP THE--
--PHONE.
THESE ARE PEOPLE I CALLED FOR MONTHS TRYING TO GET AN AUDITION. NOTHING.
BUT NOW... SUDDENLY THEY ALL WANT ME, BECAUSE EVERYONE'S TALKING ABOUT ME.
THEY DON'T WANT ME BECAUSE I'M A GOOD ACTRESS, BUT BECAUSE THEY THINK I'M POLISHING TONY STARK'S--
NOW, NOW...
...I THINK THERE'S SOME OTHER PLACE YOU MIGHT WISH TO PLACE ALL THAT PASSION.
PETER...?
YEAH, IT'S--
--MPMPRH...
...MMMMMMM...

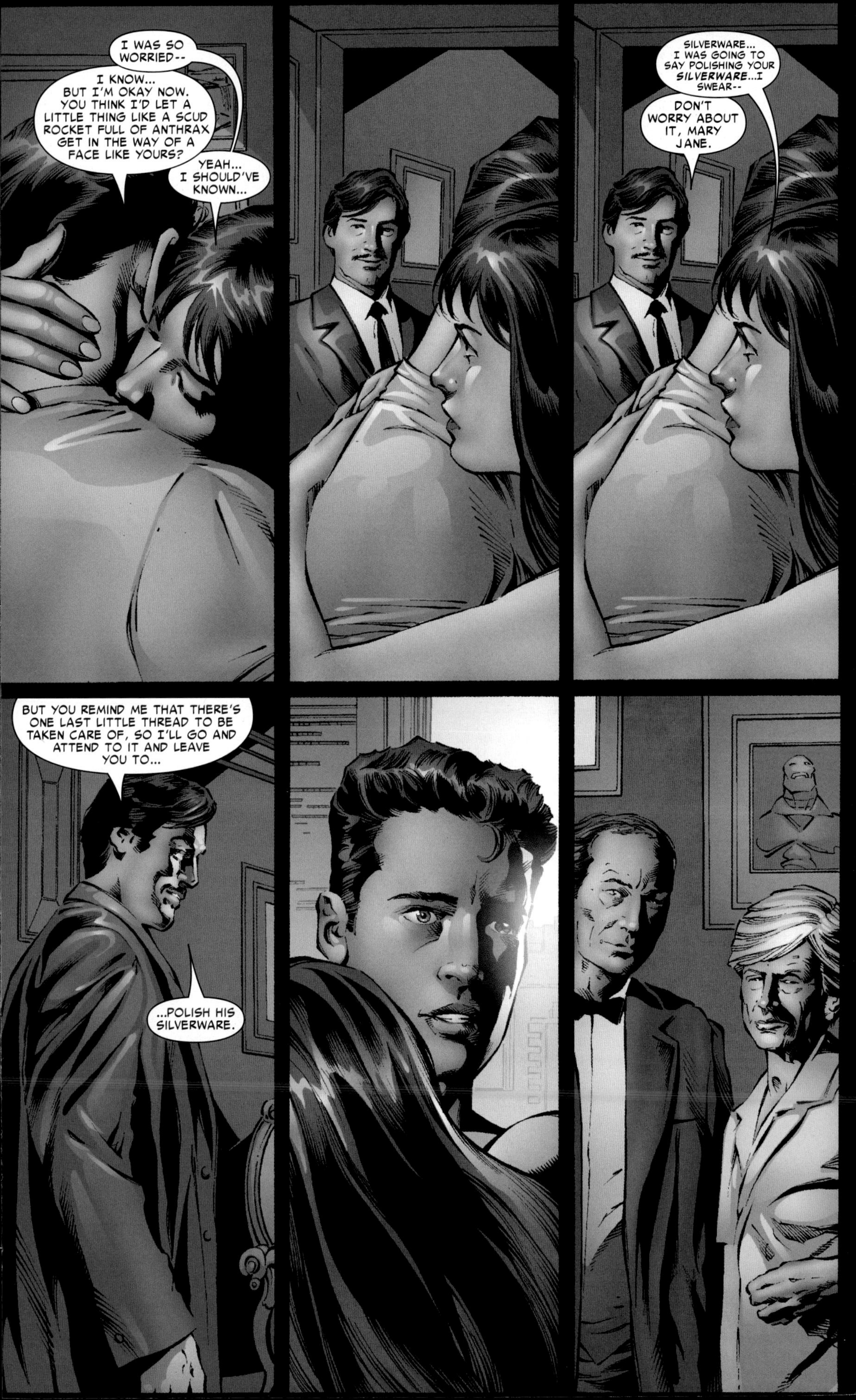
I WAS SO WORRIED--
I KNOW... BUT I'M OKAY NOW. YOU THINK I'D LET A LITTLE THING LIKE A SCUD ROCKET FULL OF ANTHRAX GET IN THE WAY OF A FACE LIKE YOURS?
YEAH... I SHOULD'VE KNOWN...
SILVERWARE... I WAS GOING TO SAY POLISHING YOUR SILVERWARE...I SWEAR--
DON'T WORRY ABOUT IT, MARY JANE.
BUT YOU REMIND ME THAT THERE'S ONE LAST LITTLE THREAD TO BE TAKEN CARE OF, SO I'LL GO AND ATTEND TO IT AND LEAVE YOU TO...
...POLISH HIS SILVERWARE.

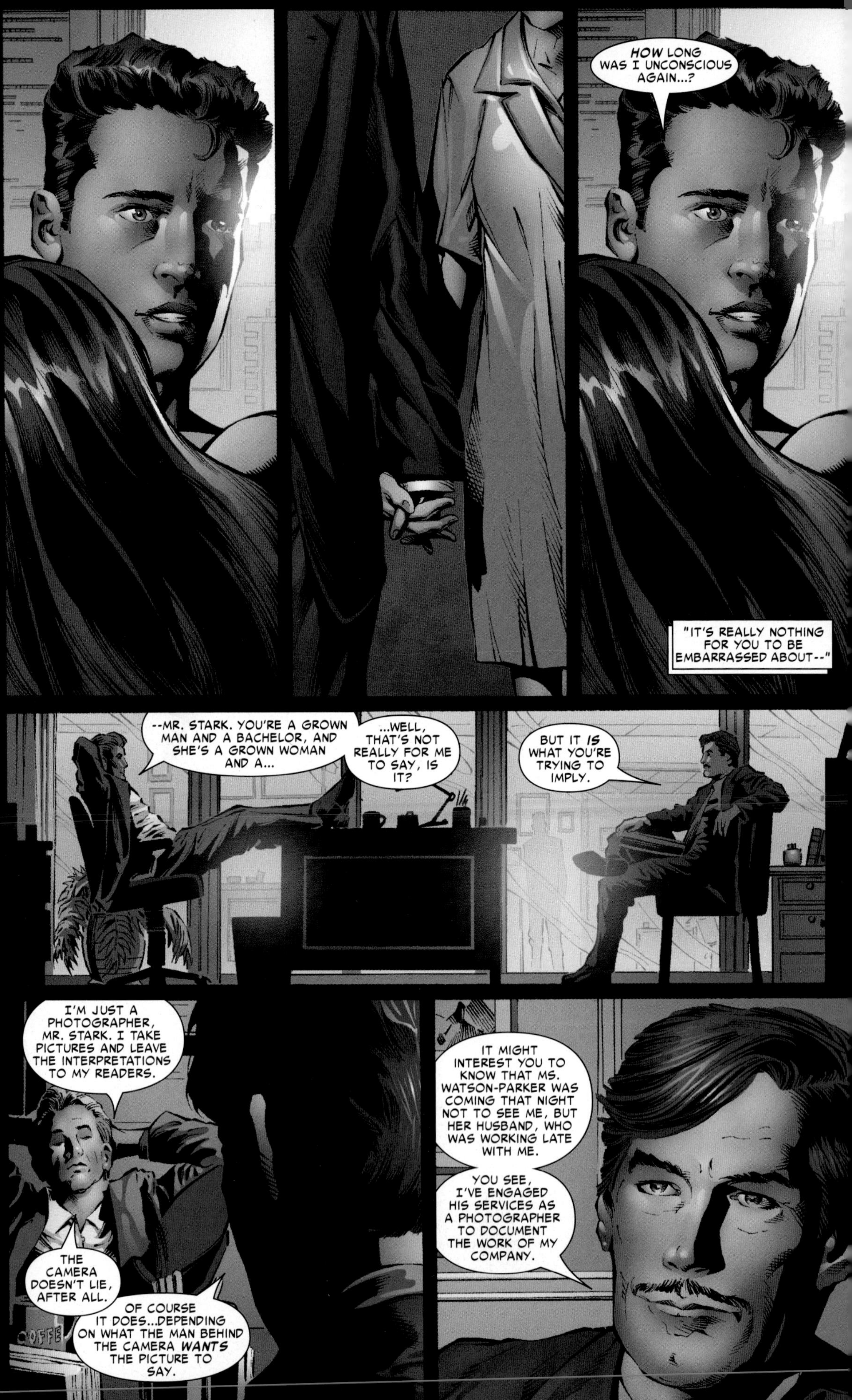
HOW LONG WAS I UNCONSCIOUS AGAIN...?
"IT'S REALLY NOTHING FOR YOU TO BE EMBARRASSED ABOUT--"
--MR. STARK. YOU'RE A GROWN MAN AND A BACHELOR, AND SHE'S A GROWN WOMAN AND A...
...WELL, THAT'S NOT REALLY FOR ME TO SAY, IS IT?
BUT IT IS WHAT YOU'RE TRYING TO IMPLY.
I'M JUST A PHOTOGRAPHER, MR. STARK. I TAKE PICTURES AND LEAVE THE INTERPRETATIONS TO MY READERS.
THE CAMERA DOESN'T LIE, AFTER ALL.
OF COURSE IT DOES...DEPENDING ON WHAT THE MAN BEHIND THE CAMERA WANTS THE PICTURE TO SAY.
IT MIGHT INTEREST YOU TO KNOW THAT MS. WATSON-PARKER WAS COMING THAT NIGHT NOT TO SEE ME, BUT HER HUSBAND, WHO WAS WORKING LATE WITH ME.
YOU SEE, I'VE ENGAGED HIS SERVICES AS A PHOTOGRAPHER TO DOCUMENT THE WORK OF MY COMPANY.

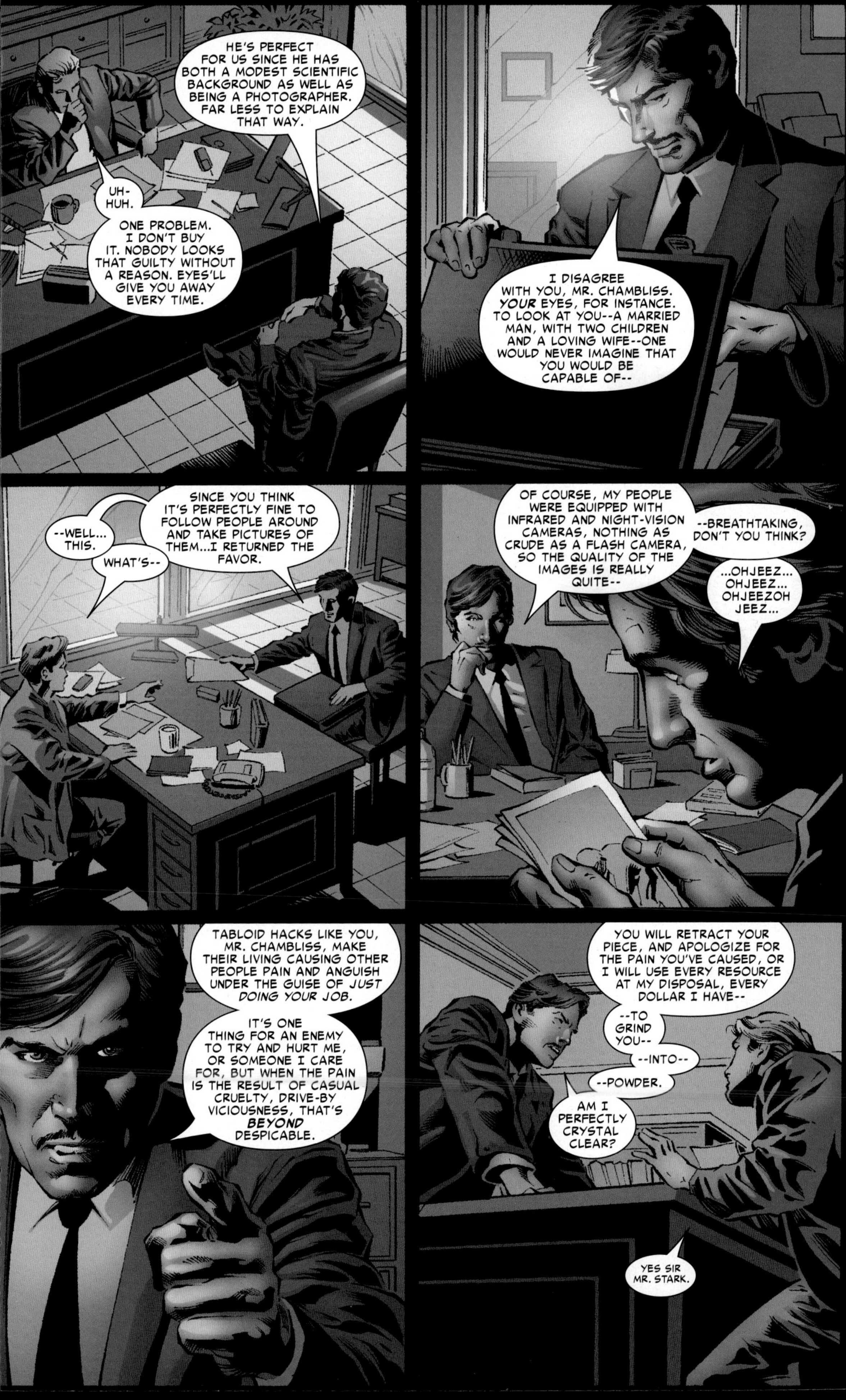
HE'S PERFECT FOR US SINCE HE HAS BOTH A MODEST SCIENTIFIC BACKGROUND AS WELL AS BEING A PHOTOGRAPHER. FAR LESS TO EXPLAIN THAT WAY.
UH-HUH.
ONE PROBLEM. I DON'T BUY IT. NOBODY LOOKS THAT GUILTY WITHOUT A REASON. EYES'LL GIVE YOU AWAY EVERY TIME.
I DISAGREE WITH YOU, MR. CHAMBLISS. *YOUR* EYES, FOR INSTANCE. TO LOOK AT YOU--A MARRIED MAN, WITH TWO CHILDREN AND A LOVING WIFE--ONE WOULD NEVER IMAGINE THAT YOU WOULD BE CAPABLE OF--
SINCE YOU THINK IT'S PERFECTLY FINE TO FOLLOW PEOPLE AROUND AND TAKE PICTURES OF THEM...I RETURNED THE FAVOR.
WHAT'S--
--WELL... THIS.
OF COURSE, MY PEOPLE WERE EQUIPPED WITH INFRARED AND NIGHT-VISION CAMERAS, NOTHING AS CRUDE AS A FLASH CAMERA, SO THE QUALITY OF THE IMAGES IS REALLY QUITE--
--BREATHTAKING, DON'T YOU THINK?
...OHJEEZ... OHJEEZ... OHJEEZOH JEEZ...
TABLOID HACKS LIKE YOU, MR. CHAMBLISS, MAKE THEIR LIVING CAUSING OTHER PEOPLE PAIN AND ANGUISH UNDER THE GUISE OF *JUST DOING YOUR JOB*.
IT'S ONE THING FOR AN ENEMY TO TRY AND HURT ME, OR SOMEONE I CARE FOR, BUT WHEN THE PAIN IS THE RESULT OF CASUAL CRUELTY, DRIVE-BY VICIOUSNESS, THAT'S ***BEYOND*** DESPICABLE.
YOU WILL RETRACT YOUR PIECE, AND APOLOGIZE FOR THE PAIN YOU'VE CAUSED, OR I WILL USE EVERY RESOURCE AT MY DISPOSAL, EVERY DOLLAR I HAVE--
--TO GRIND YOU--
--INTO--
--POWDER.
AM I PERFECTLY CRYSTAL CLEAR?
YES SIR MR. STARK.

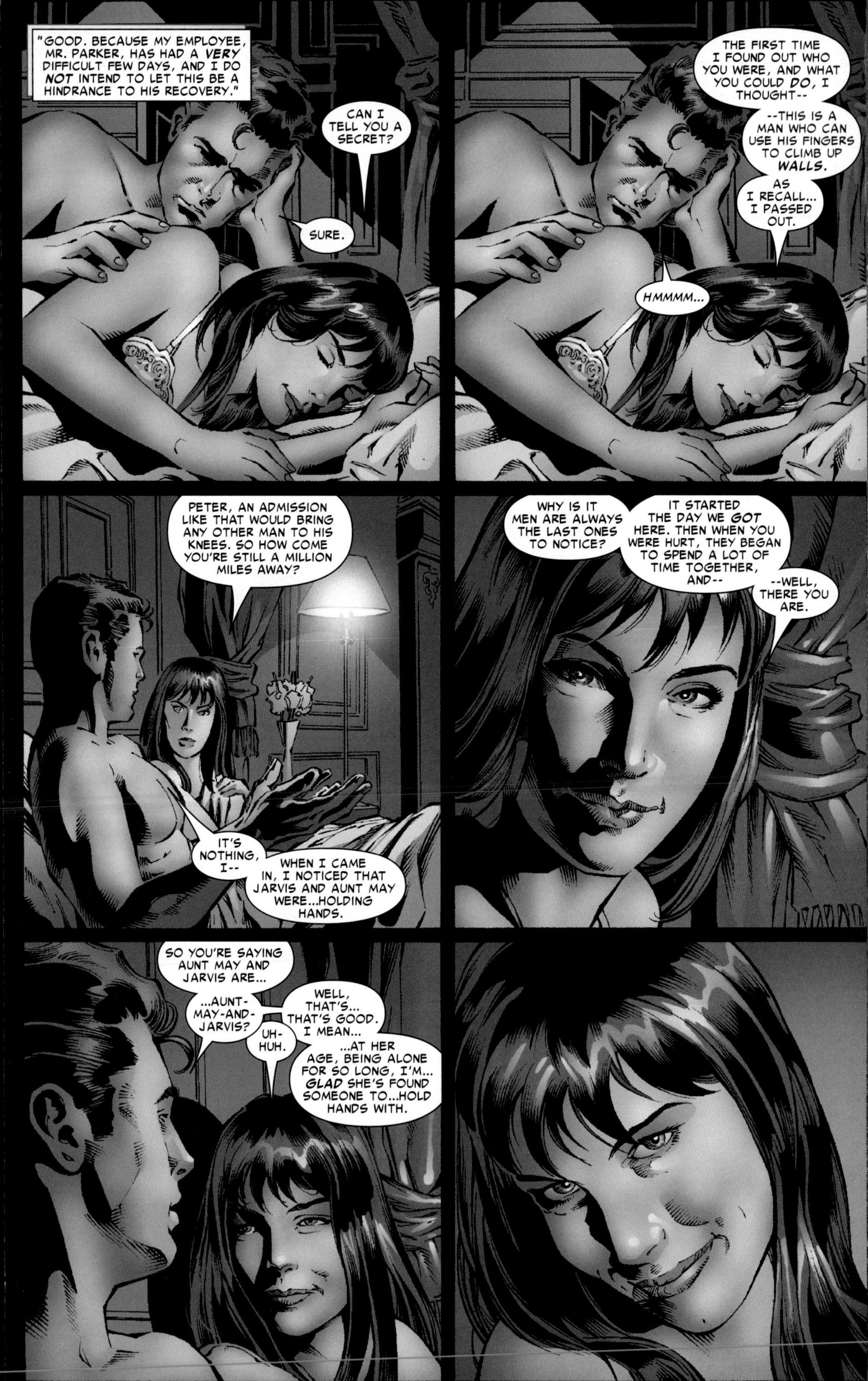
"GOOD. BECAUSE MY EMPLOYEE, MR. PARKER, HAS HAD A VERY DIFFICULT FEW DAYS, AND I DO NOT INTEND TO LET THIS BE A HINDRANCE TO HIS RECOVERY."
CAN I TELL YOU A SECRET?
SURE.
THE FIRST TIME I FOUND OUT WHO YOU WERE, AND WHAT YOU COULD DO, I THOUGHT--
--THIS IS A MAN WHO CAN USE HIS FINGERS TO CLIMB UP WALLS.
AS I RECALL... I PASSED OUT.
HMMMM...
PETER, AN ADMISSION LIKE THAT WOULD BRING ANY OTHER MAN TO HIS KNEES. SO HOW COME YOU'RE STILL A MILLION MILES AWAY?
IT'S NOTHING, I--
WHEN I CAME IN, I NOTICED THAT JARVIS AND AUNT MAY WERE...HOLDING HANDS.
WHY IS IT MEN ARE ALWAYS THE LAST ONES TO NOTICE?
IT STARTED THE DAY WE GOT HERE. THEN WHEN YOU WERE HURT, THEY BEGAN TO SPEND A LOT OF TIME TOGETHER, AND--
--WELL, THERE YOU ARE.
SO YOU'RE SAYING AUNT MAY AND JARVIS ARE...
...AUNT-MAY-AND-JARVIS?
UH-HUH.
WELL, THAT'S... THAT'S GOOD. I MEAN...
...AT HER AGE, BEING ALONE FOR SO LONG, I'M... GLAD SHE'S FOUND SOMEONE TO...HOLD HANDS WITH.

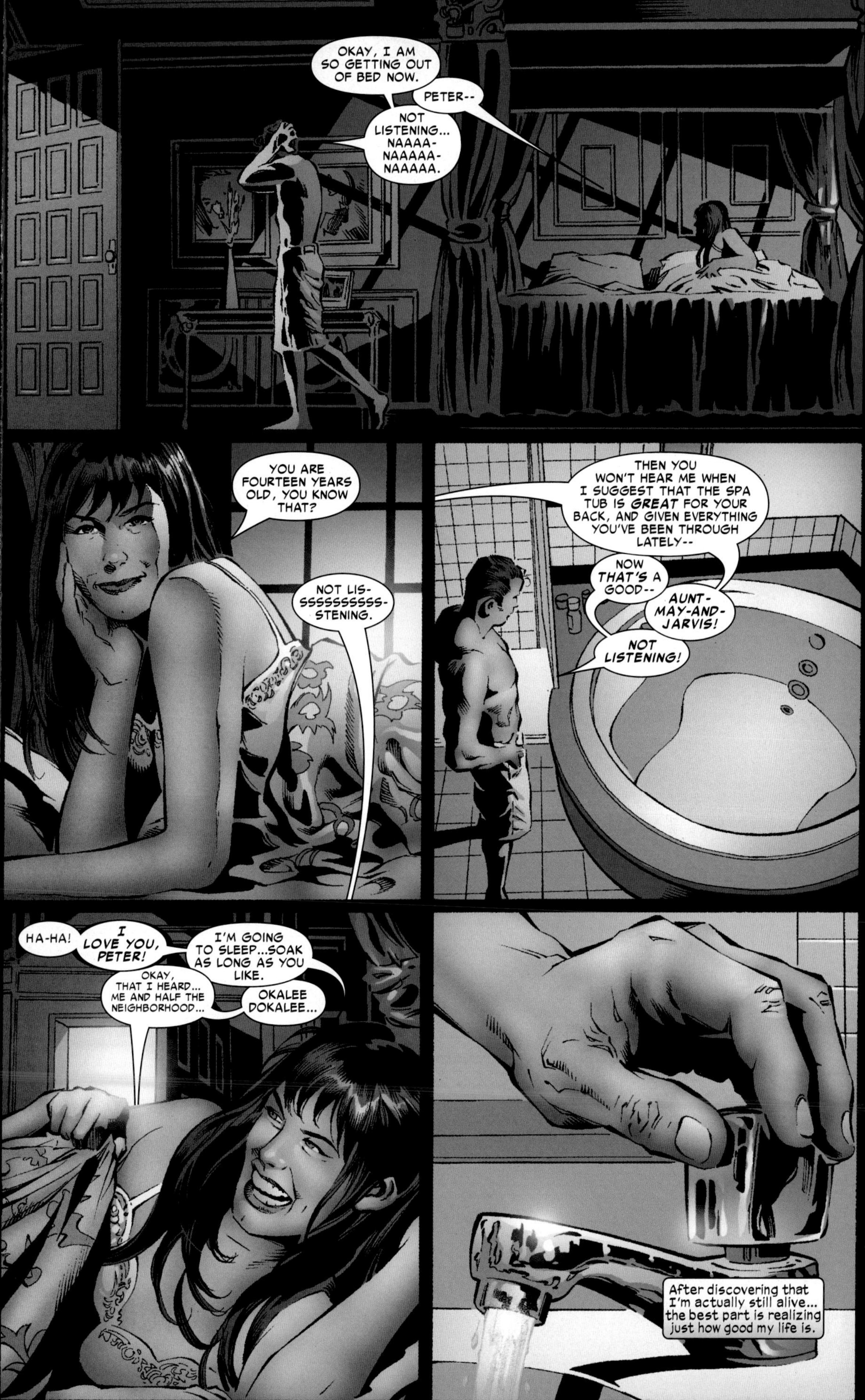

OKAY, I AM SO GETTING OUT OF BED NOW.
PETER--
NOT LISTENING... NAAAA-NAAAAA-NAAAAA.
YOU ARE FOURTEEN YEARS OLD, YOU KNOW THAT?
NOT LIS-SSSSSSSSSS-STENING.
THEN YOU WON'T HEAR ME WHEN I SUGGEST THAT THE SPA TUB IS GREAT FOR YOUR BACK, AND GIVEN EVERYTHING YOU'VE BEEN THROUGH LATELY--
NOW THAT'S A GOOD--
AUNT-MAY-AND-JARVIS!
NOT LISTENING!
HA-HA!
I LOVE YOU, PETER!
I'M GOING TO SLEEP...SOAK AS LONG AS YOU LIKE.
OKAY, THAT I HEARD... ME AND HALF THE NEIGHBORHOOD...
OKALEE DOKALEE...
After discovering that I'm actually still alive... the best part is realizing just how good my life is.

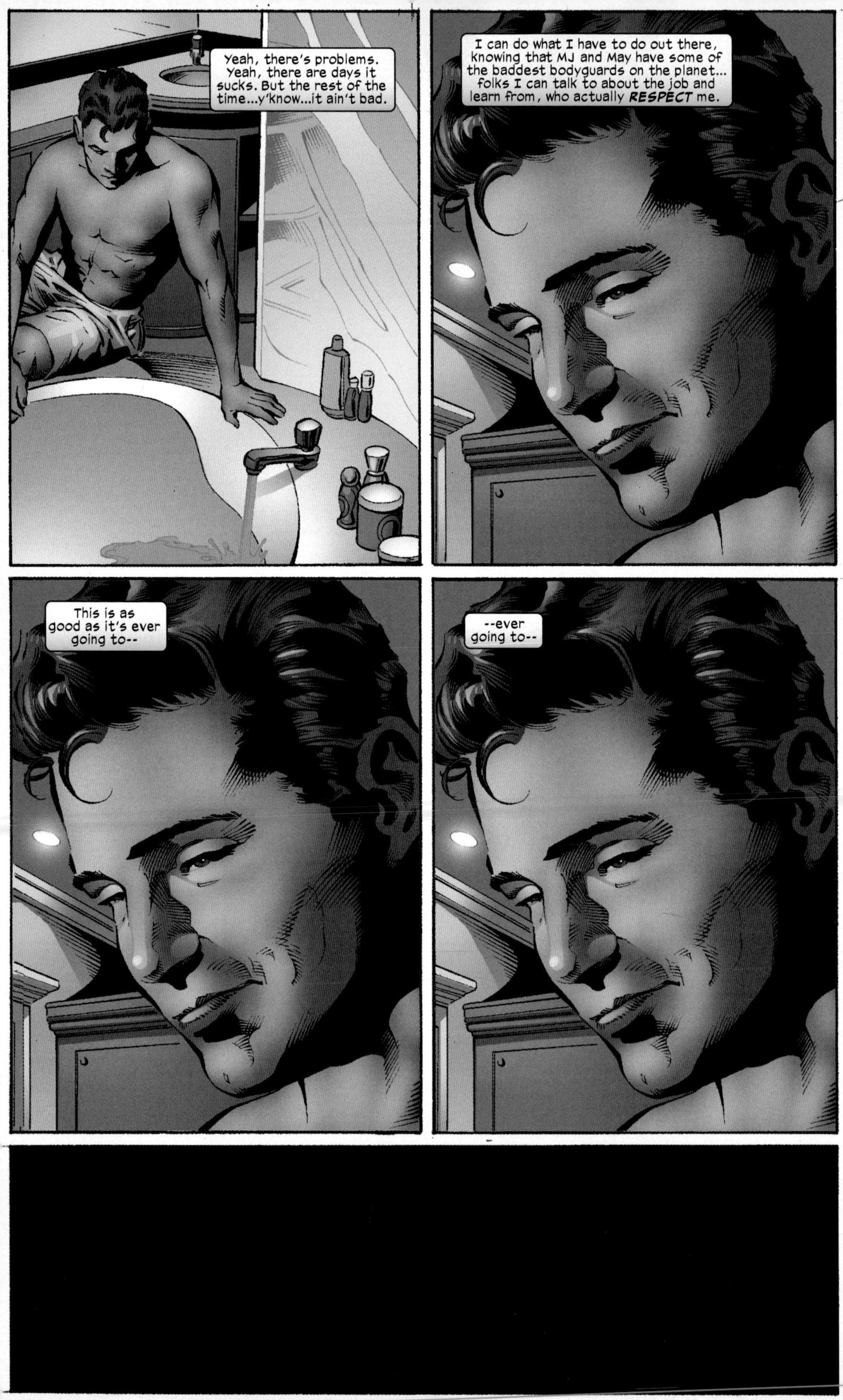
Yeah, there's problems. Yeah, there are days it sucks. But the rest of the time...y'know...it ain't bad.
I can do what I have to do out there, knowing that MJ and May have some of the baddest bodyguards on the planet... folks I can talk to about the job and learn from, who actually RESPECT me.
This is as good as it's ever going to--
--ever going to--

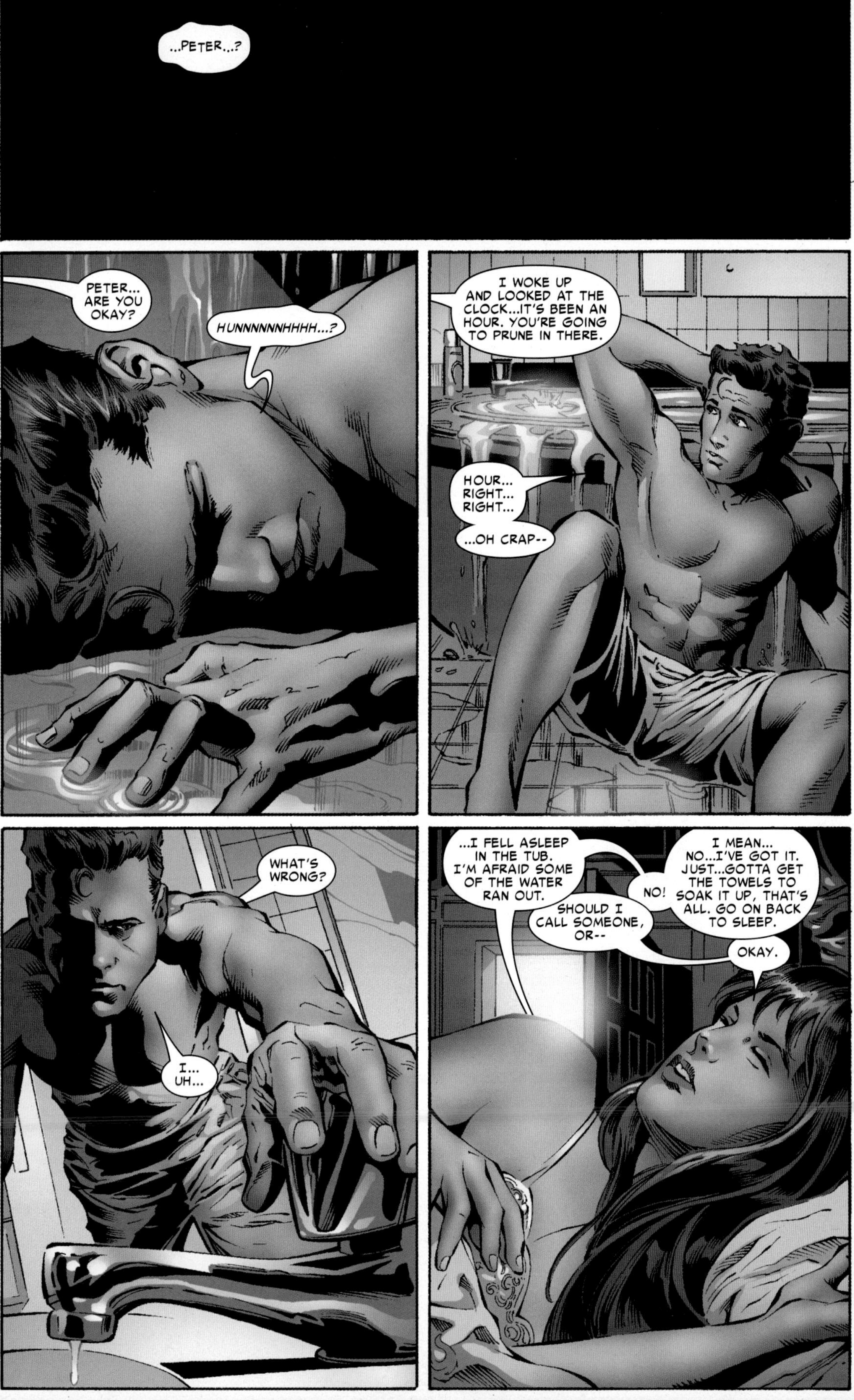
...PETER...?
PETER... ARE YOU OKAY?
HUNNNNNNHHHH...?
I WOKE UP AND LOOKED AT THE CLOCK...IT'S BEEN AN HOUR. YOU'RE GOING TO PRUNE IN THERE.
HOUR... RIGHT... RIGHT...
...OH CRAP--
WHAT'S WRONG?
I... UH...
...I FELL ASLEEP IN THE TUB. I'M AFRAID SOME OF THE WATER RAN OUT.
SHOULD I CALL SOMEONE, OR--
NO!
I MEAN... NO...I'VE GOT IT. JUST...GOTTA GET THE TOWELS TO SOAK IT UP, THAT'S ALL. GO ON BACK TO SLEEP.
OKAY.

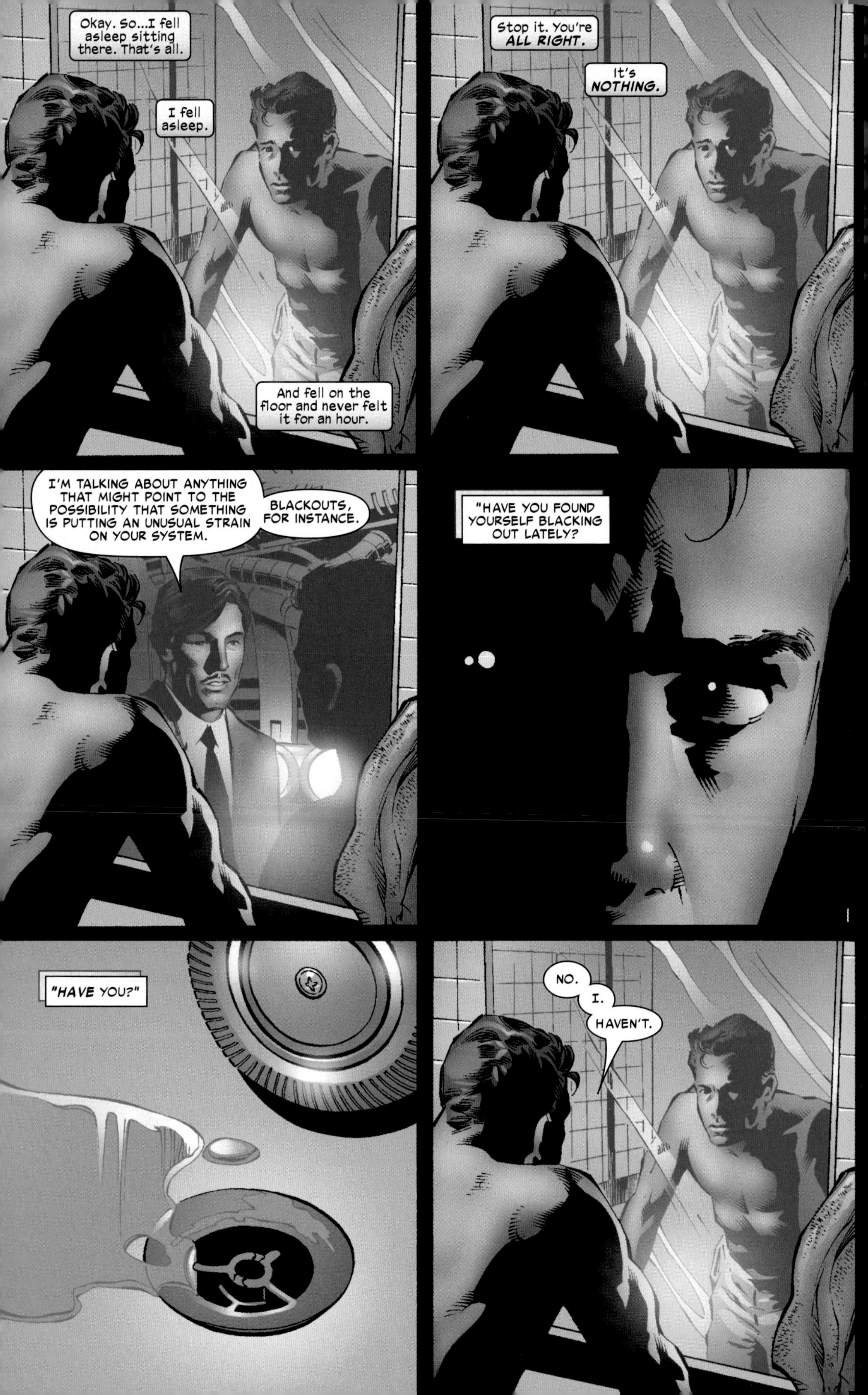
Okay. So...I fell asleep sitting there. That's all.
I fell asleep.
And fell on the floor and never felt it for an hour.
Stop it. You're ALL RIGHT.
It's NOTHING.
I'M TALKING ABOUT ANYTHING THAT MIGHT POINT TO THE POSSIBILITY THAT SOMETHING IS PUTTING AN UNUSUAL STRAIN ON YOUR SYSTEM.
BLACKOUTS, FOR INSTANCE.
"HAVE YOU FOUND YOURSELF BLACKING OUT LATELY?
"HAVE YOU?"
NO.
I.
HAVEN'T.

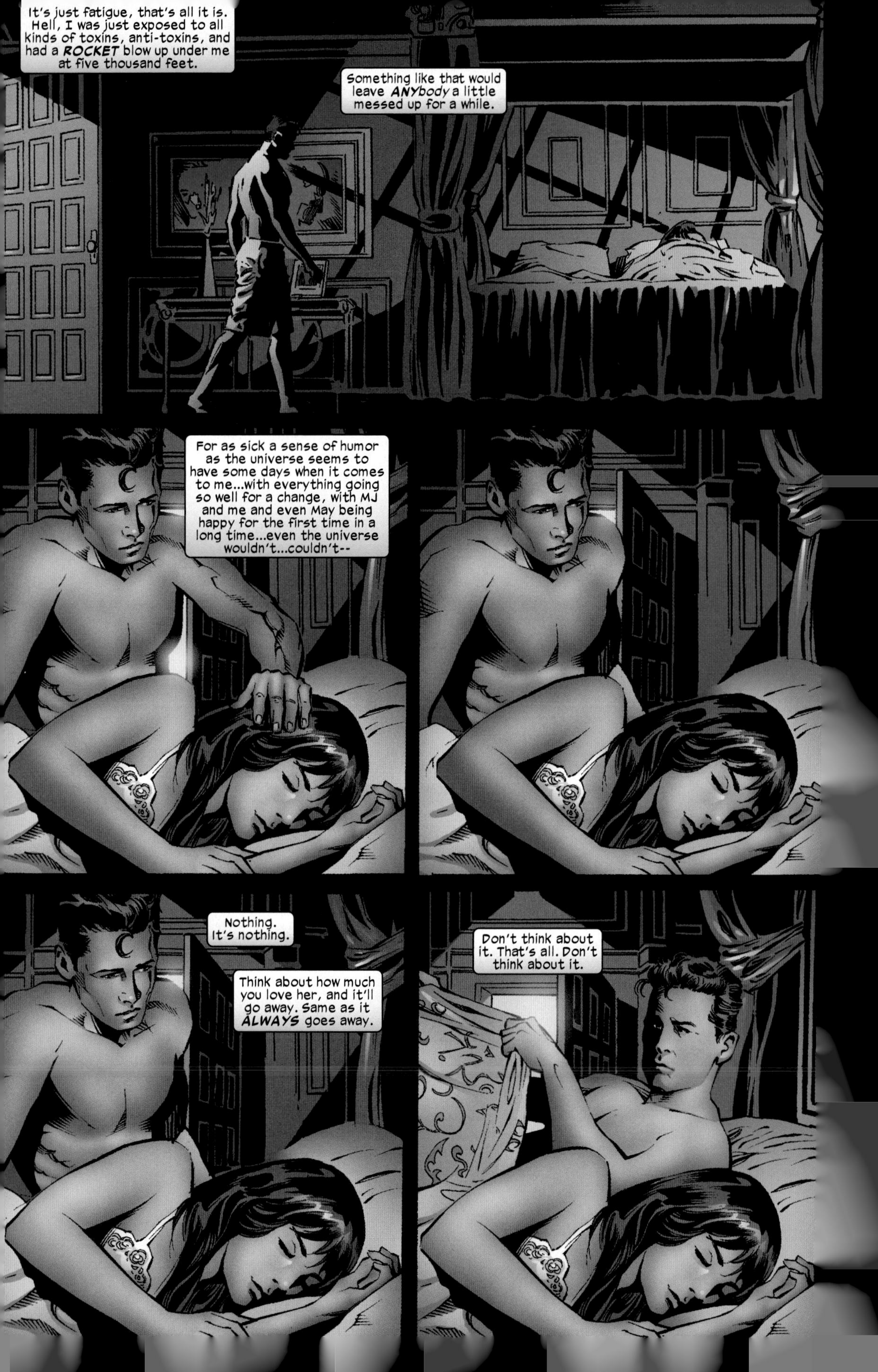
It's just fatigue, that's all it is. Hell, I was just exposed to all kinds of toxins, anti-toxins, and had a ROCKET blow up under me at five thousand feet.
Something like that would leave ANYbody a little messed up for a while.
For as sick a sense of humor as the universe seems to have some days when it comes to me...with everything going so well for a change, with MJ and me and even May being happy for the first time in a long time...even the universe wouldn't...couldn't--
Nothing. It's nothing.
Think about how much you love her, and it'll go away. Same as it ALWAYS goes away.
Don't think about it. That's all. Don't think about it.

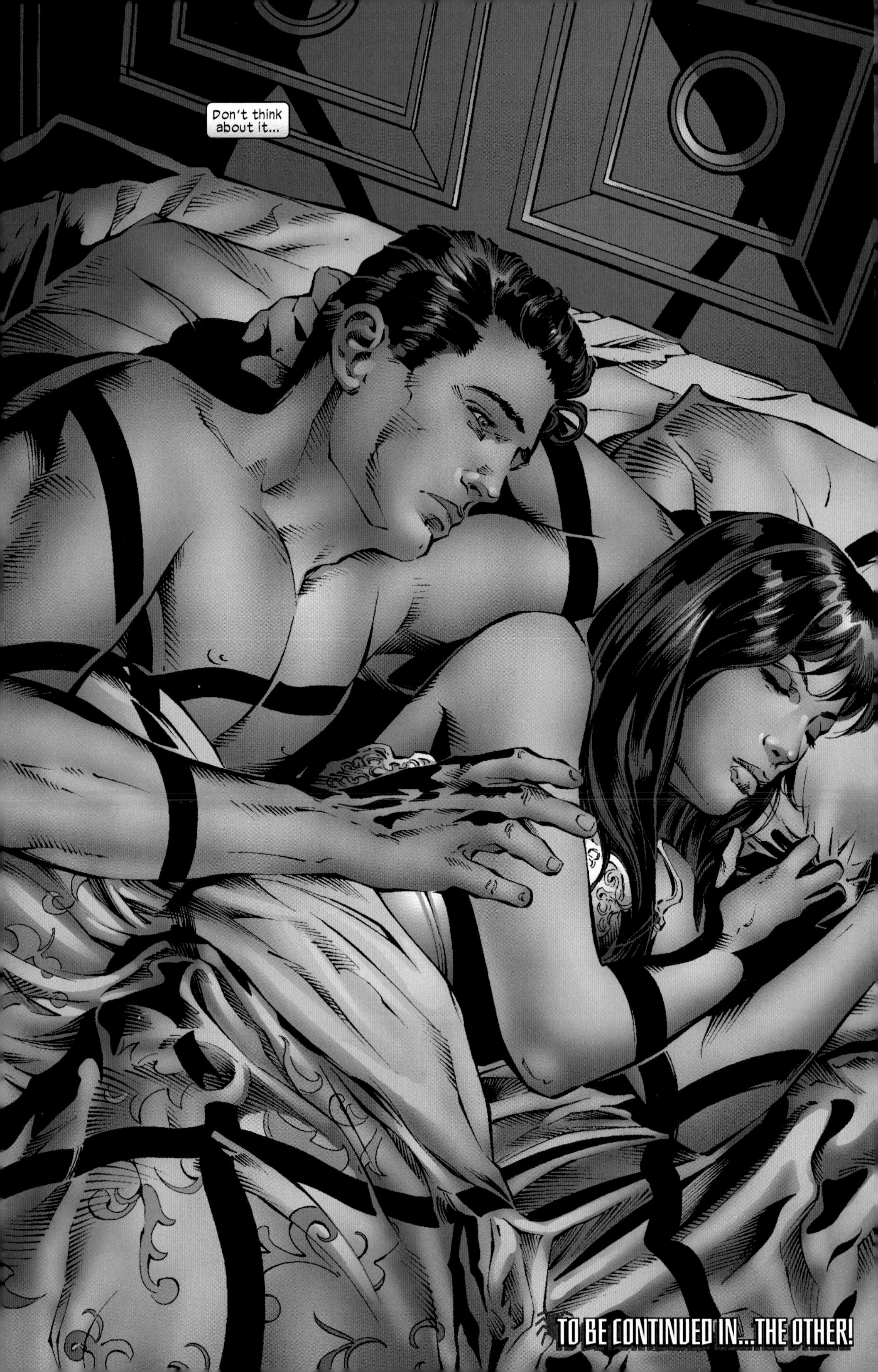
Don't think about it...
TO BE CONTINUED IN...THE OTHER!

ISSUE #520 COVER PROCESS BY MIKE DEODATO JR.

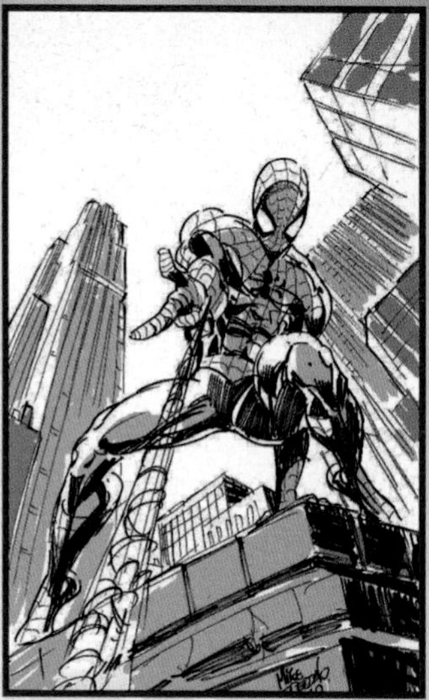

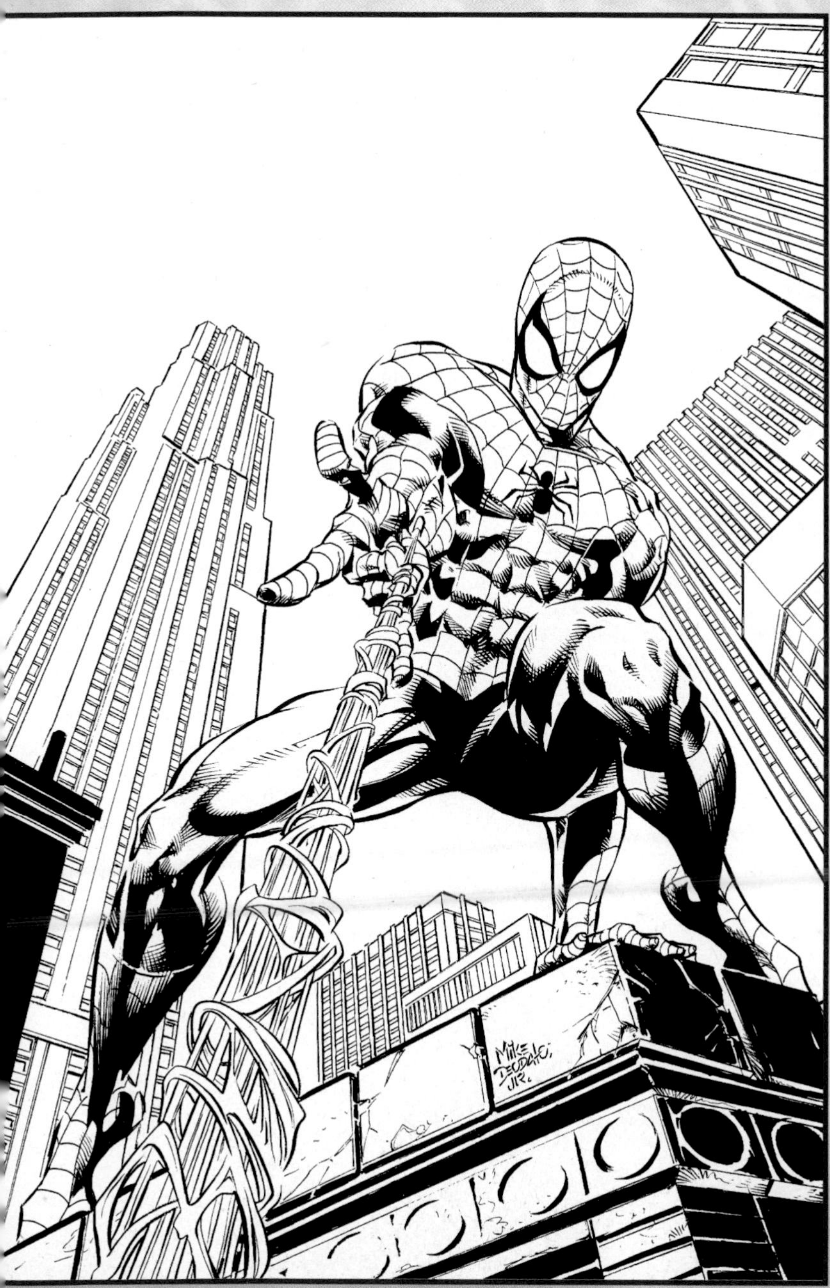
MIKE DEODATO, JR.

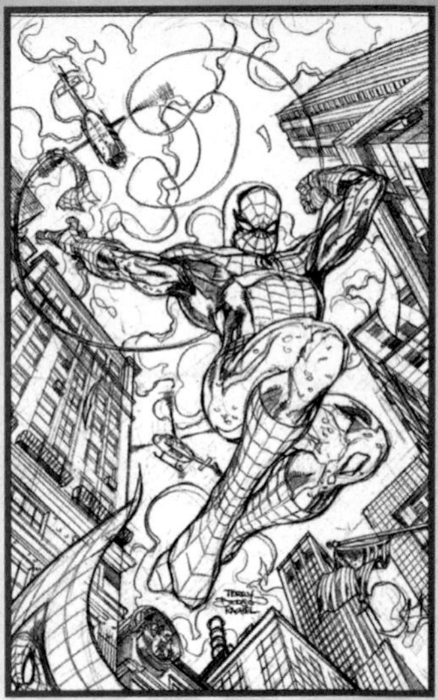

ISSUE #523 COVER PROCESS BY TERRY DODSON

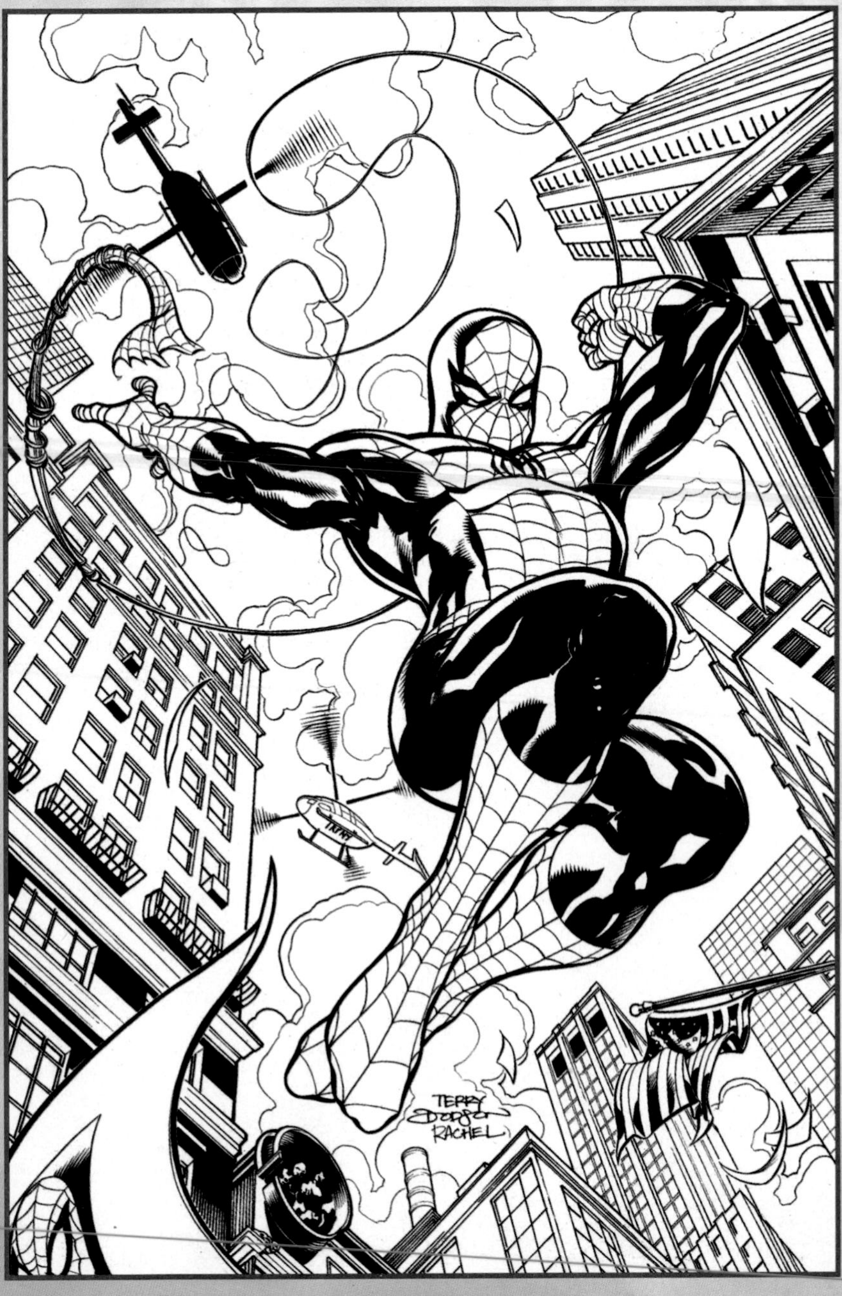
TERRY
DODSON
RACHEL